Advance Praise Digital Storytelling in the Classroom

"A very important resource for twenty-first-century teaching and learning. Ohler's ability to distill the elements of good storytelling down to simple, clearly communicable ideas will prove beneficial for teachers and students alike, regardless of experience or technological knowledge."

—Nikos Theodosakis, Director, author of *Director in the Classroom*

"Jason Ohler writes with clarity, wit, and passion about topics that are central to the enterprise of educating. He demonstrates how each student can become an active and more confident meaning-maker by using the tools that make stories powerful aids to understanding in all areas of the curriculum."

—Kieran Egan, Professor of Education, author of *The Educated Mind*

"Ohler's latest book is a godsend to all of us working with teachers and digital media. This book makes stories work."

—Michael Hallisey, Director of Learning, Digital Hub, Ireland

"The book builds and unfolds fluidly. You can see the practical progression of ideas on digital storytelling, which is wonderful because the reader can conceptualize what should happen."

—Amanda Mayeaux, Teacher

"Ohler continues to be witty, wise, and indispensable. Pedagogy that resonates, teamed with a practical road map for teachers exploring the digital frontier—the best new media guide for teachers by far!"

—Suzi Gould, Director, Story Express, New Zealand

"I haven't seen concrete examples like these in any educational book I've read. Throughout this book, my reactions ranged from 'awesome' to 'wow,' and I had many ideas for implementing the ideas in my own classroom. I love it!"

—Michael Fisher, Critical Thinking Specialist

"Essential for integrating learning, literacy, and new media in and out of the classroom. Jason Ohler is a world leader in digital storytelling, a master teacher, and a global communicator."

—Bernard J. Luskin, professor and Director of
Media Programs, Fielding Graduate University

"The visual representations from the charts and graphics are wonderful. I love the connections to current research because they give credence to the material and allow teachers to connect research to everyday strategies."

—Patricia Baker, Gifted Education Instructor

"Jason Ohler's new book is a must-read for any educator interested in harnessing the tools of digital technology to teach students to be creative and powerful storytellers. Original, accessible, and thought provoking for technophobes and technophiles alike."

—Steven Goodman, author of *Teaching Youth Media:
A Critical Guide to Teaching Literacy, Video and Social Change*

"All the elements of classical rhetoric are reinvigorated, from invention to decorum, to memory, to delivery of the story. This useful book places these traditional skills in the digital milieu."

—Eric McLuhan, Media Ecologist, author of *Electric Language*

"Ohler illuminates the very heart of learning and digital technology: storytelling. His is the story of how the networked computer amplifies our human capacity to learn through tools of expression."

—Walter Bender, President
One Laptop Per Child Foundation

"I definitely recommend this book. Many teachers do not have the expertise to plan an undertaking like this, but really want to try something new and exciting with their students. Trying new and creative activities makes teaching interesting and challenging."

—William Fitzhugh, Fifth-Grade Teacher

JASON OHLER

DIGITAL Storytelling
in the Classroom

New Media Pathways to
LITERACY, LEARNING, and CREATIVITY

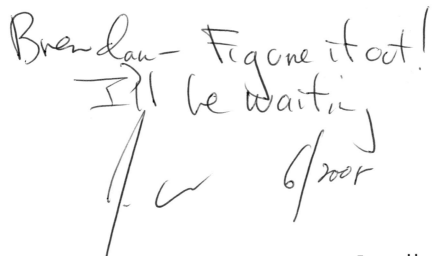

Foreword by
DAVID THORNBURG

CORWIN PRESS
A SAGE Publications Company
Thousand Oaks, CA 91320

Copyright © 2008 by Corwin Press

For information:

Corwin Press
A Sage Publications Company
2455 Teller Road
Thousand Oaks, California 91320
www.corwinpress.com

Sage Publications Ltd.
1 Oliver's Yard
55 City Road
London EC1Y 1SP
United Kingdom

Sage Publications India Pvt. Ltd.
B 1/I 1 Mohan Cooperative
  Industrial Area
Mathura Road, New Delhi 110 044
India

Sage Publications Asia-Pacific Pte. Ltd.
33 Pekin Street #02-01
Far East Square
Singapore 048763

Printed in the United States of America

Library of Congress Cataloging-in-Publication Data

Ohler, Jason.
Digital storytelling in the classroom: new media pathways to literacy, learning, and creativity/Jason Ohler.
    p. cm.
Includes bibliographical references and index.
ISBN 978-1-4129-3849-5 (cloth)
ISBN 978-1-4129-3850-1 (pbk.)
  1. Storytelling—Data processing. 2. Literature and technology. 3. Internet in education. I. Title.

LB1042.O37 2008
372.67′70285—dc22   2007010021

This book is printed on acid-free paper.

07 08 09 10 11   10 9 8 7 6 5 4 3 2 1

Acquisitions Editor:	Elizabeth Brenkus
Editorial Assistants:	Desirée Enayati and Ena Rosen
Production Editor:	Jenn Reese
Copy Editor:	Kevin Beck and Barbara Coster
Typesetter:	C&M Digitals (P) Ltd.
Proofreader:	Emily Rose
Indexer:	Nara Wood
Cover Designer:	Michael Dubowe
Graphic Artist:	Lisa Riley

 Contents

Foreword

I was blessed to hear Gregory Bateson give a presentation one time in which he started as follows:

A man walked up to a powerful computer and typed in a question, using his very best Fortran (I heard this *many* years ago). The question was: "Do you suppose someday computers will think like humans?"

After a pause to parse the question, using every ounce of artificial intelligence the computer could muster, the printer sprang to life, typing out a single line: "That reminds me of a story."

When Bateson (and numerous others) were pondering the essence of humanity, one view that received attention was that humans derived their power from their opposable thumbs—a perspective that tied in to the idea that we were the creators and users of tools. But at the same time, another anthropological perspective was emerging, encapsulated in the modern view of Jennifer James that "we are the stories we tell about ourselves."

The notion that we *are* our stories carries with it great power. Instead of stories recording our lives, they (it is suggested) have the power to shape our reality—to shape our lives!

Our children are growing up in a world of chaotic change, drowning in a growing mountain of facts. In the United States, we have decided that the measure of educational success is the extent to which these facts can be imparted to students so they can be tested on an annual basis. In this world, the future is preordained and creativity vanishes. And yet we gather around the watering hole (or water cooler or copying machine) to share our stories, whether they start with "A strange thing happened last week when I . . ." or even "A horse walks into a bar and . . ."

No matter how detached we are from deep meaning in the curriculum du jour, we stay in touch with our stories because they shape us in deep ways. Gregory Bateson knew this. So did his former wife, Margaret Mead. And so did Marshall McLuhan (although he had the grace to land on both sides of many issues, proving that consistency was for little minds).

And from the wealth of thinking on the topic of stories in education, pioneered by folks like Kieran Egan and others, we enter the world of digital storytelling and the subject of this book.

Digital storytelling, as you will see, is first, storytelling and second, digital. The point of technology is not for it to tell the stories for us but to allow us to craft stories that engage people on many levels. This can involve images, video clips, music, narration. It can be as complex as a short film or as simple as a narrated slide show. The goal is the same, no matter the medium. Find a topic you want to share with others and convey that topic as richly as possible, engaging not only the conscious mind but the emotions as well.

Recently, my wife and I went to a concert by John Fogerty (of Creedence Clearwater Revival fame). One of his songs, "Deja vu," was accompanied by a slide show contrasting the U.S. involvement in Vietnam with that in Iraq. The words by themselves were amazingly powerful, but the impact was amplified through his judicious use of images and video clips. Now, for those of you who haven't been to one of his concerts, you should know that John is a dynamic performer perfectly capable of holding an audience with his songs alone. He added other media because he wanted to amplify the impact of this powerful song.

And that is a key to understanding what Jason Ohler has done in writing this book for you. He has provided a guide to building digital story amplifiers. Of course, as he is quick to point out, imagine what happens when you give a bad guitarist a bigger amplifier! Digital storytelling will not fix a bad story—it will only make its defects more apparent.

Instead of digital storytelling, perhaps we should call it story digitalizing, or something else that puts story first, where it belongs.

Each of us has stories to tell. That includes children as well as adults. For thousands of years we gathered around the fire to share our stories. Now that the fire has become the glow of a computer monitor, we must ensure that the stories told around this new light are as powerful as those told around the old.

Through the book you now hold, Jason provides a map; it is up to you to chart your own course.

—David Thornburg

Preface

I have one word for anyone who wants to tell a story—whether it's with computers, with pictures scratched in the sand, or solely with the language of the body and the sounds of the human voice; whether it's the story of a quest to find one's holy grail, to find oneself, or simply to find a way to tell one's story; whether it's a long story, a short story, or a story that never really ends; whether it's told on the silver screen, in a circle of one's closest friends, upon the great virtual stage of the World Wide Web, or on a hill in full view of the gathered public; whether it's a personal story, a universal story, someone else's story, or a story that can be understood only by the culture that tells it; whether it's schoolwork, a work of art, art for work, or simply something that has to be said; whether it's for you, for your friends, for your community, or for those you will never meet; whether it's a personal journey, a scientific adventure, a fantasy of the mind, or a memory collage of one's ancestors; whether it exists as invisible bits of a digital file, as words on paper, as a TV rerun, or only as memories in the hearts and minds of elders; whether it never changes, changes every time it is told, or changes so slowly that no one notices. I have one word for anyone who wants to tell a story, and that word is "welcome."

Who Is This Book For?

I wrote this book so that it could be used by any teacher, regardless of technical experience, who wants help using technology effectively, creatively, and wisely in the classroom. Whether you're a beginning computer user or a seasoned expert, this book will meet you where you are and help you take your next steps.

Toward that end, this book approaches storytelling and digital media production from a generalist perspective in ways that can be adapted for use by teachers at most grade levels in most content areas. I assume that the reader's attitude toward the digital age classroom is a mixture of inspiration, intimidation, and confusion. I hope that by the end of the book, readers will find life in the digital age classroom more manageable, productive, and fun.

This book is particularly concerned with helping teachers do the following:

- Understand the value of storytelling in education, regardless of the media used in the storytelling process.

- Help themselves and their students create digital stories that employ effective principles of storytelling, technology application, and media technique.
- Use digital storytelling as a tool to promote the development of emerging literacies, such as digital and media literacy, as well as traditional literacies, such as reading, writing, speaking, and art.
- Help students use digital storytelling as an academic tool to explore content and to communicate what they understand.
- Understand the importance of combining the power of story and critical thinking as an approach to teaching and learning.
- Leverage students' imagination and help them develop their own voices as storytellers, digital media artists, and learning community members.
- Evaluate digital stories in ways that are helpful to students, parents, and the community, so that digital storytelling can be a valuable learning tool, as well as an effective use of classroom time.
- Develop a sense of media grammar so they can help guide students in the development of new media.
- Understand the basics of media persuasion and bias and how to make media literacy a part of new media production with their students.
- Understand the importance of copyright and fair use in protecting and incentivizing creative content developers, including themselves and their students, and apply that understanding to student use of material in new media projects.

Above all, this book is for teachers who want to better understand the world that often seems so foreign to them but that their students call normal. For those teachers who fear their obsolescence in the digital age, fear not. The more digital the world becomes, the more your students will need you, not for your keystrokes and technical know-how, but for your guidance and wisdom.

❧ How Is the Book Organized?

I have organized the book into three parts.

❧ Part I: Storytelling, Education, and the New Media

Are you a teacher wondering why you should consider trying one more new thing in your classroom when you're already overwhelmed trying to meet your own learning objectives, as well as the demands of your school district and your state and federal departments of education? Are you a school administrator wondering why digital storytelling should receive your support in an era of No Child Left Behind? Are you a parent, voter, or concerned citizen wondering why art and new media literacy should be valued as literacies on par with the three R's? Part I should help address your questions. It explains how digital storytelling can be used in the classroom as an academic tool to engage digital age students in constructivist learning. In addition, you will see how new media narrative promotes traditional and emerging literacies, helps students meet academic standards in a number of content areas, and gives students a chance to demonstrate their understanding of the world in their own language.

✦ Part II: The Art and Practice of Storytelling

Whether you consider yourself a high-tech, a low-tech, or a no-tech teacher, there is one common denominator for every successful storytelling project: a good story. This part of the book addresses ways to help students understand, plan, and tell stories that have the qualities of good narrative, such as conflict/resolution, character transformation, and audience engagement. In addition, it shows how to use storytelling as a tool for teaching, learning, and personal expression. The fundamental principles of storytelling explained in this part of the book can be used to develop stories for any purpose and are not limited to storytelling in education.

✦ Part III: Going Digital

If you're a little queasy about using computers and other digital technology, Part III of this book should help set your mind at ease. I provide a step-by-step approach to developing media-based stories that focuses on the teacher's role as a skill manager rather than a media specialist—*as the guide on the side, rather than the technician magician.* In addition, I provide a detailed description of software, hardware, and the media production process in layperson's terms. My focus is always on using the "low end"—hardware that is commonly available and software that is free or inexpensive. What you will discover is that the costs involved in doing digital storytelling are minimal. You will also discover that your technical skill level doesn't matter nearly as much as you thought, and you can apply the knowledge you currently have about classroom activity planning to digital storytelling. I also include a chapter on media grammar that will help you provide useful feedback to your students about creating media projects that communicate effectively, as well as a chapter on copyright and fair use, to help you and your students use media legally and ethically.

▓ How Best to Use This Book

I have written this book to be used in a number of ways.

First, you can simply read it from beginning to end—like a story. It will take you on a journey that explores the role of digital narrative in your students' lives and shows you how to plan, create, and perform digital stories that are meaningful to you and your students.

Second, it's written as a quick reference. I have separated the book into the three distinct parts described earlier and have further subdivided these into specific areas of interest. You should be able to find information quickly as specific needs arise in your classroom.

Third, it's a philosophical manifesto of sorts. This book is not just about how to do digital storytelling, but also why to do it and how it can add value to your classroom. It is about how to help students understand the opportunities and responsibilities that accompany using powerful digital technology. And it is about the important role that story and storytelling can play in the lives of your students, both within and beyond your classroom.

And last, it's a how-to storytelling book. As I said earlier, you can use what you find here to help your students tell many kinds of stories, from simple, traditional stories that use no technology at all to elaborately produced stories that use the latest gear—to everything in between. However, my target audience is the vast majority of teachers who have limited access to technology. Most of the teachers with whom I work have small budgets, very little time in their schedules, minimal training, and access to only average, conventional equipment—just like you.

▓ What Kind of Technology Do You Need?

You need only conventional equipment, including the following:

- As of 2007, either Macintosh computers running iMovie software (which is free) or Windows machines running Movie Maker software (also free). You should have a way to burn CDs or DVDs to both show your stories to others and move your stories off the computer in order to save hard drive space and provide permanent backup copies of student work. Many conventional computers have this capability.
- A flatbed scanner (under $100) to scan objects and documents. Ask around in your district before you buy one. They are quite common these days.
- A bare-bones digital camera ($200 and up). Again, ask around, because they are also quite common these days, especially given that people

like to upgrade their cameras and have older ones they aren't using that are quite adequate. You do not need the latest and greatest, just a camera that will take decent pictures that you can download to your computer. Most digital cameras have these capabilities.

- A microphone (about $20). Many computers have built-in mikes these days that work just fine. If your computer doesn't, then check around your school or district for microphones you can borrow before buying one.
- If you're doing green screen performance-based storytelling (explained in detail in this book), then you need a consumer-level video camera with an external microphone jack ($300–$500) and a wireless microphone (about $100). Again, check around your district before buying these, as they are often available. In addition you need special green screen software, which is as inexpensive as $30 these days.

If you're interested in what to purchase, check jasonohler.com/ storytelling, where I post a list of inexpensive hardware and software. Check back often, as it changes frequently.

⚏ How Much Technology Do You Need?

Ideally, you need one computer and microphone per storyteller and one scanner and one camera per 5 to 10 students. If you're doing green screen storytelling, one video camera and wireless mike per classroom is sufficient.

This doesn't mean you need 30 computers for 30 students. It means that if you have only five computers, then you will need to set up your storytelling project so that only five students need them at a time. Same for scanners or cameras—set up the project so that there is not a bottleneck to use the resources you have. When equipment is scarce, planning becomes key.

Can you have students work on joint projects, so that small groups can share one computer? Yes. The world of professional media production is a very teamwork-oriented world, and having students work together helps them develop important group process skills needed for media development projects as well as many other ventures in life. But it has been my experience that students approach digital stories very personally and they will want—and should have—control over all aspects of at least their first journey into producing new media narrative. In the process, they will develop an understanding of the many facets of digital storytelling production and, as a result, will be more effective team members in group projects.

For more information about storytelling, as well as telling stories with digital technology, go to www.jasonohler.com/storytelling.

Acknowledgments

Thanks to Brett Dillingham for the gift of the Visual Portrait of a Story and ongoing inspiration in the world of storytelling; to Glen Bledsoe for continuing to provide so much inspiration through his work and the work of his students in the world of new media in education; to Dr. Howard Pitler, Director of Educational Technology at McREL, and Dr. James Boyle from the Duke University Law School for their invaluable input about copyright and fair use in the classroom; to Robert McKee for the use of his inspiring story maps and diagrams; to Joseph Campbell and his wise words about the nature of stories; to brothers Rick and Mike always, for the stories we share; to the people at the Center for Digital Storytelling, Suzi Gould, Judy Halasek and other digital storytellers from Scott County, Kentucky, and many others whose work in digital storytelling has informed my own; to David Hunsaker, Scott Christian, and Ishmael Hope for their help and input; to University of Alaska (UA) President Mark Hamilton, UA Vice President Dr. James Johnsen, UA Geography Program Director Dr. Mike Sfraga, University of Alaska Southeast (UAS) Chancellor John Pugh, and UAS Provost Dr. Roberta Stell for their support for this project; to the many, many teachers, students, and others who have worked with me and talked to me about digital storytelling and new media narrative over the years, especially Hannah Davis, Dana Scofield, Skip Rice, and Lori Hoover; to Bethany Stringer for "Captain Obvious"; to everyone at Budzo Manor who tell all manner of stories; to Carmen Davis for allowing me to use references to the wonderful storytelling work created by her daughter, Hannah; to Steven Goodman, Kenn Adams, Bernie Luskin, and Walter Bender for their inspirational work; to Red Boucher for the vision, heart, and soul he brings to Alaska; to Eric McLuhan for helping me to distinguish figure from ground. Many thanks especially to Ernestine Hayes, whose guidance and wisdom has informed my sense of story in profound ways, and to Kieran Egan, for believing in the imagination of children.

Corwin Press gratefully acknowledges the contributions of the following individuals:

Sara Armstrong
Educational Consultant
Sara Armstrong Consulting
Berkeley, CA

Patricia Baker
National Board Certified Teacher
Mary Walter Elementary School
Bealeton, VA

Diane Baumstark
National Board Certified Teacher
Priest Elementary School
Detroit, MI

Jeanne Biddle
Director of Technology
Scott County Schools
Georgetown, KY

Cathleen J. Chamberlain
   Assistant Superintendent
Oswego City School District
Oswego, NY

Michael L. Fisher
Critical Thinking Specialist
Starpoint Middle School
Lockport, NY

William Fitzhugh
Fifth-Grade Teacher
Reisterstown
   Elementary School
Reisterstown, MD

Jacqueline Jacobs
Professor
Educational Leadership
   and Foundations
Western Carolina
   University
Cullowhee, NC

Amanda S. Mayeaux
Assistant Principal
Dutchtown
   Middle School
Geismar, LA

Nancy Yost
Professor
Indiana University of
   Pennsylvania
Indiana, PA

To my wife, Terri. Life with her is a wonderful story indeed.

About the Author

Jason Ohler is a speaker, writer, teacher, researcher, and lifelong digital humanist who is well known for the passion, insight, and humor he brings to his presentations, projects, and writings. Combining 25 years of experience in the educational technology field with an eye for the future, he connects with people where they are and helps them understand how they can impact living, learning, and working in the digital age in ways that support their vision for the future. Although he is called a futurist, he considers himself a nowist, working nationally and internationally to help educators and the public use today's tools to create living environments that they are proud to call home.

He continues to enjoy working directly with teachers and students in K–12 classrooms, joining them in their quest to use digital tools to explore ideas, create learning communities, and tell stories. He is the author of numerous articles, books, and teacher resources (www.jasonohler.com/storytelling), all of which are devoted to digital humanism—the quest to live humanly in a digitally deluged world. First and foremost he is a storyteller, telling tales of the future that are grounded in the past. He clearly loves what he does and loves sharing what he knows with others.

"The goal is the effective, creative, and wise use of technology . . . to bring together technology, community, and learning in ways that work. And while we are at it, to have fun."

Are there rules about digital storytelling? Perhaps one: story without digital works, but digital without story doesn't.

Part I

Storytelling, Education, and the New Media

1

Confessions of a Digital Storytelling Teacher

Twenty Revelations About Digital Storytelling in Education

Once upon a time, long ago, during the early, dark days of the digital age (circa 1980), when the Internet was a secret information club for government officials, icons were religious symbols, and iPods were something peas came in, the early adopters of digital technology began using the crude tools of their day to create what we now recognize as digital stories.

Decades later, most of us are involved in digital storytelling (DST), often unconsciously, as we use the powerful new tools we take for granted to satisfy our ancient need to give voice to our narrative. Digital stories are simply the latest manifestation of one of humankind's oldest activities: storytelling. As we are continually swept away by the latest wave of leading-edge innovation, it's reassuring to know that some things don't change. From the age of prehistoric cave dwellers to the age of postmodern computer digitalists, our need to tell stories is one of those things.

My Cell Phone Tells Stories

In fact, the only thing I know for certain about the technologies that await us in the future is that we will find ways to tell stories with them. The cell phone clipped to my belt is a good case in point. When it rings, it plays music I created while displaying a slide show that tells a simple story of a trip my wife and I took in southeast Alaska. There is no question that this is something very new. In fact, if I had told people 25 years ago that I would have such a thing 25 years hence, most would have told me I was crazy. Three hundred years ago, and I would have been burned at the stake for being a witch.

But the fact that I have found a way to use my cell phone to tell a story should also seem ancient, predictable, and comforting. We are, above all, storytelling creatures who use stories to do many essential things, like teach each other practical skills, build communities, entertain ourselves, make peace with the world, and cultivate a sense of personal identity. Technologies will come and go, but stories are forever. And as we shall see, in many senses what makes stories effective has also been very consistent throughout the ages, a fact that can help ground us when engaging in a form of storytelling that involves a lot of potentially distracting technology. Part II of this book addresses how to tell an effective story, a skill that will only become more important as the technology becomes more powerful.

> **Revelation #1**
>
> I know only one thing for certain about the technologies that await us in the future: we will find ways to tell stories with them.

▓ The Early Days of Digital Storytelling

Even though we were telling stories with digital technology in the early days of the information age, it wasn't easy. I think it's fair to say that early microcomputers weren't story friendly. The Apple IIe computers that my students and I were using in the early 1980s booted up in the BASIC programming language. That is, when you turned them on, a cursor sat there blinking at you, waiting for you to write lines of programming code to create a computer application from scratch. There was a good deal that needed to be created, because software as we know it today didn't really exist then.

> **Revelation #2**
>
> The digital revolution would have been a storytelling revolution if early computers had booted up in a word processor instead of a programming language.

▓ Imagine Computers Without Software

It's hard to imagine, but in the early 1980s there wasn't really much software! The tool software that we take for granted today, like word processors, spreadsheets, and image-editing programs, were still far into the future. But even though programming was a calling few of us had, that didn't stop me from using computers as storytelling machines. One of the first computer assignments I gave my high school students was to write a computer program that told a story about the values and principles that guided their lives. Despite clunky keyboards, fuzzy screens, and truly inelegant software, the light of their stories shone through. I have been involved with DST since the earliest days of personal computing, and although the tools have changed dramatically over the years, the nature of a good story—as well as the need to tell a good story—has not.

▓ An Age of Assistive Technology Dawns

Revelation #3

Digital technology is assistive technology for the artistically challenged.

I like to think of the tools of the digital age as being "assistive technologies for the artistically challenged." They give the rest of us who didn't learn how to use a typewriter or play a piano or wield a paintbrush a chance to tell a story.

In fact, if I had to summarize the digital age in a sentence it would be this: Finally, we all get to tell our own story in our own way. Digital cameras, painting programs, music keyboards, and word processors—as well as all those technologies just around the corner that we can't even imagine right now—give us new ways to personalize the methods of self-expression. We get to explore new communication forms with relative impunity, because we can try out an idea and then, through the miracle of editing, change our minds, something that's hard to do using a typewriter or a paintbrush. And thanks to Web 2.0 (O'Reilly)—the name often used to describe the current evolutionary status of the Internet as a distributed, collaborative, participatory commons— we have an international stage for the stories we tell.

Revelation #4

The digital revolution in a sentence: Finally, we all get to tell our own story in our own way.

▓ Art Finds Its Place as the Fourth R

In fact, it's largely because of the Internet and the need for an international Esperanto for our global village that art is becoming the fourth R and "story" is becoming a key format for global communication. Because we now expect students to produce multimedia homework assignments, including Web pages, PowerPoint presentations, and digital stories, the language of art and design is taking center stage. Once a hard sell to a practical public, art is becoming as important for workplace success and personal fulfillment as the other three R's.

Revelation #5

Art is the fourth R.

For more about this, I invite you to go to the Art the 4th R Web site (www.jasonohler.com/fourthr).

Seeing the Digital Revolution Through the Creative Process

Do you know those moments in your life when suddenly everything changes? Like when you realize that your parents were actually your age at one time? Or the pet you love will someday leave you and go to pet heaven? Being a DST teacher has provided a number of such moments that have changed me deeply and irrevocably, as a teacher, friend, researcher, citizen, creative content developer, and digital humanist.

First, a little background.

Fuzzy Screens and Loud Keyboards

In 1981 I encountered my first personal computers as a teacher. They weren't really computers; they were more like small army tanks. Their keyboards sounded like jackhammers, and the monitors were so fuzzy that people with perfect vision thought they needed glasses. But they worked and provided the beginning of an exciting journey in the development of personal expression tools. The distance we have come in just two decades has been miraculous.

While I have welcomed the increased expression that the evolution of graphic, audiovisual, and other tools have brought to DST students, many years ago I realized something very interesting: as the technology became stronger, many of my students' stories became weaker. Some students seemed to have an intuitive grasp of using new technology powerfully and artfully, while others didn't. In fact, for them the story components of their digital stories were getting worse. I could hear the words of my teacher Marshall McLuhan as held forth in the classroom echoing in my mind: technology is an amplifier.

McLuhan Is Ever Present

On the upside, a car amplifies our backs by allowing us to carry more; it amplifies our feet by allowing us to travel faster; it amplifies our night vision by giving us headlights. But on the downside, it amplifies our ability to pollute, generate noise, and ignore our immediate surroundings because we move way too fast to interact with them. Technology amplifies the upside and the downside of what it is to be human. And what I was watching in my DST class was a good example of the upsides and downsides of technology in action.

As a teacher, my immediate concern was to help those who were struggling. As I worked with them, a revelation hit me like a ton of bits: if you

> **Revelation #6**
>
> What happens when you give a bad guitar player a bigger amplifier?

don't have a good story to tell, the technology just makes it more obvious. Or to put this in language that anyone who grew up during the 1960s (and beyond) can relate to, What happens when you give a bad guitar player a bigger amplifier?

Don't get me wrong—I really enjoyed music in the 1960s. But a lot of it was loud and pretty bad. I know because I contributed to it. I formed my first band in 1965 when I was 12. We were called Jason and the Argonauts. We were loud. And we were beyond bad.

▓ Finding the Story, Despite the Technology

It became my goal many years ago as a DST teacher to make sure that I wasn't enabling the technophile at the expense of the storyteller in my students. That is, I wanted to make sure that my

> **Revelation #7**
>
> It is the special responsibility of teachers to ensure that students use technology to serve the story and not the other way around.

students knew what a good story was before they sat down behind all the wonderfully empowering and distracting technology they had at their disposal. I began by incorporating storytelling basics into every class in which telling a story was a focus. I even brought in an oral storyteller to help my students learn how to tell stories in front of people in traditional oral fashion. I then helped my students transition from oral to digital stories, applying the tools in service of the story rather than vice versa. And lo, the quality of my students' digital stories rose dramatically. As a result of this discovery, I have included some form of storytelling training in my DST workshops ever since.

▓ The Importance of Learning Communities

Naturally, I wanted to tell others about my discovery. One day, as I was trying to explain my experiences to a group of educators, I realized I was using stories to do so. When educators pushed back on my ideas, they did so

> **Revelation #8**
>
> Learning communities are storytelling communities.

by telling me stories, most of which, from their perspective, were failure stories about trying new technology and teaching techniques. No one was quoting research; instead, everyone was telling stories.

That's when another revelation hit me: learning communities are primarily storytelling communities. Stories permeate our social fabric and have the primary function of teaching others, whether formally or informally. When you get right down to it, much of the communication that transpires among people, whether in classrooms, offices, living rooms, or the online communities that permeate the Internet, consists of telling stories. I began to see and hear stories all around me, like a kind of social, emotional, psychological, and spiritual air we all breathed to stay alive. It become clear to me that our dependence on stories was deep and pervasive and that storytelling with technology merely amplified that fact.

The next revelation came shortly thereafter and had to do with our relationship with information flow in the digital age in two respects: the rate of information change and the inherent conflictual nature of the information we consume in the "infosphere," that great amalgam of information resources (the Internet, TV, radio, etc.) in which we are immersed and which we take for granted—a lot like air. These points deserve some attention.

⚑ Lifelong Learning and the Prodigious Rate of Information Change

There is a relatively new term in wide use today that is directly related to the accelerated rate of change of life in the digital age: lifelong learning. It implies that we can never stop learning, because the rate of change won't let us. But the fact is that lifelong learning has always been a way of life. Even 50 years ago, people were learning all the time. However, the rate of change was much slower, and therefore the need to learn new things was far less demanding. When little changes, there is little to learn. The slow rate of change assured the status quo a position of supremacy in the scheme of things.

But not anymore. Because the Internet and traditional media forms like radio, TV, newspapers, and magazines continue to crank like there's no tomorrow, lifelong learning has become a pervasive, immediate, and ongoing lifestyle. The result is that the attitude has become the aptitude. That is, your attitude toward learning new things—as well as your willingness to let go of obsolete information—plays an important role in determining your aptitude and intelligence. Digital storytelling represented one of those areas that tested educators' attitudes about the

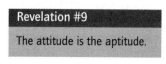

Revelation #9

The attitude is the aptitude.

nature of learning not only in terms of tools but also in terms of the kinds of literacy and classroom communities they wanted to support. For the unadventurous, DST was at best a confusing waste of time, at worst, a serious threat to the status quo. It's all a matter of attitude.

⚑ Information Conflict Leads to Story Diversity

Information 50 years ago not only changed more slowly but was also much less conflictual in nature. The information we consumed from the very few sources we had access to fit much better into a consistent schema of how life worked. Want to know how to behave? Pick up a newspaper, watch *Leave It to Beaver* on one of the three channels of network television available to you, talk to your parents. There was, compared to today, relative consistency among the social behavioral norms portrayed by the few information sources available to us. It was as though a singular world outlook had been coordinated by the few who controlled the distribution of information. If I were paranoid by nature, I would suspect conspiracy.

But that singular outlook has evaporated. The information we have access to is much more liberated and conflictual. Pick a topic, any topic, and head out into the infosphere, where you will find as many different ways to look at it as there are people who care to voice their opinion about it through Web sites, chat rooms, video cams, and the zillion other ways we exchange information. What happened to the consistent social schema our parents depended on? Gone, given way to our right to be informed, overwhelmed, and free to choose our own paths. In an age of conflictual information, being able to critically assess information, rather than trust it without question, has become a survival skill. The social expectation of children being seen but not heard has given way to the expectation that they become critical thinkers and creative problem solvers largely because the conflictual nature of information demands it.

▩ People in Conflict Need to Tell Their Stories

An automatic result of living with information conflict in the digital age is our need to tell stories. As we shall see later in this book, the heartbeat of most good stories is conflict resolution. As each of us struggles to make sense out of the cacophony of information that bombards us, the need to construct personal, clarifying narrative that is connected to the world we live in becomes critical. In story parlance, each one of us needs to become the hero of our own life story in which cutting through the clutter of the infosphere becomes our quest as we resolve the issues that face us. In the process we can expect to spend lots of time and energy slaying the multiheaded dragons of fear, ignorance, and distraction.

Thus, it became clear to me that "the story" had become the metaphor for our time—not just for education, business, and entertainment, but also for our personal lives as we adapt to life in the digital age. The same story structure that frames much of our popular media can be used to understand and resolve conflict, mine opportunities, and overcome obstacles.

Revelation #10

Stories help us make sense out of the chaos of life.

⚍ Stories Help Us Survive

In other words, stories are more than just good for us—they are essential to survival. I have come to believe, on a very basic level that feels biological to me, that we need stories. Without them, life is just too overwhelming to piece together from scratch each day. Stories allow us to take snippets of life and put them together in ways that make it possible for us to learn and remember new things. They give communities coherence and our lives meaning. They make order out of what would otherwise be the ongoing chaos of life and help each of us create a sense of personal identity in relation to our communities and the world in which we live. In short, storytelling is far more than entertainment. It's a set of practical processes that can be adapted to a wide range of issues, both personal and professional.

> **Revelation #11**
>
> Story provides a powerful metaphor, framework, and set of practical processes for resolving issues, educating ourselves, and pursuing our goals.

For an educator, understanding story as a structure and process with practical benefits has profound implications. The story form becomes a way to shape curricula, build units of instruction, and frame academic arguments. Above all, stories become the cornerstone of constructivist learning, in which students become heroes of their own learning adventures. This happens academically, with students building stories around academic pursuits. But it also happens personally. One of the most powerful stories a teacher can have students tell is the story of their future selves, in which they become heroes of the lives they want to live. If they are not heroes of their lives, then they become victims of them. Helping students understand this will pay dividends for a lifetime.

> **Revelation #12**
>
> Students need to become heroes of their own learning stories as well as of the stories they tell with their own lives.

⚍ Stories Organize Information

It was the practical value of storytelling that ultimately led me to see its utility as a learning tool. Story's structure and rhythm, as well as the emotional involvement it encourages, can help us remember important information that might be forgotten if it's delivered to us in the form of reports, lectures, or isolated bits of information. It is precisely this quality of story, covered in detail in Part II, that makes it so useful as an information organizer. While this quality has always been a hallmark of stories, it's particularly poignant now because we desperately need tools to navigate and coordinate the immense amount of information available to us.

> **Revelation #13**
>
> Stories help us remember.

▦ Stories Can Be Dangerous

But stories come with a price. Because engaging with them demands that we willingly suspend our disbelief (Coleridge), we let our guard down and tend to consume the story experience with little critical assessment. In fact, a successful story is one that essentially hypnotizes us. When we look up from the movie we have been watching or the novel we have been reading and realize that two hours have passed, we rightfully consider this the hallmark of a successful story. For entertainment, this is fine. But for education, we need more than hypnosis. We need intellectual engagement.

> **Revelation #14**
>
> Combining storytelling and critical thinking defines an important pedagogical frontier.

To illuminate this potential danger of story, Apple Fellow Alan Kay (1996) compares going to the theater with attending a political rally. The two experiences look similar—they both have orators, happen on a stage, and employ theatrical production values. But whereas we need to suspend our disbelief at the theater, we want to do the opposite at the rally. We want our critical judgment in high gear at the rally, asking all sorts of questions about what is really going on. If we asked the same questions while watching a play, it would ruin the experience.

Clearly we need to blend the power and engagement of storytelling with the skills and perspective that insight and critical assessment offer. In fact, blending these two educational strategies is one of the most exciting pedagogical frontiers that awaits us. We need to engage all of ourselves—left brain and right brain, researcher and narrator, critical thinker and storyteller/ listener. Doing so offers the power to engage and educate in ways that resonate with the media culture our students understand while providing them the tools necessary to navigate within it wisely.

▦ Digital Storytelling Allows Today's Students to Speak in Their Own Language

In fact, it's in the academic arena that the greatest potential for DST lies, primarily because it provides digital natives (Prensky, 2001) an opportunity to speak their own language. Students inhabit a largely oral and digital world, then sit in classrooms where the printed word is the primary medium in play. Digital storytelling allows them to express content-area understanding in ways that are familiar. I have seen digital stories that do everything from explain math, science, and literature concepts to illuminate the interior landscapes of cultural, artistic, and personal

> **Revelation #15**
>
> Digital stories allow today's students to pursue academic content in their own language.

perspective. Students today are not the passive media consumers of the past. While they consume their share of TV, they also use the Internet to develop and share original video, photography, music, chatter, and other digital creations. For many, digital is the language they speak, media is the environment in which they feel comfortable, and the multimedia collage is the new global language. For them, Web 2.0 is a highly creative social space.

Along with the development of content understanding, digital storytellers also develop planning skills that are immensely useful and transferable. Digital stories require students to create storyboards, story maps, scripts, media lists, and other planning products that have wide application. They require students to engage in what those in the creative content world call "the media production process," a process (covered in detail in Part III) that can be applied to any endeavor that involves creating, editing, and sharing original work. Media production is not something that works if students shoot from the hip. It requires them to zoom out, slow down, take the long view, and ask themselves, "Where am I going and what steps do I need to take to get there?" Most important, the media production process requires students to synthesize imagination, creativity, research, and critical thinking in order to translate their ideas into some form of media-based expression. The personal growth that occurs during this process is as profound as it is practical.

> **Revelation #16**
>
> Digital storytelling helps students develop planning skills that are transferable to many endeavors.

❊ It's All About Literacy

The next two revelations have to do with literacy. Simply put, I have found no better vehicle for blending traditional and emerging literacy development than DST. With DST, good old-fashioned, clear, expository writing is key. "If it ain't on the page, then it ain't on the stage" is as true of a digital story as it is of a movie or Broadway play. Many teachers have told me that media projects are a great way to sneak writing in under the radar. Students who have no taste for the planning and execution of an essay attack the planning and narration of a digital story with gusto.

My approach to DST also involves, whenever possible, other literacies such as art and speaking, as well as writing and digital production. The actual digital story is the tip of the iceberg, below which are a number of artifacts for the assessment of literacy, including planning documents, scripted narratives, treatments, storyboards, and self-assessments, as well as music, art, taped oral presentations, and other prized examples of student

> **Revelation #17**
>
> Digital stories combine traditional and emerging literacies, engaging otherwise reluctant students in literacy development.

work. A digital story project can literally be a portfolio unto itself of great depth and breadth.

❧ Understanding Media Persuasion

Digital storytelling is also an effective vehicle for teaching another kind of literacy that is becoming increasingly important as our students spend more and more time in a media-saturated culture: media literacy. While there is a good deal of debate about what media literacy is, I define it simply as having the skills necessary to recognize, evaluate, and apply the persuasive techniques of media.

Our students live in a world overwhelmed by story-based media that often view them in terms of commercial market share. For that reason, we want students not only to learn with media but also to learn about media. We want students to understand that the difference between a successful story and an effective advertisement is largely one of purpose. This is true whether students are using just print or the full arsenal of digital tools at their disposal. In the words of Steve Goodman (2003), "Media is a filter while pretending to be a clear window" (p. 6). We want students to understand how a filter can be made to seem like a window.

> **Revelation #18**
>
> Digital story creation offers an effective means to teach media literacy.

The reality is that until students become persuaders themselves, the persuasion of media remains hidden to them. Digital story development provides powerful media-literacy learning opportunities when teachers involve students in the analysis of media technique and grammar and can relate it to other media in their lives. Doing so helps students detect how and when they are themselves being persuaded. In much the same way that we want students to be effective writers because it helps them become better communicators and critical thinkers, we want them to be effective media users so that they can tell their story and understand the true nature of the stories that others are telling them.

❧ Creativity: The Most Practical Skill of All

The next revelation has to do with creativity, that touchstone of the human experience that seems to come in and out of favor in the world of education as often as wide ties do in the world of fashion. On the one hand, it seems to be out of place in the world of No Child Left Behind and standardized testing. This induces parents, teachers, and school boards to devalue it. On the other hand, there seems to be a general understanding that students who do not cultivate imagination and creativity have very limited options in our innovation-driven world.

> **Revelation #19**
>
> Digital storytelling helps students develop creativity and innovation skills needed to solve important problems in imaginative ways.

After 25 years in educational technology it's my belief that the heart and soul of success in the digital age—both personal and professional—lie in understanding that digital technology provides one of the greatest imagination creativity amplifiers humankind has ever designed. To use new media technology to do the work of previous generations is to miss the opportunities that it presents in education, the workplace, and our personal lives.

To date, I haven't seen an activity that allows students to blend design, creativity, thoughtful expression, and technology skills as well as DST does. It compels students to think out of the box while focusing on goals that have real human value. It brings out the practical artist in students while helping them to practice creativity as a skill that is marketable, personally rewarding, and good for the communities in which they live. If you want to encourage your students to think creatively while demonstrating their ability to communicate and solve problems, DST is an extremely effective way to do so.

Teachers Are More Important Than Ever

The last revelation has to do with helping teachers find their bearings in the digital age classroom. As a way to stimulate discussion about new media production among teachers, quite often I will show them a sampling of digital stories created by students and peers. While some teachers are genuinely excited and interested in what they see, there are always those who are moved to call their retirement system to find out when they can leave the profession. It is my fervent hope that they don't leave. Their students need them now more than ever.

> **Revelation #20**
>
> Technology doesn't make teachers obsolete. Quite the opposite. More than ever, students need the guidance and wisdom that teachers offer to help them use technology with care and to tell their stories with clarity and humanity.

It's not important that teachers be advanced technicians. Their students will cover that for them. Students have the luxury of time and well-developed informal learning communities to keep up on the latest and greatest happenings in the technology world. What is important is that teachers be advanced managers of their students' talents, time, and productivity. They need to be the guide on the side rather than the technician magician.

The idea that technology is making teachers obsolete is 180 degrees wrong. More than ever, students need teachers who can help them sort through choices, apply technology wisely, and tell their stories clearly and with humanity. More than ever, students living in the overwhelming and often distracting world of technical possibility need the clear voice of a teacher who can help guide them through the learning process. More than ever, students will need teachers for their wisdom. And what sage advice do I recommend teachers give to their DST students? Focus on story first, technology second, and everything will fall into place.

2

Defining and Discussing Digital Storytelling

Helping Teachers See, Think, and Talk About Digital Storytelling

Defining Digital Story

Ohler's axiom of vagueness states that combining two vague, expansive concepts produces something that is at best only slightly less vague and expansive than either one individually. Such is the case with combining "digital" and "story." "Digital" refers to literally anything associated with the information age, and "story" means so many things to so many people that it defies strict definition. Combining the two terms covers a good deal of territory and evokes the following description rather than definition: digital storytelling (DST) uses personal digital technology to combine a number of media into a coherent narrative.

As we see DST play out in classrooms, the following characteristics are also usually implied: digital stories in education are typically driven by an academic goal, use low-end technology that is commonly available

> **How big is Story?**
>
> Ask your coworkers to tell you the first thing that comes to mind when you say the word "story." I did, and here's what they said: fairy tale, excuse for not doing something, news, you (apparently because I tell lots of stories), great book I just read, movie I saw, trying to get out of trouble, too confusing, important to Native culture, floor of a building, how we learn, cucumber (huh?), what's personal and important to me, never ending (the arc). It's unanimous: story is big!

15

to students, and usually are in the form of short (two- to four-minute) quasi movies that an audience watches via computer or other digital means.

Later in this chapter I describe a number of stories, most of which use a very common DST format: voice-over narration supported by still pictures, music, and titles, reminiscent of a Ken Burns documentary. But others use video performance, animation, and other technologies and techniques. At the end of this chapter I take a look at the future of DST and how new technological developments and evolving social needs will impact the development of this field.

⬚ Digital Storytelling and New Media Narrative

Within the discussion of DST in this book, I use another term: "new media." This is a broad-reaching term that roughly refers to any digital media production beyond print: video, image development, audio production, and basically all of the things we have been creating with microcomputers for the past 20 years, with the possible exception of simple word processed documents. Basically, the word of new media is the world of multimedia.

I think it's fair to say that while every digital story qualifies as a new media production, not every new media production is a digital story. The key determinant is *story* and what it means to you as a teacher and audience member. In turn, how you define story will shape the requirements you want to establish for the digital stories you assign students to create. In Part II, I cover guidelines for creating effective stories in some detail, regardless of the media you use, which should prove helpful in addressing this issue.

There is also a third term I use that I often find more helpful in describing the world of personal media production than DST: "new media narrative." Narrative is a bit broader in its implications than story and captures better the diverse nature of the world of individual media expression. And whereas the word "digital" implies technical methodology, the word "media" more importantly implies expressing oneself before an audience. Furthermore, the term "new media" captures the decentralized spirit of the current revolution, in which media production and distribution is available to the general public. But I elected to use the term "digital storytelling" in this book because it's recognizable to so many. However, it's all new media narrative to me.

⬚ Teachers Talk About Digital Storytelling

To many teachers, the rapid evolution of digital technology is both exciting and inspiring, as well as intimidating and confusing. As teachers watch students create new media with handheld technology, navigate the "tEcosystem" with ease, and treat today's technology like intelligent furniture, they struggle to understand their role in their students' lives. This is why I try to create a space for teachers during my workshops to simply talk about their hopes and fears about student media production in education. They usually welcome the opportunity, noting that while they know how important the topic is, there is very little time or encouragement to discuss it within their professional environments.

> **tEcosystem:**
> Ecosystem with a T. It's the ecosystem created by humans consisting of digital technology, connectivity, and the flow of communication they facilitate.

It's important to note that most teachers who attend my workshops are creating their first and last digital story. I've found that most come to learn enough to be helpful to their students and to be able to understand DST as a classroom activity rather than as a technical event—both very laudable goals. That is why discussing the value and limitations of DST is so important.

To facilitate their dialogue, I usually begin workshops by showing a series of student- or teacher-developed projects that have been identified as digital stories or new media productions by their creators. After each showing, I ask teachers to do a "quick write" focused on the following questions, with their responses serving as the basis for the discussion that follows:

> *What are your overall impressions of what you just saw?* This encourages them to see digital stories openly, free from "shoulds" about what a piece of new media ought to look like.
>
> *How could it be used in education?* This encourages them to see digital stories within the context of education in general terms.
>
> *How would you assess what you saw?* This encourages them to see them in practical terms as a classroom teacher who needs to determine their utility in meeting curricular objectives.

Most participants have never had an opportunity to look at new media production in a focused, reflective manner among colleagues. Conversations are fascinating, insightful, and often spirited. Most conversations focus in some way on the topic of assessing digital stories. That is, teachers want to understand how to evaluate new media in ways that make sense to them and their students within the professional contexts of their school, district, and state and federal mandates.

▓ Digital Story Examples

What follows are descriptions of some of the digital stories I show during workshops. Following the descriptions, I will try to capture a number of the more interesting and helpful discussions I've had with teachers about these stories in particular and about the nature and utility of new media production in the classroom in general terms.

❈ Fox Becomes a Better Person

This story was created and performed by Hannah, a fourth grader in the Native immersion program in Juneau, Alaska. It's a story about a fox who was too mean to have friends and who turned to the neighborhood dove for personal counseling. Hannah's performance was videotaped in front of a green wall, which allowed her original crayon artwork to be added behind her in postproduction using the same kind of chroma-key editing used in weather shows and professional cinema production, like any of the Harry Potter movies. The result is Hannah telling her story in front of her own artwork. It is interesting to note that had all of the technology failed, the project still would have been successful as a performance. However, the students would not have had any of the digital or media literacy opportunities that chroma-key editing provided. Length: Five minutes.

❈ A Day at School

A student with severe physical challenges narrates an average day at school presented as a series of pictures that she has asked others to take of her. Because of her disabilities, she is unable to speak unaided, so her voice-over narration comes through a message communication system. Emotional instrumental music plays throughout the entire piece. Length: One minute.

❈ My Piano

A teacher tells the story of what the piano has meant to her throughout her life, beginning with her parents requiring her to learn to play the piano as a child, largely against her will, and ending with her feelings of gratitude toward her parents for making music a part of her life. She used scanned images, old photos, and herself playing simple piano music as she narrated the story. Length: Four minutes.

❈ Super Bugs

To demonstrate their understanding of drug-resistant bacteria called super bugs, two students created a digital story in which Bobbi tries to discover why he can't manage to shake his illness despite treatment from his doctor. It turns out that Bobbi did not complete his full course of antibiotics and has created a colony of super bugs that are resistant to his medication. Bobbi's doctor explains how super bugs are created and ends with this admonition: don't mess around with antibiotics. The students used graphs and scientific illustrations that were narrated by a conversation between the two of them. Length: Four minutes.

▓ School Train

Glen Bledsoe's fourth graders created this in response to a language arts assignment requiring them to show that they understood the concept of metaphor. In this unique new media project, the students used sophisticated music and editing techniques as they compared going to school with riding on a train. The narrative is challenging because it doesn't so much tell a story as simply present the similarities between the two experiences, rather matter of factly and with no sense of plot or expectation. The unusual music and use of graphics gives the feeling of being on a train. It's the kind of media piece that tends to either excite traditional educators about education in the digital age or inspire them to consider retirement. Narration is told by a number of students in both English and Spanish. Length: Four minutes.

▓ Next Exit

This is by Dana Atchley, one of the original founders of the digital story movement who tragically died in 2000 but left behind a body of work and a legacy that help define the possibilities of DST. On the Web, *Next Exit* is an interactive digital story, which allows viewers to choose between a number of stories Dana tells about his life. I saw a video recording of a live performance of *Next Exit* in which Dana told stories in traditional oral fashion while a computer-generated environment that he created played behind him. Of particular note was a digitally produced campfire, creating a high-tech version of an old-time campfire storytelling experience. Length: Variable, because it's user driven.

▓ Making a Ball Roll

This was created by fourth-grade mathematics students at Mollala Elementary School under the direction of technology teacher Glen Bledsoe. The students used animation software to create a story about how to make a ball roll on a beach. As the story unfolds, the narration explains a problem that has occurred: the ball skids along the sand instead of rolling. The students clearly explain their error and describe how they developed a more mathematically sound approach to their project. In the end, the ball rolls. The animation is accompanied by subtle background music. The voice-over narration is told by a number of students. Animation includes creating a beach and the rolling ball, as well as drawing mathematical models. Length: Two minutes.

Creative Awakening

This is a personal journey through two decades of wrestling with the ebb and flow of personal creativity in the storyteller's life that leads to the eventual rediscovery of the artist within. The storyteller used still images, including a number of images of her artwork, voice-over narration, and standard kinds of titling and transitions. No music was added, which, counterintuitively, actually adds to the story's power. Length: Eight minutes.

Eddie the Grape

A story about how Eddie the Grape and his friends rescue Grandpa Grape, who gets scooped up by a cereal company. The characters in the story are actually green grapes sporting faces drawn with magic marker. The format is a series of still images of the grapes, and voice-over narration. It's light, fun, and interesting. Length: Five minutes.

My Life

This story is told by a teenager in drug recovery who struggles to live with a parent who also has substance abuse problems. One day she's on a hike and witnesses one animal attacking another and compares herself to being the animal who loses the fight. This compelling piece uses still images, voice-over narration, and music from her generation. Length: Two minutes.

Dialoguing About Digital Stories—What Teachers Talk About

For most teachers, watching the stories is largely an exercise in seeing. They find themselves confronted by truly new material that challenges their preconceptions about student work in content areas. As a result they struggle, often enthusiastically, to grasp what they are watching.

The conversations that follow viewing the stories are often filled with the feelings associated with discovering new territory: excitement about being in a foreign land, anxiety about not understanding the native language, in this case the language of media, and frustration as they struggle to remain open-minded. It is my job to act as a guide, explaining digital stories in terms of their historical perspective, points of interest, component parts, and connections with their own personal and professional lives.

I've grouped the discussion topics into three categories: (1) story type, purpose, or impact, (2) story elements, and (3) story production. A continuum accompanies each topic that describes a range of consideration. In all cases the traits represent questions teachers can ask themselves or perspectives they can consider before assigning a DST project to their students. While these traits overlap and can often defy strict definition, they have great utility in terms of helping teachers frame what it is they are seeking in student projects and what is desirable and manageable within the constraints of their curricula and classrooms.

Category 1: Story Type, Purpose, or Impact

Given the need to have digital stories driven by academic goals, teachers talked about the different kinds of stories they watched and how seeing stories in terms of their type, purpose, or overall impact could help them determine how to approach DST in content areas. What follows are the basic topic areas that emerged from that discussion.

Essay Versus Poem

I've found that the most important aspect of a DST assignment that teachers need to address when articulating project expectations can be summarized symbolically by the following question: Are students expected to create an essay, a poem, or something in between?

Clear, like an essay	Where? ▼	Challenging, like a poem
	← ——————————————→	

The significance of essay versus poem as it's used here has to do with audience expectation. Readers expect essayists to work hard to make their points clearly so that they can read without interruption. Good prose should pass through the eyes and into the mind fairly effortlessly on a mechanical level. That is, we may be challenged by the ideas but not by the writing. On the other hand, readers expect to be challenged by poetry. When we read poetry, we often assume we'll need to read things more than once, and that ambiguity and imagery, frowned upon in essay writing, are often used by poets to convey insight and meaning. In short, we expect to work harder to understand a poem than we do to understand an essay. Thus, the continuum for this trait is bounded by "clear, like an essay" on one end and "challenging, like a poem" on the other.

Bottom line: If students are creating a digital story as an essay, then assessment simplifies tremendously: if the story is not intelligible to the evaluator, then it needs more work, regardless of whether or not the creator agrees. However, we always have to keep in mind that unlike the written language, which has had centuries to evolve in terms of syntax and expression, new media expression is in a constant state of flux. Thus teachers also need to decide how much of the responsibility they want to assume in not understanding material presented via digital story. If students are writing "poetry" as the metaphor has been used here, then teachers need to use other assessment yardsticks, presumably with more latitude.

⚏ Choosing Your Metaphor or Genre

To help orient teachers to the world of DST, I sometimes ask them to choose the appropriate metaphor for each story we watch. Is the digital story a historical documentary? A short action movie? A teaching story? A fantasy? A visual poem? A personal story? *Super Bugs* is pretty much a teaching story. *Eddie the Grape* is a short action movie. *A Day at School* and *My Piano* are both personal stories, although *My Piano* also functions as a documentary, and so on. Identifying a metaphor allows teachers to use some of the tools they have already developed when assessing student work created with more traditional media. Thinking in terms of metaphor can also be helpful when aligning story type with curricular goals. A theme that runs throughout my workshops is that digital stories are very new adaptations of an ancient activity. Seeing what is old is a safe and instructive place to start.

Another way to view metaphor is in terms of genre. In *Story,* the bible of aspiring screenwriters, author McKee (1997) says that when writing a movie story, writers have to select a genre and stay within it or else risk audience alienation. That is, a serious murder mystery can't suddenly turn into a hilarious farce, an action movie can't suddenly morph completely into a romantic comedy, and so on. The same is roughly true for digital stories. Genre consistency helps create an effective story.

Bottom line: Thinking about project requirements in terms of metaphor or genre can help teachers focus on the best way for students to approach creating a story for digital production. Having students identify a metaphor or genre in the planning stages of story development provides a handy metric for teachers to use to determine whether students are on track.

Resonant Versus Nonresonant Stories

One of my favorite questions to ask teachers after watching a digital story is simply, "So, how did that work for you as a story?"

It's a trick question, of course, because story means different things to different people. But conversations typically merge on the idea of resonance in one form or another.

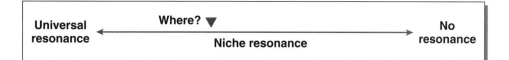

Simply put, a story resonates when others can relate to it. While a story may involve experiences that are completely foreign to listeners, it can still act as a lens that helps listeners see themselves more clearly. In short, a story resonates when it reminds listeners of their own stories. This is certainly the case with *A Day at School* and *My Life,* though their struggles often made mine seem insignificant. *My Piano* tends to remind everyone of something their parents made them do for which they are now grateful. *Creative Awakening* stimulates reflection about following our own path of awakening, and so on.

Stories might resonate because they are universal, a concept discussed in Part II. If that is the case, then, by definition, they should resonate with everyone. Sometimes in workshops I find this to be the case. But other times, a story resonates with some and not with others—a kind of niche resonance. This helps define the audience that can relate to and benefit from the story.

Bear in mind that stories can satisfy listeners for reasons other than resonance, such as simply being interesting or helpful. But resonance is linked to memorability. When a story resonates, it tends to stick with us long after we hear it.

Bottom line: Memorable stories resonate by allowing listeners to relate to them. When assigning digital stories to students, teachers need to decide whether resonance—universal or niche—is important and, if so, how to determine whether resonance has been achieved. In the section on story elements, I discuss a number of the story qualities that can contribute to resonance.

Story Versus Report

Earlier I noted that one of the hallmarks of a good story is that you don't really notice it, at least not while you're watching it. This begs the question, What is the role of active, critical thinking in the pedagogy of storytelling? In fact, combining the engagement of stories with the reflection encouraged by less emotionally involving kinds of media, such as reports and essays, is one of the most exciting and interesting challenges facing teaching digital age students. As students blend storytelling and analysis, they will have the best of both worlds. Bear in mind that engagement may be in full play as students research reports, just as analysis may be a key component in developing a story. In this trait I'm talking about story presentation, not preparation.

As teachers discussed this aspect of DST, I recommended that they not think about story versus report in either-or terms, because most school media projects have the potential to be some combination of the two. Instead, it's more effective to think about media in terms of where they fall on the continuum shown here. *My Life* is a documentary with first-person reflection, *Super Bugs* is a story designed to report about a particular medical phenomenon, *Making a Ball Roll* could have been just a report, but because the students encountered a mystery they had to solve, was part story, and so on.

Incidentally, this continuum can also be used to frame discussions of professional media, especially the news. Ideally, if the goal of news is a presentation of the facts, then it should be all report and no story. Yet most of us wouldn't watch news that was presented in such a manner. What does this say about the nature of reporting that we depend on for our window into the world?

Bottom line: When planning student media projects, it can be helpful for teachers to identify a point on the continuum that they want students to aim for: Half report/half story? All story? Mostly story, but with academic information embedded in the plot? Similarly, when students analyze media, it can be helpful to have them identify where on the continuum particular media pieces fall. As a rule of thumb, I advise teachers who are interested in academic storytelling to aim for the middle of the continuum, combining the engagement of the story form with the application of academic focus in equal measure.

Passive Viewing Versus Active Viewing

Another way to frame the discussion of critical thinking and media production is passive viewing versus active media viewing from the story listener's perspective. Passive viewing can be thought of as story mode, or to others, entertainment mode, in which students view media without reflection, both during and afterward.

Active viewing is the opposite and typically involves engaging students in the following ways: (1) assigning them questions to address based on the viewing, (2) requiring them to take notes during the viewing, (3) providing them time to reflect on and write about the assigned questions directly following the viewing, and (4) engaging them in a class discussion following their reflective writing. Active viewing feels very much like an unnatural act for TV watchers, but it opens up a more effective way to mine video, movie, and television material for academic utility. Teachers may want to consider where on the viewing continuum they want students' projects to fall when creating digital stories from the listener's perspective.

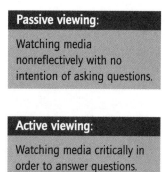

Passive viewing: Watching media nonreflectively with no intention of asking questions.

Active viewing: Watching media critically in order to answer questions.

Bottom line: Decide whether you want students to create a story that is intended to be actively viewed. If so, include the development of active viewing questions as part of the assignment.

Teaching About Myself Versus Myself Teaching About Something

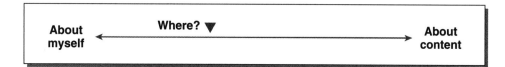

A variation of the theme "story versus report" is "teaching about myself versus myself teaching about something." Teachers are always moved by students telling personal stories in their own words and images, like *A Day at School, Creative Awakening,* and *My Life.* These kinds of stories can reflect assignments in language arts, history, geography, and culture studies. But within an educational context teachers may want students to demonstrate their understanding of content-area material, which is why I also show them "myself teaching about something" stories like *Super Bugs*, *Making a Ball Roll*, and *School Train*. These kinds of stories seem to be of more interest to science and math teachers, who I've found are typically less likely to make a connection between storytelling and classroom activities.

Bottom line: The natural propensity is for students to tell personal stories rather than academically oriented stories. Deciding how important content is, and where on the continuum you want students to aim, can be very helpful in explaining story expectations. Also keep in mind that telling stories that are both personal and academic is an exciting academic frontier that most certainly will develop in the coming years.

❧ Category 2: Story Elements

This category addresses the story traits that teachers found important in the stories I showed them. Most of these traits will not be new to language arts teachers, as they are typically addressed in any creative writing class. They also mirror many of the digital story traits addressed by Lambert (2003) in *Digital Storytelling Cookbook and Traveling Companion*, a good source for this topic.

❧ Point of View

Teachers often note the many different points of view employed in the stories I show them. *Fox Becomes a Better Person* uses what I call third-person magical, in which animals assume human qualities and tell their story with the help of an omniscient narrator. *Making a Ball Roll* uses third-person plural as the students talk in terms of "we" doing and discovering things; *My Life* and *Creative Awakening* are told in first person in a highly personal way; *Eddie the Grape* uses the omniscient narrator; *Super Bugs* uses a didactic conversation between two people who speak in the first person; *A Day at School* is in first person with overtones of third-person narration as she reports about the events of her day; and so on.

Bottom line: The range of points of view that can be employed in digital stories is vast and is constrained only by whatever perspective teachers want to impose. Teachers may want students to create a very personal reflection in language arts class versus a more objective documentary about a local historical event in social studies. Or they may simply want to throw it open to students to choose their own point of view, as long as they meet the goals of the assignment.

Emotionally engaged ← Where? ▼ → Detached, objective

Emotional Engagement

Emotional engagement is always a topic teachers like to discuss, often emotionally, when debriefing about the stories they watch. Initially, teachers tend to have the same expectations of digital stories that they have of any media production: if they are not moved by what they watch, then the piece has failed on some level. However, I purposefully show a number of different kinds of stories, from the detached to the emotionally overwhelming, in order to help teachers expand their notion of story value.

A Day at School is overwhelmingly an emotional experience as we listen to a physically challenged elementary school student speak through a voice machine about the simple pleasures of a day at school while heart-wrenching music plays in the background. On the other end of the spectrum, *Super Bugs* is pleasant but far less emotional, aiming for engagement through content. In the middle but leaning toward the emotional end of the spectrum is *My Piano*, which engages listeners by reminding them of their struggles of being pressured by their parents to do something they didn't want to do but eventually appreciated. Also in the middle but leaning toward the less emotional end of the spectrum is *Making a Ball Roll*. Watching kids figure something out always has emotional appeal at some level. An interesting aside about this piece: the storytellers' use of music is not emotional in a typical sense but is very captivating. It's so subtle that it can generally be detected only on a second viewing.

Sometimes teachers speak in terms of emotional versus intellectual engagement. That is, some of the less emotionally engaging stories are nevertheless interesting enough to sustain their attention. To me, this translates into a story having a good story core (discussed in Part II) and the teller having enough finesse to make story listeners want to know what was going to happen next.

Bottom line: Most of us are unconsciously inclined to judge digital stories the same way we judge entertainment media—in terms of their emotional engagement. That is, the more emotionally engaging a media piece is, the better. We do this largely because most of our experience with media has been watching entertainment material in passive viewing mode. However, teachers need to determine how much emotional engagement and how much objective argument is appropriate for the projects they assign. I've been part of a number of fascinating conversations about how emotionally engaging stories *should* be, particularly in the areas of math and science. Teachers have a very real concern about whether the standards that drive consumer media should also be used for media created within an educational context. Also, teachers may want to outlaw what I call cheap shots—music or images that will evoke strong emotions regardless of the strength of the story. More about this later when I discuss the grammar of media.

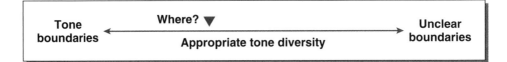

▓ Tone

Teachers typically like to talk about the different tones that are employed in the digital stories I show. *Eddie the Grape* is humorous, *My Life* is edgy, *Creative Awakening* is introspective and a bit sad, *Super Bugs* is upbeat, and so on. Teachers tend to feel that much of what would be acceptable in a writing class regarding tone is also applicable to digital stories. Usually this means that it's important that students write within tone boundaries, aiming for consistency rather than diversity in tone. Switching tones successfully within any piece of narrative is hard to do, no matter what medium is used.

Bottom line: Like working within a genre, adopting a tone provides a handy yardstick for students and teachers to use to determine whether they are on target or not. Teachers may want to have students choose a tone at the outset or simply assign students to practice storying using a particular tone: Somber? Straightforward? Detached? Introspective? Sarcastic? Funny? Gut wrenching? An interplay of one or more of these?

▓ Spoken Narrative

A fair amount of assessment talk focuses on how well the narrative worked, and with good reason: narrative in digital stories, whether spoken or performed, tends to carry the story. Incidentally, the emphasis on the narrative is nearly universal among teachers in my workshops; math teachers are just as interested in it as language arts teachers and are equally demanding about the need for focused narrative that is clear and articulate.

It's always interesting to listen to teachers compare written narrative with the spoken narrative they hear in digital stories. Some aspects carry forward easily from writing, like tone and pacing. Others do not, like inflection and mixing voice with music. Also interesting are the conversations that inevitably occur about more technical aspects of voice recording and how they impact the quality of the story. More about this in Chapter 14. All of this is relatively new territory for most teachers and is very important, given that all the digital stories I show them involve a spoken audio component, whether as voice-over narration or the audio component of a video recording. While spoken narrative is not mandatory in digital stories, it's almost always present.

The conversation also tends to address the link between written and spoken narrative and the writing opportunities that scripted narration provides. In fact, a recurring area of interest is whether scripting should be required or whether students should be allowed to just speak extemporaneously. While unscripted conversation can certainly be useful, I recommend teachers include writing whenever possible, because it encourages reflection, which results in better work. Writing also produces artifacts for assessment purposes.

Bottom line: Narrative is the foundation of most digital stories. Therefore, teachers should be interested in whether students give narrative the appropriate amount of focus in their stories. Fortunately, teachers feel comfortable focusing on its importance largely because it's an element that is shared between digital and nondigital stories. Teachers should determine how they are going to assess narrative before assigning a digital story project. I recommend that written components of a digital story be included in the story's overall portfolio.

▨ Soundtrack Music

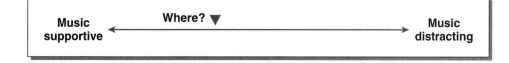

The audio component of the story usually also includes music, which introduces both opportunities and problems. On the one hand, music is very compelling. On the other, it can be so emotionally engaging all on its own that it can easily overwhelm a story, or worse, compensate for the lack of a story. Developing an overdependence on music is a convenient way for students to become lazy about articulating their stories. This is usually unconscious laziness. In their minds, the music evokes the feeling they are trying to convey. Therefore, the reflection, scripting, and story production that teachers might want to emphasize seem superfluous. But if students allow the music to generate the impact for them, then they are effectively allowing someone else to tell their story for them. Consider this interesting reference point: *Creative Awakening* is eight minutes long and is all about a personal journey to overcome personal insecurities in order to reconnect with the artist within. It uses no music at all yet is extremely powerful.

A note about music videos. If students are assigned to create music videos, rather than more traditional digital stories, then the relationship between music and narrative reverses. That is, narrative serves the music. However, in the absence of a specific musical focus, music should serve the narrative.

Bottom line: Teachers need to address how much music they will allow in the digital stories they assign and how much sway it's allowed to have over the narrative. I encourage teachers to experiment with the entire length of the continuum and especially to challenge students to use no music at all as a litmus test for the quality of their stories. Teachers should feel free to challenge students on whether they have used music in an appropriately supportive role. Also, mixing music effectively, so that it doesn't drown out the voice narrative (a common problem), should be addressed in the assignment expectations. I discuss this and other aspects of producing effective soundtracks in Chapter 14 on media grammar.

▓ Role of Video and Performance

Note that all of the digital stories I described involve the use of still images accompanied by narration and music, while only two of them have strong video-recorded performance components. The use of still images with voice-over narration, and the exclusion of video material, is a common format for digital stories for a number of reasons, including simplicity and low cost.

Performance, video info	Where? ▼	Still images, voice over

For the uninitiated, I've found that the difficulties in using video in DST can only truly be understood through direct experience. Using video tends to be more complex, time consuming, and costly to create and edit than other DST approaches, such as the use of still images and voice-over narration. As video becomes easier to use and edit, this situation will certainly change. But until it does, as a teacher you may want to limit video production simply for these reasons.

But you may also want to encourage video-recorded performance because you might want students to improve their speaking, acting, or presentation abilities. You may also want them to add speaking and performance to a portfolio to show their progress in this skill area over time. Also keep in mind that there are many sources of video other than student performances, such as interviews, community events, science experiments, and even TV and movie footage, with obvious copyright concerns (addressed in Part III).

A note about still images in digital stories. Make sure students know the gamut of still images available to them so that they can make wise choices about image use. They come in many forms—charts, graphs, original drawings and photos, scanned objects, and so on—all of which have the capacity to be useful as well as distracting. Matching media with communication goals is key.

Bottom line: Teachers should consider the kinds of visual images they want students to use and make sure they have the technology and time in their curriculum to accommodate their use. As always, the use of visuals should be driven by learning and communication goals, with particular attention paid to the decision of whether to use video. Above all, make sure the use of video provides an academic payoff that is worth the complexity it brings to the story development process.

Creativity and Originality

After showing digital stories to a group of educators, I like to ask, "Who thinks every student should be capable of this kind of media production?" Nearly every hand goes up every time. Then I ask, "How many feel you have the support to pursue that goal in your classrooms?" Very few hands go up.

Creativity, originality valued ← Where? ▼ → Not valued

The ensuing conversation often focuses on the importance of "creativity," that elusive quality that seems to be at odds with a world of standardized testing and "getting the right answer." When teachers watch digital stories, they recognize an originality of voice they don't often see in other schoolwork. They also see evidence of creativity skills important in the real world of the digital economy that are not being addressed in school.

While it might seem odd to suggest that there might be times when originality or creativity shouldn't be a focus, sometimes this may be the case. For example, some storytelling projects seek to have students capture and retell traditional stories. In this case, careful research can be more important than originality. Also, some media pieces, such as *Making a Ball Roll* and *Super Bugs,* are original in the presentation but not in their content. Thus, it's always helpful for teachers to talk to students about the parameters and objectives for using creativity in their DST work.

A note of warning: while digital tools can encourage students to find the creative storyteller within, this does not guarantee originality. I've seen stories that look like canned TV or that use images and soundtracks that are very cliché. The world of infinite possibilities includes everything from the sublime to the banal.

Bottom line: If teachers are looking for creativity and originality in student work, then they need to be clear about their expectations. One approach: teachers can require that a certain percentage of the music, photos, or other elements that students use be original. Also, they can talk about story line in terms of being original, borrowed, or something in between.

⊠ Time, Story Length, and Economy

A common first comment from teachers after watching a digital story is "How much time did that take to do?" The subtext here is that teachers are already slammed for time, and anything that is going to make that situation worse is unwelcome. Ultimately, the conversation turns to considerations of time spent versus benefits derived, which is something teachers deal with all the time as they address ever-expanding content areas and demands for student testing. I've found that if a teacher's school or district does not value digital skill building, then DST typically attracts only the innovators—that small percentage of the teachers who are willing to be excited by the possibilities of DST despite their lack of support.

There is a direct connection between the length of the stories that students produce and the amount of classroom time required to produce them. Roughly speaking, four-minute stories will take about twice as long to produce as two-minute stories. While this sounds like something Captain Obvious might say, it's nonetheless important to point out to teachers who may not have a grasp of the time involved in producing new media.

Let me be clear about my bias here. Even if classroom time were abundant, I would still prefer pieces that hover around two minutes in length because they produce economy of expression. The shorter time frame forces storytellers to weed out what isn't truly important and prioritize what is. It compels them to plan carefully, write more, and really think about what it is they're trying to say. Two minutes is also very digestible to story listeners as well as teachers who may need to assess 30 projects from a single class. For those concerned that two minutes doesn't present enough of a challenge for students, I assure you that anyone who has created a digital story would disagree.

Another way to constrain project length is to limit the input. In *Digital Storytelling Cookbook and Traveling Companion,* author Joe Lambert (2003) notes that economy is often the largest problem for storytellers, and therefore he recommends limiting the amount of media that storytellers can use. Thus, requiring that students use no more than, for example, six scanned photos will naturally limit the length of the story they tell.

Bottom line: To enforce economy and make DST work within the time constraints of classroom life, it's helpful for teachers to create specific digital story requirements about length, number of media components students can use, and other variables related to how long a project can be.

Category 3: Story Production

While the stories I show teachers may seem somewhat familiar to them as media consumers, they are quite new to them as media producers, largely because producing media is not something they have had much experience doing. This fact leads to discussions about story production and the more technical aspects of producing new media, which are addressed here. It also leads to discussions about how to address the fact that students are generally more comfortable with digital technology than teachers are and how they can best manage their students' skills within the context of a learning assignment.

Production Values

Participants often discuss the difference between the stories in terms of polish—how finished, glitzy, or professional a piece is, depending upon your viewpoint. Typically, the term used in media circles to describe this aspect of

Low production values	Where? ▼	High production values

media production is "production values." The more polished the piece, the higher the production values employed by its creators. Media productions that have high production values are directly analogous to magazine articles that have been thoroughly edited and are considered, in the parlance of the publishing world, "camera ready."

While it might seem like a no-brainer to require new media production that has high production values—after all, who wants to create or watch media that is less than it could be—there are some things for teachers to consider before doing so.

Most important, teachers need to consider that media production takes time (as does good writing), a fact that often dissuades teachers from including it in an already crowded curriculum. Furthermore, the higher the production values, the more time it takes. We're at the point with new media production technology where we were with very early word processors; media is much easier to produce than it ever has been, but it is not quite what I would call truly easy yet. Seemingly slight increments in the refinement of digital stories can often seem to take an inordinate amount of time.

As the technology gets cheaper, easier to use, more distributed, and more second nature, this will change. In the meantime, I advise teachers to consider the rule of 80/20: you can produce 80% of a high-quality, high production-value digital story in 20% of the overall time that it takes to create the entire story. The last 20% of your story—the polished, often glitzy high end of production—takes 80% of your time, attention, and aggravation (Figure 2.1). That is, after you complete your story and have done everything except apply all the polish, you've produced your story in a fraction of the time required for high production-value work. This is typically the point at which you hit the production wall. Scaling it takes a lot of work—80% more work. This begs the question: Is it worth spending 80% of the time and energy to produce the last 20% of a finished piece? Typically, I say no. That is, when the production wall looms, say "good enough."

And take heart. Not only will digital media become easier to produce as the technology becomes easier and cheaper, but also it will become an expected part of the average high school portfolio. This will make it much easier to make the case for having students create finished, digital stories, thus justifying the time and budget necessary to do so.

Bottom line: Teachers consistently cite the time required to produce new media as a reason for not considering using DST in the classroom. My advice:

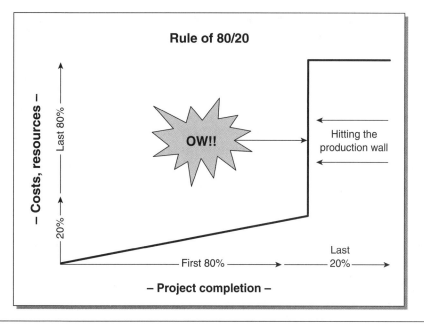

Figure 2.1

rather than not considering doing DST at all, consider forgetting the last 20% of high-end production. While the final product might be rougher than teachers and storytellers might like, "80% complete in 20% of the time" still looks good. This is an effective way for teachers to get their feet wet with media production in their classrooms and to learn how to more carefully budget their time and resources next time around.

▓ Media Grammar

In Chapter 14, I look at specific aspects of media grammar as they apply to DST. Here I introduce the topic and show how it helps facilitate a conversation about the more technical aspects of new media projects for those uncomfortable or unfamiliar with technical issues.

After watching a digital story, teachers usually want to know something about how it was made. Sometimes this is simply tech talk, but at other times it involves discussion of what I call media grammar. I usually introduce this topic by explaining that just as with writing, there are new media creation techniques that work better than others. New media has its own version of grammatical infractions like run-ons, fragments, and misspelled words as well as its own version of clear, organized presentation and effective modifier use. The use of familiar grammar terminology to discuss aspects of new media is often helpful.

However, as teachers discuss media grammar, they discover quickly that it's not nearly as well developed or as widely shared as grammar for writing. To help clarify the situation, I comment that if I were to give each of them an essay to assess, most would converge on similar—but not identical—assessments that value certain aspects of good writing that many of us have grown up with over the years. However, this does not happen when I show them a digital story. One teacher's source of confusion is another's unifying concept. That is, what is cited as a distracting or unclear digital story can vary greatly from one viewer to the next. In addition, just as poetry does not hew to the grammar of prose, some media will bend or ignore rules that apply to more straightforward media presentations. Breaking the rules effectively can be the hallmark of an emerging art form or simply an example of using one's own voice, hopefully in an effective and compelling way. But breaking the rules can also be an ineffective use of media with no particular payoff for the audience. Recall the earlier discussion about whether a digital story is, metaphorically speaking, an essay or a poem. This distinction becomes particularly important in regard to media grammar.

As we approach the area of media grammar, we need to keep in mind that most of us have developed our sense of writing grammar as both consumers (readers) and producers (writers). This is not the case with new media. Most teachers are only new media consumers and know what works for them largely from the perspective of someone who watches TV programming, movies, and Internet material. Thus, the reflective component that accompanies writing when attempting to write clearly for an audience is an experience few teachers have had with new media. The vital conversation that we need to have with peers, experts, and ourselves about communicating what we want to say with new media has not taken place.

Bottom line: The degree of importance that is attached to media grammar will vary from project to project and from teacher to teacher. However, teachers will need to teach and/or model whatever grammar they expect students to observe and make sure that students know that they are being assessed on its use.

❧ Equipment Needed

The stories I show teachers provide a rich context for the discussion of the very real issue of resources and equipment access needed for students to create digital stories. Teachers often have very limited technology budgets and want to know what hardware and software their students will need in order to create the stories they watch. Fortunately, many of the stories I show use fairly low-tech gear, such as low-budget digital cameras and scanners and free software, such as iMovie on the Mac or Movie Maker on the PC. In fact, I try to use only low-budget gear in my workshops so that teachers have a good chance of transferring what they learn to the realities of their classrooms. Take heart: in the DST world, there is a great deal you can do with very little.

Technology low end, available	←	Where? ▼	→	High end, or not available

However, stories like *School Train* and *Fox Becomes a Better Person* require extra hardware and software. While tools should not drive curricular goals, they can't help but define their possibilities. Talking about technology requirements is healthy and helps bring a sense of reality to producing new media in the classroom. It also helps teachers understand what they need to advocate for when budget talks are on the table. I provided a brief overview of the technology needed for digital stories in the Preface and discuss it in more detail in Part III.

Bottom line: Teachers need to determine what they need and what they have access to before embarking on a DST project. Typically, they need sustained equipment access for a week or two. If there are not enough computers to allow each student to work alone, then teachers need to consider staggering student projects and/or assigning team-based DST projects.

▓ Role of Help, Tech Support, and the Teacher

Teachers invariably want to know how much help students received in creating the digital stories I show them, especially for the more "wowwy" pieces like *School Train* and *Fox Becomes a Better Person*. Teachers have a number of justifiable concerns in this area.

Help is part of process	←	Where? ▼	→	Help is not allowed

First, they're concerned about students doing their own work and how much outside help is acceptable or desirable. The stories I show them represent the gamut in this regard. For most projects, students worked alone, receiving "just in time training" as needed from peers, friends, mentors, and Web sources. But other projects involved some teacher or professional help. For example, Glen Bledsoe reports that students received brief but crucial help from him to create *Making a Ball Roll.* The chroma-key editing in *Fox Becomes a Better Person* was done by editors, not the students, because we ran out of time. However, in other green screen projects, I've required students as young as fourth grade to complete all aspects of technical production, which they do with no problem and a good deal of enthusiasm. Teachers see help as everything from an acceptable part of the process to an unfair advantage that restricts learning.

Second, teachers are concerned about how to provide help to digital age students who typically know more technically than they do. I promote the use of learning communities—students helping each other by making their expertise available to each other. This exists within the classroom as an immediate learning community, as well as through learning communities facilitated by the Web. Interestingly, this conversation also leads teachers to wonder about the role of tech support at their schools. Technical support comes in many types, from fix-it help to professional development. Sometimes support is available to help teachers with projects like DST. I've found that when such support exists, it's incredibly helpful. Determining what help is available to you is definitely worth investigating.

Last, a related interest is the issue of students working alone versus working in groups. Ideally, both approaches should be used. When students create personal stories, their narrative has to be crafted individually. However, within this context students can still work collaboratively to solve each other's technical problems, review each other's work, and so on. Beyond projects of individual significance, there is great value in having students work together, particularly for longer projects, given that media projects tend to be team-based in the real world of media development.

Bottom line: Teachers need to decide to what degree seeking help is part of the process. They need to determine ahead of time what help exists in their schools or districts and how they want to structure, encourage, and reward students for helping each other with their DST projects.

▓ Emerging Digital Stories

What will be important to the future of DST in terms of story purpose, elements, and production? In addition to what I've already described, here is a glimpse:

Good, clear expository writing. This will continue to be essential to new media production far into the future. This could come in many forms, including research, story treatments, scripts, and other documents required in the media world. Whatever students produce, it must be clear, organized, and compelling.

Traditional, oral storytelling. As video technology becomes cheaper and easier to use, we will see more oral storytelling appear in digital stories.

Short movies. These will more resemble miniature movies rather than storytelling performances. There is currently surprisingly little of this in the DST world, a fact that will change as technology and interest evolve. YouTube points the way in this regard, ensuring that movies will have a place in digital storytelling.

Gaming, interactivity, and participation. Games, including educational games, already have user-directed story components, a trend that promises to continue. We should expect increased interactivity and more multiuser digital stories in which the audience participates as both story listener and story creator.

Green screen and other advanced movie techniques. We can expect students to want to use the same tools that are used to create the media they experience in their own lives, such as the use of green screen chroma-keying in *Fox Becomes a Better Person*. Green screening is just the beginning. Whatever tools the entertainment industry uses will show up in education at some point in some manner.

Animation. One of the advanced movie techniques that is becoming increasingly affordable and more common is animation. We should expect students to want to use voice-over animation, looking much like scaled-down versions of box office hits such as *Toy Story*. We should also expect stop-action animation, using real people, Claymation, and other approaches. In addition, programs like Flash are making motion-based multimedia a very useful storytelling tool.

Inclusion of original artwork and music. Copyright constraints, easy-to-use software like GarageBand, and the desire to create something truly original will compel digital storytellers to include more and more original work. The eventual recognition of the importance of art and design literacy—art being the fourth R (www.jasonohler.com/fourthr)—will also help this along. This will include semioriginal artwork, the domain of the mashup.

Art stories. It was McLuhan (1964) who noted that new media are used to do the work of old media until we figure out what the new media offer the world of communication that is truly new. When we do, we verge on a new art form. One kind of digital story that promises to increase is—for lack of a better phrase—the art story. I don't mean artistically told conventional stories, but truly new creations. We can guess what these might look like, but in many cases we don't know what they are until they arrive. Increasingly, art and media classes will look to the DST format as a canvas, voice, and stage.

VR, holography, haptics, and other advanced technologies. As I noted earlier, I know only one thing about the technologies that await us in the future: we will find ways to tell stories with them. Every new technology that reaches a classroom (or that students import into the classroom from their personal lives) will be used by digital storytellers. In fact, digital innovators who want to discover the capabilities of new software and hardware would do well to give it to DST students and ask them to create something with it.

Advanced editing techniques. Earlier I noted that we should expect to see more video material in digital stories as it becomes cheaper and easier to use. While this is true, we should also expect technique creep. That is, what passes as acceptable edited video today won't pass tomorrow. Recall how quickly dot-matrix printouts fell out of favor. As our capabilities advance, so do our expectations. The result is that the leading edge becomes cliché very quickly in the tEcosystem. Editing as an art form will continue to grow, much as it has in print media. Also, keep an eye out for self-editing technology that will adjust images on the fly to make you look better or make your story look, ironically, more realistic.

Distributed, collaborative, shared stories and story spaces. The Internet provides an international stage for digital storytellers. As it morphs into Web 2.0, it also facilitates interactivity and participation locally and at a distance, allowing students to share and collaborate on digital stories. A special form of distributed, shared stories will occur in story spaces, specialized electronic communities that specialize in storytelling. They will be facilitated through the use of avatars and other virtual representational entities. This is already happening to some extent and will continue to grow in popularity. We should also expect projected "real" performances using video techniques such as green screening. "Beam me up" may be a ways off, but "project me there" is already here.

Role blur. Podcasting suggests that the same thing will happen to storytellers that has happened to artists and musicians: the division between artist, producer, and distributor will blur beyond recognition. While role blur gives artists more to do, it also gives them more control over what they do and how they distribute their work. Storytelling becomes the entire process, from conception to development to distribution and performance and everything in between.

A good story. All of the technology that is coming down the pike should be both exciting and worrisome. With each advance in DST tools, we also advance our ability to say less with more. Beginning with a good story will become more important than ever in DST. Telling stories effectively, regardless of the media, will be crucial. Within our classrooms, it will be up to teachers to help students ensure that the technology serves the story and not the other way around.

3

Digital Storytelling as an Educational Tool

Standards, Planning, and Literacy

There has been very little research conducted on the value of digital storytelling (DST) in education. But I wouldn't let that bother you. Much has been written about the effectiveness of storytelling in education as well as the importance of digital skills to today's students. The two complement and reinforce each other quite naturally.

However, it's worth discussing the value of DST in relation to some of the broad areas of concern that emerge in the public discussion of education. Toward that end, let's consider DST within the context of standards, instructional design, and literacy.

Digital Storytelling and Standards

My consideration of standards is concerned with how they can be used to help teachers better understand what DST offers classroom instruction. To facilitate this discussion, I consider standards in three areas: (1) content, (2) technology, and (3) language arts.

1. Content Standards

Standards exist for all K–12 content areas commonly addressed in schools. Standards typically address what is important for students to understand within a content area and at what grade level. In most cases, standards exist at both the national and state levels; in some cases they even exist at the district or school level. For the most part, content standards address outcomes more than methodology. Because DST is viewed primarily as methodology it might therefore seem outside the scope of our discussion. However, it does seem reasonable to ask whether DST has any limitations that might preclude it from being used as a methodology to address the curriculum goals that are developed in response to content standards. Clearly, this does not seem to be the case. The examples I described earlier included stories about math, science, and language arts concepts, as well as stories of cultural and personal significance. It is reasonable to infer from the wide variety of topics addressed by these stories that DST has wide application and can be used by students in most, if not all, content areas. It also seems reasonable to infer that DST can be used to address most topics within content areas as long as the time, technology access, and technology training exist to support it. As always, this assumes a fertile and supportive educational environment to be successful.

✦ 2. Technology Standards

The K–12 world has embraced the educational technology standards developed by the International Society for Technology in Education (ISTE). As of this writing, these standards can be accessed at the ISTE Web site: www.iste.org.

Even though ISTE has created separate technology standards for teachers, students, and administrators, they embrace a common core of concern and concepts. Teacher standards are listed in Table 3.1.

I debated whether to address the ISTE standards in depth, given that new media embody the standards in such obvious ways. I decided to simply let the standards speak for themselves and add the few points that appear below that might otherwise fall below the radar. Beyond this, I recommend that teachers consult the ISTE standards, which are clear and well documented. Using the ISTE standards to drive DST projects is a no-brainer. Every DST project I have participated in involves most ISTE standards in some way.

How techie a teacher do I need to be? Standards I and V (technology operation and concepts; productivity and professional practice) are either directly or indirectly concerned with teachers' technical proficiency. Over the years, I have come to appreciate that this is an aspect of teaching that every teacher makes peace with in a very personal way. The question that each teacher needs to address is simple in concept yet complicated in application: How technically capable do I feel I need to be to use new media in my curriculum?

There are a number of responses to this, all of which are quite workable. Teachers can opt to simply manage the talents of their students, an approach

Table 3.1   ISTE NETS Standards for Teachers

Standard I	Technology operation and concepts
Standard II	Planning and designing learning environments and experiences
Standard III	Teaching, learning, and the curriculum
Standard IV	Assessment and evaluation
Standard V	Productivity and professional practice
Standard VI	Social, ethical, legal, and human issues

SOURCE: Retrieved from http://cnets.iste.org/teachers/t_stands.html. ISTE Teacher NETS standards are reprinted with permission from National Educational Technology Standards for Teachers: Preparing Teachers to Use Technology, © 2002, ISTE ® (International Society for Technology in Education), iste@iste.org, www.iste.org. All Rights Reserved.

that opens the door for nontechnical educators to include DST in classroom activities. A nontechnically oriented teacher with an open mind and good classroom management skills can be very successful in a digital age classroom. On the other end of the spectrum, teachers can decide that they need to have an advanced understanding of new media in order to be truly responsible and helpful. As long as they see themselves as a resource and not a gateway through which students need to pass to gain access to resources and knowledge, they too can be very successful. And then there is everything in between. After 25 years of advising teachers to be the guide on the side rather than the technician magician, I can tell you that the teachers who thrive are those who do what they genuinely feel comfortable doing but aren't afraid of their next steps. I can also tell you that if teachers decide to take their next steps, then they need to have access to the professional development necessary to do so. Often the most helpful thing a district office can do for teachers is to make sure such professional development is available and encourage and incentivize teachers to use it.

Teachers can't require what they can't evaluate. Standards II, III, and IV (planning and designing learning environments and experiences; teaching, learning, and the curriculum; and assessment and evaluation) address the essence of the learning experience, whether it's approached low tech, no tech, or high tech. Of particular interest here is evaluation. As I say at a few points in this book, one of the most significant barriers preventing teachers from requiring more new media projects of their students is that they don't feel comfortable assessing them. This is understandable, given that the primary media that most of today's teachers have produced is text, a fact that is rapidly changing as the workforce becomes younger. In an era of No Child Left Behind and an already jam-packed curriculum, teachers need assistance assessing schoolwork in forms that are unfamiliar to them. Hopefully this book will provide help in this area.

Social impacts and media literacy. Last, the issues addressed by Standard VI (social, ethical, legal, and human issues) become extremely important within the context of new media production. Students live in a world of very persuasive media, much of which goes undetected by them. Students, as well as the rest of us, are much like the proverbial fish that are unable to see the water they swim in. Having students create digital media provides the ultimate media literacy opportunity. As teachers oversee students creating their own media, they can help them see the water by deconstructing media and the many persuasive techniques media producers use to "pierce the neocortex and connect with people's feelings" (www.jasonohler.com/storytelling). I think one of the most important questions on teachers' minds is simply this: What are the legal and ethical parameters that I need to consider if my students want to download media from the Web and include it in their digital stories? The chapter on copyright issues should help answer this question.

▧ 3. Language Arts Standards

Two reasons inspire me to provide the following analysis of how and why the standards developed by the National Council of Teachers of English (NCTE) and the International Reading Association (IRA) are an effective vantage point from which to view the importance of new media in the classroom. First, they deal directly with the production and understanding of narrative. In so doing, they offer a helpful perspective from which to view the extension of text into the digital domain and the expansion of concepts like reading, writing, and grammar that have come about owing to emerging technologies, literacies, and practices such as DST. Web 2.0 is, above all, a narrative environment. Second, DST is new to many teachers and policymakers. Thus, how it impacts the world of language arts may not be apparent. Even if readers already understand the connections between language arts and student-based new media production, they may benefit from the extra arguments they find here. However, if readers aren't in need of any further argument in this area, then I invite them to skip ahead in the book. This section is for those who have questions about this topic.

To structure my analysis, I use the Standards for the English Language Arts developed by IRA and NCTE (1996), which appear on the NCTE Web site: www.ncte.org.

Before proceeding, three elements of DST that I have previously identified bear repeating here for the purpose of this discussion:

1. Successful DST depends upon traditional writing and the literacies associated with it in the development of scripts, narrative, and other planning instruments.

2. DST integrates traditional and emerging literacies while pursuing content-area learning.

3. DST is, above all, storytelling. As such it has many of the educational benefits of traditional storytelling, as well as some new ones.

With this in mind, let's consider how the standards are introduced on the NCTE Web site. The introduction begins as follows:

> The vision guiding these standards is that all students must have the opportunities and resources to develop the language skills they need to pursue life's goals and to participate fully as informed, productive members of society. (NCTE, 2006, n.p.)

The current de facto language is the multimedia collage. Consider the average Web page. It's a mix of text, graphics, video, sound, and other elements of communication arranged to maximize aesthetics and effectiveness. Informed and productive members of society need traditional and emerging literacy skills in order to read, write, and navigate Web information, which, incidentally, are the same literacy skills needed to develop effective digital stories. The world of Web 2.0 is a social environment connected and facilitated by narrative, which depends upon the literacy skills of its participants to be effective. I discuss the nature of these literacies, and the part they play in DST, in the next section. The introduction continues:

> These standards assume that literacy growth begins before children enter school as they experience and experiment with literacy activities—reading and writing, and associating spoken words with their graphic representations. (NCTE, 2006, n.p.)

Basic new media literacy begins at an ever-younger age. First-generation digital kids send text messages, take pictures with cell phones, and personalize their own Web spaces without training or trouble. To them, the technology is largely just intelligent furniture. DST is an effective vehicle to use to help students continue the literacy growth they have begun outside school while giving it shape and academic purpose. The introduction continues:

> Recognizing this fact, these standards encourage the development of curriculum and instruction that make productive use of the emerging literacy abilities that children bring to school. Furthermore, the

standards provide ample room for the innovation and creativity essential to teaching and learning. They are not prescriptions for particular curriculum or instruction. Although we present these standards as a list, we want to emphasize that they are not distinct and separable; they are, in fact, interrelated and should be considered as a whole. (NCTE, 2006, n.p.)

Two important points arise from this passage, the first of which is about story. In his book *Teaching as Story Telling*, Kieran Egan (1989) notes that kids come to school already understanding the story form. Yet what they encounter is information in report form, which lacks the rhythm and imagination that makes stories so involving. The result is cognitive dissonance as kids try to bridge the worlds of preschool and school. If we view storytelling as an emerging ability, and seek to nurture it when children enter school, we can tap into communication structures they already understand. Digital storytelling provides one avenue to do this, a concept I explore more deeply in Part II of this book.

Second, with a little wordsmithing, this passage could easily be adapted as an inspirational vision statement for a school's educational technology plan or digital literacy scope and sequence. The phrase "emerging literacy abilities" effectively describes the skills and understandings young people are developing as they begin to use new media. DST not only provides ample room for "innovation and creativity" but expects it, anticipates it, and depends on it, largely because the tEcosystem and the participatory world of Web 2.0 facilitates it so naturally and pervasively. As I detail in the next section, DST interrelates standards, literacies, and content in truly unique ways.

Now let's consider DST within the context of each language arts standard. As you will see, it's not difficult to do, which is a testimony to the insight embedded in the standards, as well as to the utility of DST within a language arts context. In most cases, my comments merely point out ways that new media, and DST in particular, can be considered as natural extensions of language arts. As extensions they bring with them some new considerations about language.

Standard 1. Students read a wide range of print and nonprint texts to build an understanding of texts, of themselves, and of the cultures of the United States and the world; to acquire new information; to respond to the needs and demands of society and the workplace; and for personal fulfillment. Among these texts are fiction and nonfiction, classic and contemporary works.

The range of text now available to students spans not only literary genres and cultures but nonprint media forms as well. Students need to be able to "read" TV programming, digital stories, online discussions, and other kinds of media collages that consume much of the bandwidth in their tEcosystem. We owe it to language arts students to present them with a scenario in which conventional and emerging texts complement and challenge rather than collide with each other. Having students blend reading the classics in print with experiencing more contemporary works in new media form ideally situates them to be literate in the most useful, contemporary sense.

Being able to read new media is not just a matter of literacy, it's also a matter of survival, for two primary reasons. First, reading new text is the basis of the kind of critical thinking needed for workplace success in an information economy. It is commonplace for employees at many levels of an organization to be required to acquire new information by searching the multimedia environment of the World Wide Web and analyzing and applying what they find. It is also commonplace for them to be asked to participate in online communities for the purposes of collaborative problem solving and data mining. Such communities are rapidly adopting the multimedia collage as the de facto communication format, merging text and nontext sources into expressions of new media.

Second, while we want students to read new media for personal fulfillment, we also want them to read it in order to understand how it can be used to persuade its readership in powerful and often subtle ways. In an age in which media companies see young people largely in terms of market share, having the ability to read print and nonprint text critically is a matter of survival.

While this standard focuses on reading rather than writing, it's important to point out that just as with literacy associated with conventional texts, literacy involved with new media texts is an interplay between production and consumption. That is, the most effective way for students to learn how to read new media is to create it. Conversely, the most effective way for them to create effective new media is to be able to read, deconstruct, and analyze what they're creating. DST is as much a reading process as a writing process.

> **Standard 2.** Students read a wide range of literature from many periods in many genres to build an understanding of the many dimensions (e.g., philosophical, ethical, aesthetic) of human experience.

Blending literary tradition with new media texts provides a range of reading experience previously unfathomable in language arts. In the hands of a skilled teacher, the variety within this range provides a way to explore how much has changed yet remained consistent about human nature over the centuries, despite the evolution of language tools.

It's important to note that the world of digital stories has expanded the philosophical, ethical, and aesthetic dimensions of the human experience beyond the famous to the masses of the great unknown. There are many Web sites and other online environments that host digital stories by people with seemingly ordinary lives. It can be a great source of inspiration to students to know that what may seem common is actually special when explored with appropriate reflection and expressed in the language of their generation.

DST is not only personally empowering but also widely applicable across genres and academic areas. I've seen compelling new media pieces produced by students that explicate the works of authors as diverse as Shakespeare and Sylvia Plath. The new media documentary is rapidly becoming a respected and even expected format for student presentation.

> **Standard 3.** Students apply a wide range of strategies to comprehend, interpret, evaluate, and appreciate texts. They draw on their prior experience, their interactions with other readers and writers, their knowledge of word meaning and of other texts, their word identification strategies, and their understanding of textual features (e.g., sound-letter correspondence, sentence structure, context, graphics).

We saw earlier that teachers used a number of strategies in their evaluation of the digital stories they watched, most of which were drawn from their work analyzing more conventional texts rather than new media. This is understandable, given that their prior experience with new media was mostly as passive consumers of TV, movies, and other popular media. That is, their experience had rarely consisted of "active viewing"—a process used to deconstruct media within a media literacy context—and even more rarely of actual media production.

That is why an important aspect of the experience of viewing digital stories was teachers' interactions with each other as readers and writers of new text in a professional setting. Much of their conversation was focused on "seeing" new media and reading it with understanding, a new experience for most. These insights were then carried forward into the new media they produced in the workshop. Reading and writing new media are important abilities for teachers to have, particularly so they can teach them to students who are so immersed in the tEcosystem that new media are largely invisible to them. Standard 3 clearly supports teaching these abilities.

Standard 3 is also important with regard to the role of traditional literacy in the development of digital stories. As I stated earlier, the world of new media is built upon the written word in the form of scripts, treatments, narratives, and other planning documents, all of which require the foundational literacy skills associated with success in language arts. They are the same skills necessary to read and analyze new media as well as create it.

Standard 4. Students adjust their use of spoken, written, and visual language (e.g., conventions, style, vocabulary) to communicate effectively with a variety of audiences and for different purposes.

Standard 5. Students employ a wide range of strategies as they write and use different writing process elements appropriately to communicate with different audiences for a variety of purposes.

Standards 4 and 5 support the need to conceive new media production in terms of audience expectation and needs, recalling our earlier discussion of digital as essay versus poem. The ability to write for diverse audiences for a variety of purposes is as important in the digital domain as it is in more conventional communication environments. The world of possibility in this regard was made clear by the tremendous variety of the digital stories described earlier. We can further infer that with the appropriate motivation and imagination, digital stories can and should be developed to suit virtually any audience.

These standards are also helpful in reinforcing the potential of new media to appeal to multiple intelligences, both as a way to approach diverse audiences as well as to facilitate students seeking the most effective ways to use their many talents. Within DST, a range of communication strategies exists through the use of different media elements, including words, pictures, music, and so on, allowing creators to speak in many different languages to a wide range of listeners.

Standard 6. Students apply knowledge of language structure, language conventions (e.g., spelling and punctuation), media techniques, figurative language, and genre to create, critique, and discuss print and nonprint texts.

This standard can be used to address "language" in two senses within the context of student digital media development: conventional writing and the language of new media employed in DST and other nonprint texts.

As I mentioned earlier, conventional writing is a key component of new media development. While digital stories are typically viewed as an event on a computer screen, written work provides the foundation and blueprint needed to give them life. Students need to apply an understanding of language structure and conventions commensurate with what they are reading or producing, particularly in the following genres: stories and story treatments written in clear expository prose, narrative written in authentic vernacular, and story maps and storyboards written in concise shorthand.

New media also introduce an expanded notion of language while retaining some of the familiarity of more conventional text. Recall that when teachers analyzed digital stories, they identified traits that were familiar, like tone and point of view, as well as traits that were new, like the application of music and visuals to support spoken narrative. It is because of the overlap between conventional and emerging languages that I call my approach to new media language convention "media grammar." I find that digital stories have their own version of run-ons, fragments, weak organization, and clumsy pacing, as well as effective uses of adverbs and adjectives, character development, and flow. Media grammar allows teachers to approach the often unfamiliar language of new media using tools that are familiar and still useful for the purposes of creating, critiquing, and discussing new media text.

> **Standard 7.** Students conduct research on issues and interests by generating ideas and questions, and by posing problems. They gather, evaluate, and synthesize data from a variety of sources (e.g., print and non-print texts, artifacts, people) to communicate their discoveries in ways that suit their purpose and audience.
>
> **Standard 8.** Students use a variety of technological and information resources (e.g., libraries, databases, computer networks, video) to gather and synthesize information and to create and communicate knowledge.

Standards 7 and 8 reinforce the notion that whether students are generating traditional reports or digital stories, they need to engage in the same quality of inquiry, research, and analysis in order to be successful. What may be new for some is the use of new media texts, including TV, movies, new media work by peers, and Web-based animations, as textual sources, as well as the need for media literacy skills in order to read and analyze them. What may also be new is the participatory nature of research on the Web and how instrumental that will be as students "gather, evaluate, and synthesize data" for their projects. But regardless of the methodology, the goal of high-quality research remains.

From the examples of digital stories described earlier, we see clearly that students can use new media to communicate discovery based on research. In the small sampling of stories that I provided, students communicated their understanding of a number of academic concepts, including super bugs, metaphor, and the mathematics of a rolling ball, as well as their understanding of important personal events.

> **Standard 9.** Students develop an understanding of and respect for diversity in language use, patterns, and dialects across cultures, ethnic groups, geographic regions, and social roles.

The Web provides access to many sites that feature digital stories and other new media texts created by students from many cultures throughout the world. Their stories are highly diverse: some detail daily life; others chronicle living in a war zone. Their approach to media development is equally varied: some use no more than a cell phone, while others use sophisticated video technology. These same sites provide opportunities for students to become part of Web 2.0's global village (as well as its many subcultures and enclaves) by posting their own stories. In short, the Internet provides a reading list of a breadth and depth that was unimaginable not long ago. It also does something else that is truly unique: it provides students the opportunity to add to the global reading list itself. Blogs, YouTube, Wikipedia, and so on mark the infancy of celebrating diversity on the Web in a very grass-roots sense.

An important aspect of respecting other cultures is understanding the communication limitations imposed by the media. Some things are more faithfully reproduced in the digital domain than others. For example, the current standard of music video presentation, particularly for youth, includes a good deal of movement and razzamatazz, which may be at odds with the nature of the culture trying to present itself via digital means. As always, part of showing respect for diversity lies in trying to understand how the media distort cultural expressions and favor some cultures while disadvantaging others.

> **Standard 10**. Students whose first language is not English make use of their first language to develop competency in the English language arts and to develop understanding of content across the curriculum.

Writing for digital media projects compels students to focus on the use of language in ways that they don't necessarily focus on when writing is the only final product. Because digital stories often employ spoken narrative, students get to hear what their writing sounds like by recording it and listening to it as many times as they like. It is not uncommon for students who are crafting a short narrative to labor over phrases that don't sound quite right. In much the same way that good writing is rewriting, good narration is renarration. Because of the interplay between writing, speaking, and listening, DST has great potential to help students learn language.

It is worth mentioning here the "translative" benefits of DST. In order for students to translate something from one language to another successfully, they need a firm understanding of the content. I used to require my ed tech students to translate technical information into plain English for this reason. DST has great value in this regard, because it compels students to go from script to new media, a language translation process we are just beginning to appreciate. This potential for second language speakers to use this process to develop first language skills—as well as media literacy skills—is very great.

> **Standard 11.** Students participate as knowledgeable, reflective, creative, and critical members of a variety of literacy communities.

Reflective communities are part of DST in many ways, two of which are particularly important here. First, reflective learning communities are primarily storytelling communities. As I walk among students in a DST workshop engaged in the creative process, whether they are huddled over paper during the planning stages or are at their computers during production, I often hear them helping each other by telling their own stories of success and failure. As I sit with students individually, I hear them reflect on the story, the process, and their technique, looking for the insights that will help put on the screen what they think and feel. Effectively, they are teaching each other new media literacy through trial and error, peer assessment, and the media production process. In addition, the Internet hosts a number of resource communities that can help students learn about everything from telling stories to using technology to do so. Second, once their stories are completed, students have to share them to complete them—a story is not done until it has been told. This happens within class and often in the broader context of school and community in "literacy communities" devoted, often informally, to sharing and critically assessing new media in terms of story and technique.

> **Standard 12.** Students use spoken, written, and visual language to accomplish their own purposes (e.g., for learning, enjoyment, persuasion, and the exchange of information).

Outside the academic arena, students engage with new media because they enjoy it and because it has great practical value to them as communicators. Digital media extends the hours of the school hallway, provides a collective canvas for emerging artists, and puts young people at the helm of a culture creation engine that is constantly surprising all of us with its potential. The result is that in the less formal, less school-oriented context of text messaging, cell phone chatting, online community discourse, and the many other things that young people digitally do, students are already producing digital stories of a sort. Language arts provide them with many ways to create their own voice. They are first-generation digital. This is how they speak.

✦ Instructional Design: Stories, Inquiry, and Backward Design

In Part II of this book I discuss in detail what makes a story memorable and effective. Suffice it to say for now that stories usually work when they have at their heart an effective story core: a central character (which can be anything from a person to a group of people to an inanimate object) that undergoes a transformation in order to solve a problem, answer a question, meet a goal, resolve an issue, or realize the potential of an opportunity. Note how similar this is to inquiry-based education, in which students are presented with a problem or essential question that they address through learning and other activities of discovery. In many ways, a memorable story and an effective unit of instruction are very similar. When students become heroes of their own learning stories, success occurs through a learning process in which they are transformed by becoming smarter, more aware, more skilled, or more developed in some regard.

In *Understanding by Design,* Wiggins and McTighe (2001) add a clear and helpful voice to the public discussion of effective learning processes by focusing on, from my perspective as a storyteller, the transformation component of the story core. They shift from activity-based to outcome-based lesson design by employing the backward planning model: understand the goal first and then build a learning process that leads to it. They capture the essence of the instructional design process in three essential questions: (1) What is important for students to understand? (2) What is acceptable evidence of this understanding? (3) What learning experiences can promote this understanding? I adapt these three questions to a story context in the following way: (1) What transformation do students, as heroes of their own learning stories, need to undergo? What discoveries do they need to make to successfully conclude their quest? (2) How can students, by the end of the story, prove to themselves and their evaluators that they internalized their transformation and discovery in an authentic manner? (3) What adventures, either of their own creation or designed by the teacher, should students undergo to make sure this happens?

Shifting from unit form to story form is largely a matter of perspective. As I pointed out earlier, Kieran Egan (1989) notes that kids come to school well versed in the story form and instinctively look for it in what is presented at school. When they don't find it, boredom or disorientation ensues. The primary difference between the two forms is the rhythm of their respective internal structures. Units of instruction can often be episodic, consisting of a series of events that may be logical but don't employ tension/resolution and other elements of story that involve story listeners through a rhythm of anticipation. The result is that to students, the information in a unit of instruction can feel disconnected, while the same information within a story context can feel organized. The tools needed to add these elements to an otherwise sound unit of instruction are covered in Part II.

▓ Digital Storytelling and Literacy Development

Traditional storytelling is highly regarded as a powerful tool for helping students develop literacy skills. DST merely extends this into the digital domain. In the process, it usually integrates a number of traditional and emerging literacies into the storytelling process.

In its minimalist form, a digital story consists of still pictures, voice-over narration, and perhaps music, titles, and transitions. Most of the stories I described earlier were of this kind. Teachers who require students to write their narratives and rehearse their recitations involve them in oral and written literacies. If they include photography, drawing, or even music development, then they expand literacy development into the domain of art and design as well. If students perform their stories, as is the case with *Fox Becomes a Better Person*, they involve what storytelling expert Brett Dillingham (2005) calls "performance literacy." Of course, the tools and skills that make much of this possible fall under the heading of digital literacy.

Figure 3.1 The DAOW of Literacy

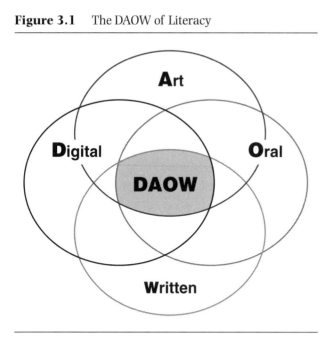

As we shall see, an important component of this is media literacy, which can roughly be defined as recognizing, evaluating, and applying the methods of media persuasion.

I call what DST offers the world of literacy and learning the DAOW (pronounced "DOW") of literacy, an acronym arising from the four major literacies it most often involves: digital, art, oral, and writing. In the pages that follow, I address how each literacy is involved in the creation of digital stories and how each adds an important dimension to the overall domain of literacy development.

🏮 The Value of Digital Literacy (the D of DAOW)

Pointing out that digital literacy is an important component of DST truly sounds like something Captain Obvious would say. Yet the reality is that while the importance of digital literacy might seem obvious, how it should be approached might not. The nature of digital literacy covers a vast area of concern and has been debated without resolution since the first desktop computers showed up in schools. Many books, articles, and technology planning meetings have been devoted to a very simple question that drives public concern in this area: What is important for our students to understand about using digital technology? For many years my mantra as an educational technologist has been simply this: students need to be able to use technology effectively, creatively, and wisely. These characteristics play out in DST in the following ways:

Effective use of digital technology. Obviously, we want our students to use digital tools effectively. That is, we want them to use digital tools intelligently and proficiently. This includes knowing how to push the right buttons, use the Web efficiently as an information resource and collaboration tool, apply technical skills to problems with proficiency, and transfer learning from one situation to another. Effective use addresses the domain of know-how and applied know-how. Digital storytelling is quite demanding in this regard. Students have to be able to use and apply a variety of digital tools in some depth if they are to be successful. The skills they develop in creating digital stories are widely applicable to a number of endeavors.

Creative use of technology. Beyond effective use lies the creative domain of technology application. This involves not just all those attributes associated with "art the 4th R" discussed next but also those associated with using technology as an imagination amplifier to solve seemingly mundane problems. We want students to be able to use technology as a lever that, combined with their own insight, creative problem solving, and critical thinking, can address issues and create opportunities that they would not have seen before. DST offers tremendous opportunity in this area.

Wise use of technology. Last, we want students to be able to evaluate technology and its impacts within the larger picture of community. The wisdom we want our students to cultivate is both practical and theoretical. Practically speaking, we want them to be media literate—to be able to recognize, evaluate, and apply the persuasive power of technology and media, much of which flies beneath their radars unless they are actively looking for it. Perhaps more theoretically, we want students to be able to zoom out and place digital technology in the larger perspective of personal, social, and environmental impacts. Having students use DST for important purposes, particularly those that extend beyond themselves and attempt to provide connections with the world, helps cultivate this wisdom. The interplay of theoretical and practical wisdom compels us to think globally while acting locally and to balance our personal needs with those of our community.

▓ The Value of Art Literacy (the A of DAOW)

Before addressing art's value in DST, I am saddened to report that even in the year 2007, I still need to address its value in education at all. But there is hope. Art, long considered in our schools as an elective at best, superfluous fluff at worst, has taken center stage, because the multimedia tEcosystem we inhabit is largely based on the language of art and design. Art has indeed become the fourth R, a literacy in a very practical sense, as important as reading, writing, and arithmetic. While there are many reasons for this, three in particular make our need to adopt art as a literacy particularly urgent:

Digital tools provide assistive technology for the art-challenged. Today's relatively affordable, easy-to-use, multimedia technology acts as assistive technology for the artistically challenged. In the same way that word processing opened up the world of the writer, multimedia technology has opened up the world of the artist. Today, anyone who can move a mouse can jump in and give it a go.

Art is an international language. The Web uses the multimedia collage as its Esperanto, spreading the language of digital media throughout the global world of the Internet. In retrospect, it seems inevitable that citizens of the internationally networked world would move away from text-centric communication and toward pictures, diagrams, sound, movement, and other more universal forms of communication.

Art is real work for real pay. Just 10 years ago some of the words most feared by parents were "Mom, Dad, I'm marrying an artist." They shouldn't be anymore. Artists now have real work for real pay. Businesses are desperate for the artist's design eye and know-how to provide them a professional, effective presence on the Web. Artists are sought after because they are literate in the language of imagery and design that is so prevalent in the physical and virtual worlds we construct but which is still largely not valued in our schools. The value of this language is not merely aesthetic. It also helps navigation, orientation, and other aspects of the media collage associated with getting the job done.

How does art literacy impinge on DST? In several ways. Here are some of the most important:

- *Art creator.* Digital storytellers are often required to create artistic material. In some cases, it's taking pictures. In others, it's actually creating original paintings, music, video, and other work. In the absence of artistic production values, such work lacks communication impact, just as poor writing does. Note that having students create their own work is the most effective way to address the legal morass associated with copyright and fair use.
- *Art manager.* When not required to create original material, digital storytellers are required to manage artistic material created by others. Selecting, editing, and mixing material requires art literacy to be effective.
- *Art producer.* Whether students are creating or managing art material, they need to apply it to their projects with the skills of a producer. DST is essentially an artistic endeavor, requiring storytellers to write, direct, and create a multimedia dramatic production. They are required to blend text, images, video, music, sounds, animation, and other media sources into a unified, seamless whole according to the grammar of design. Effectively, digital storytellers enter the world of the producer, painting with a wide brush.

Seeing DST as an artistic activity is the antidote to seeing it as a technical event. All too often I see syllabi for DST courses that look like software training sessions. When digital storytellers begin with the story and proceed as artists, the technology falls into place.

🎴 The Value of Oral Literacy (the O of DAOW)

Oral literacy—or oracy—is often defined simply as the ability to understand and use spoken language. DST provides opportunities to do both.

Most of the DST I am involved in falls into two categories, both of which rely heavily on speaking and listening:

1. *Computer-based DST.* This is the traditional storytelling I have already described. Looking somewhat like a typical documentary, it is built upon a voice-over narration, to which are added images, music, and so on. Most of the stories I described earlier were in this form. In this kind of DST, the writing process becomes the renarration process, as students write out their narrative, record it, listen to it, and then rewrite and/or rerecord it.

2. *Performance-based green screen storytelling.* A good example is Hannah Davis's story, which I described earlier. In it she performed in front of a green screen, allowing original artwork to be added in after production.

Both approaches to DST require an attention to the spoken word that simply is not found in conventional approaches to written literacy. In both cases, students hear themselves via recorded media for the purpose of listening, self-assessment, and rewriting and/or speaking or recording—the renarration process. The power of hearing oneself for self-assessment purposes can't be underestimated. It's as though the process of getting words out of one's head and into the open air exposes them to a quality of critique not available within the confines of one's internal landscape, even if the only people reviewing the narratives are the authors themselves. In addition, we value oral literacy in the DST process for the following reasons:

- Oral storytelling is how storytelling began and has endured for millennia. It has a history that is rich in timeless skills, perspective, and sense of audience. Good teaching is often a matter of good storytelling. No matter how high tech we become, telling stories orally will endure as one of our primary and most powerful forms of communication. It will always be an important skill to have in the workplace, in our communities, and in our schools. As we become overwhelmed by media, speaking effectively becomes an important way to cut through the clutter to make a point.
- Oral storytelling provides a skill set that can be used regardless of the kind of storytelling students are doing. It informs storytelling activities whether they involve high, low, or no technology.
- Oral storytelling is an effective tool to improve writing.
- As a preproduction exercise in the development of a digital story, oral storytelling is an effective way for students to develop their own voice and determine what is important to include in their stories.
- Including oral storytelling within a school project provides a rich teachable moment for students to explore historical connections between their activities as digital storytellers and storytelling as an ancient and timeless means of education, communication, and entertainment.
- Video material of people acting as well as telling oral stories will become increasingly important in DST as shooting and editing video becomes cheaper and easier.
- Students are required to tell stories with media accompaniment as a matter of course these days. Delivering a PowerPoint presentation is a good example. The average audience now expects a blend of media and oral presentation.

We've been telling stories with just our voices and bodies for many years. We will continue to do so, presumably forever. Involving oral storytelling can only be helpful to students, no matter what kind of storytelling project they're developing.

The Value of Writing (the W of DAOW)

Those worried about the fate of written literacy in an era of DST will be happy to know that writing is more important than ever for the following reasons:

> Having students write for media is an effective way of slipping writing in under the radar.

- As I mentioned earlier, while writing may not be the final product of a digital story, it's an important part of the process students must use to create it. The saying "If it ain't on the page, then it ain't on the stage" is just as true for DST as it is for projects created for theater and movies. Recently I watched an HBO documentary in which actors, directors, and producers were interviewed about what made great movies. Several interviewees made the point that a good script was absolutely essential and that no amount of good acting or special effects could compensate for the lack of one. Good new media rests on the foundation of solid writing.
- Media production is an effective way to engage kids in writing in an authentic way. Anecdotally, I have heard from teachers that students who don't want to write school reports or essays are happy to write media plans and narratives, because doing so is not perceived as schoolwork but as "scripting." Many teachers refer to their use of scripting as "slipping writing in under the radar." Students who are attitudinally predisposed not to like writing can develop a taste for it as well as the writing abilities they don't often use.
- The writing skills that students employ in the process of creating their digital stories embrace many aspects of writing that are considered important in school as well as the world outside school. Of particular note is the fact that digital stories require students to synthesize the techniques of both creative and expository writing in order to produce an effective piece of media.
- The deep processing for which writing is so often noted is crucial to the DST process because it engages storytellers in personal reflection prior to their using technology that has the potential to distract them from the intent of their project. It's simple: when students write, they think.

No matter how sophisticated our technology becomes, the future of DST will involve writing and conventional forms of literacy. It is our job as educators to make clear to parents and the public that DST is an effective way to pursue traditional literacy as well as emerging literacies. They need to understand that students are not giving up traditional literacy; they are simply expanding its utility while developing new literacies they need in the digital world.

⬚ A Letter to Parents About the Value of Digital Storytelling

Now let's imagine using DST in practical terms. Suppose you're interested in including DST in a class project and feel the need to explain to parents why you're doing so. You decide to send a letter home to parents to explain what you're doing and why you feel it's important. You know it needs to be short and compelling and needs to mention how DST addresses academic standards and literacy. Here's a rough draft you can modify for your own use.

Dear parents:

(Note to teachers: I provide you two different openings, depending on the kind of digital storytelling project you are doing. For performance-based digital storytelling, use this paragraph:

I'm happy to announce that students in my class will be part of a digital storytelling project. In this project, students will be creating original stories and telling them in front of a green surface, like the weather announcer uses. Students will then create their own artwork and add it behind their performances using a technique called chroma-key editing. The result is students performing their own stories in front of their own artwork.)

(For computer-based digital storytelling, use this paragraph:
I'm happy to announce that students in my class will be part of a digital storytelling project. In this project, students will be using the computer to create a short movie or documentary.)
Here is some important information that I thought you would like to know about this project.

- Students will engage in a good deal of writing. A goal of this project is to improve students' writing and communication skills.
- This is a classroom-based project, and will be used to support [teacher's name] as she [he] addresses research, content understanding, and skill building with her [his] students.
- Students will be developing a number of technology and media production skills they can use in pursuing important schoolwork.
- Students will learn how to create stories that are engaging and meaningful.
- *(Note to teachers: you may want to exclude this for computer-based digital storytelling)* Students will be learning how to tell stories in front of an audience. This helps them develop presentation skills and self-confidence.
- Students will be developing artwork to support their stories. In the visual world of the digital age, art has become the fourth R. This project helps them develop art and creativity skills that can be used to communicate ideas and support project goals.
- Students will be involved as "producers and directors" of a media project. Kids are very involved in media these days, and helping them develop skills in this area is becoming an important part of their education.

I also wanted to let you know that this project will require parent permission because we will be recording students and showing their performances to others. I will be sending home a permission slip for this.

> When the digital stories are done, we hope you will join us for Digital Storytelling Day on _____ . Students will then complete a DVD containing all students' stories. All parents and students will receive one.
>
> We are very excited about this project and welcome any comments you have. If you have any questions, feel free to contact me.
>
> Sincerely,
>
> [Teacher's name]

This letter has evolved over the years. Feel free to adapt it however you wish. To see the most recent version, go to www.jasonohler.com/storytelling.

❁ Permission Slips

Note that I did not include a permission slip template in this book, simply because parent permission requirements can vary from district to district. Ask your administrator for the standard media release form to use for recording and distributing student work. When in doubt, always ask an administrator or your district's legal counsel for clarification. The release must be signed by a parent or guardian, or the student can't participate.

❁ A Word About Multiple Intelligences

It's fitting to end this chapter with a nod to Howard Gardner (1983) and his theory of multiple intelligences that has generated so much enthusiasm in educational circles.

Although the significance of multiple intelligences is usually reserved for discussions of student learning styles within education environments, the reality is that we live in a multiple intelligences world outside school as well. That is, the real world communicates using the intelligences that Gardner identifies. If this were not the case, then they would not be so highly prized in education.

DST is a veritable cornucopia of intelligences, particularly if blended with the DAOW of literacy. Like traditional literacy, DST is widely applicable across the curriculum. Unlike traditional literacy, it taps skills and talents that might otherwise lie dormant in many students. Most of Gardner's intelligences, from the linguistic and the musical to the kinesthetic and intrapersonal, are important in digital stories if we understand how to teach DST effectively. It is our job as educators to deliberately include as many intelligences as possible in DST assignments. We need to do this not just to provide students an opportunity to engage the intelligences but also to allow them to see how they are at work in the world, particularly the world of media.

4

Assessing Digital Stories

The Opportunities and Challenges of New Media Evaluation

In many ways, assessment is a pivotal point in the education process. It is how we determine how our students are doing as learners and how we are doing as teachers. It is also how we communicate with the public about the status of education in our communities. If we're going to include digital storytelling (DST) in the curriculum, then we need to be able to show why. Parents, school board members, and education officials will want to know how DST impacts learning and instruction. Teachers will need to be able to explain the assessment strategies they use and what these strategies will tell us about student learning.

Previously I addressed helping teachers "see digital stories." By showing teachers a number of examples of digital stories and guiding them through a tour of this new pedagogical landscape, I was able to help them identify a number of considerations, concerns, and opportunities, both practical and theoretical, about using DST in their classrooms. Ultimately, this conversation leads us to assessment considerations, which I address in this chapter. However, I need to frame my comments within the overall context of assessing new media in education and the shifting bell curve with regard to using technology in teaching and learning.

Shifting Bell Curve

Mainstream education currently doesn't encourage, and rarely requires, students to produce schoolwork in "new media" format such as digital stories. Time requirements as well as technology availability are certainly reasons for this. But even if time was abundant and technology was cheap (of note, MIT has developed a $100 laptop), another reason would prevent this from happening: traditional educators aren't new media literate and thus don't feel comfortable assessing new media projects, a point that I mentioned earlier in my discussion of new media grammar and that

> **Parents will understandably ask:**
>
> Why did you have my child create a digital story, and how did you grade it?

will be addressed in great detail later in Chapter 14. In an era of No Child Left Behind, there is little incentive for teachers to branch out into new areas of literacy or content exploration unless they feel comfortable assessing the student work that such new ventures will produce.

To me, the center of the bell curve has shifted in terms of mainstream education's attitude toward technology in learning. It has gone from fear of the unknown to being overwhelmed by the sort-of-known to being somewhat enamored of the somewhat known, to being grudgingly accepting of what won't go away, and to where we are now: resigned to the fact that kids speak new media, while being honestly confused about how to assess what they create with it. Without a practical, meaningful way to assess new media, teachers are understandably reluctant to include it in the curriculum. If we don't find a way to help them do so, DST is in jeopardy of becoming just another flash in the pedagogical pan and one more thing that kids will do anyway, with or without the involvement of the educational system. As I tell my graduate education students, imagine you're at parent-teacher night. After you show parents a digital story their child has created, they ask, "So, why is my child doing this and how did you grade it?" Educators need to be able to respond reasonably and meaningfully to that question.

Stalled on the technology assessment issue. Technology in education is stalled on the assessment issue, largely because the public has been led to believe that using technology should somehow make us smarter. Clearly, technology doesn't do this, especially when the metric used to determine intelligence is the standardized test. Meanwhile, as this debate rages on, our kids are showing up at school with laptops, personal digital assistants (PDAs), and other powerful technology, demonstrating skills, creativity, and literacies that the present schooling system can't accommodate. If we want our kids to be "smarter," and if what we mean by that is more useful in the real world, then we need to recognize that a large part of the real world consists of the tEcosystem. Thus, if learning how to read and write passes muster as intelligence, learning how to understand and create new media—that is, learning how to read and write new media narrative—should as well.

A little historical perspective will help here. We forget that at one point books were considered heretical new media. Like our new media of today, they came with many downsides: they challenged authority, diminished human memory, and substituted book reading for real experience and community storytelling, to name but a few. Yet we didn't shy away from using them in our educational systems for one compelling reason that has little to do with academics: their pervasive presence in everyday life mandated that we learn how to use them within schools so that our students might better use them outside of school. We have been debating how to assess the literacies associated with books—reading and writing—ever since.

Clearly, when we know how to create and assess new media projects such as digital stories, we will find a place for them in the curriculum, just as we have for more traditional media. But to put things in perspective, we need to remember that even though we have had centuries to get used to traditional literacy, books and articles continue to appear every year about how to improve traditional literacy assessment. Therefore, we shouldn't expect to understand how to assess new media in education so soon after its arrival. But that shouldn't stop us from beginning the process.

Three compelling reasons to assess new media. In fact, there are three compelling reasons to move forward with understanding new media assessment now. First, as explained earlier, new media includes the use of old media. Traditional literacy is very much a part of new media production and provides a way to interest media-savvy students in reading and writing. Second, being able to create and understand new media is going to become part of what it means to be literate, a reality we can approach reactively or proactively. We have the luxury of a little bit of time right now to think about the kinds of literacy standards we want. In the very near future, however, we'll just be playing a game of catch-up.

And last, with or without us, our students leave school every day and enter a tEcosystem that provides them many kinds of learning opportunities that they don't find in school. In fact, more and more students are bringing their tEcosystems with them to school in the form of cell phones, laptops, and other kinds of personalized, networked technology. The net result is that they can leave school once they arrive! As Web 2.0 evolves, students will bypass parts of school altogether, using the tEcosystem as their main source of information, education, and social interaction. We can choose to become part of their world so we can guide how and what they learn or ignore it at everyone's peril, including our own.

▒ Assessment Considerations

I'm always reluctant to propose specific evaluation rubrics for others to use. There are two reasons for this. First, each teacher has his or her own way of doing things, most of which work just fine. If I employ a scale or assessment approach that they don't like, then the rubric can be dismissed in its entirety. That's why I tend to share the traits that I consider for DST projects, which can then be adapted to any assessment system. Second, given that DST is so new and the assessment territory associated with it so uncharted, I don't want to suggest structures that restrict rather than broaden. What I see in this vast new land may not be what others see. That's why I include ongoing rubric development as a component of the DST workshops I conduct for teachers. As teachers learn about DST throughout the workshop, they refine and broaden their approach to evaluation.

In the meantime, here are some issues to consider before going forward. They should make clear that while new assessment strategies and considerations may be required for DST, more traditional considerations are still applicable and important. Following this discussion I describe my own very simple approach to assessing digital stories that are created by students.

Set clear goals. Were your goals clear and did your students meet them? I appreciate that this sounds like something Captain Obvious might ask, but I've found that this is particularly important for teachers who are trying to assess new media projects. It's easy for the technologically underskilled (i.e., most teachers working in a classroom today) to get lost in the new environment of the digital landscape and fall victim to what I call "giving an A for Anything." That is, because teachers aren't new media literate, they give an inflated grade rather than risk being unfair to students or risk doing a poor assessment job because of their unfamiliarity with the genre of new media.

Consider this in terms of assessing conventional schoolwork. When teachers aren't clear about the goals of a traditional assignment, they can always evaluate the quality of student writing as a fallback assessment strategy. However, teachers with limited new media assessment skills must depend heavily on evaluation tied to project goals when evaluating digital stories. Thus two points emerge: (1) goals must be very clear when giving digital story assignments and (2) it's imperative that we pursue new media assessment with vigor.

Assess the story. In Part II, I talk about effective storytelling and provide some ideas about what to include in such an assessment. Suffice it say for now that assessing a digital story based solely on a student's command of the technology is like assessing a student's short story based solely on his or her command of grammar.

Assess all the artifacts students create to develop the digital story, especially the written work. As I discussed earlier, students generate a number of documents and media pieces on their way to creating the final product we see on the screen. My recommendation is that teachers assess all of them and make sure that students know they are doing so. This provides an opportunity to assess writing, planning, art, and media production as well as content understanding.

> Story creation produces a cornucopia of assessable material, much of which is "traditional" in nature.

Assess student planning and process. Some of the most transferable skills derived from DST projects are planning skills. In Part III, I address the media production process, which I recommend teachers require students to follow. Besides providing students with a time-honored approach to media creation that will be understood anywhere in the world of media production, it also provides built-in assessment criteria as well as an assessment schedule.

Assess media grammar and student use of media. Admittedly, this is where it gets tricky. One person's photo collage is another person's waste of time. But recall the earlier discussion about digital stories as "essays versus poetry." If you want students to produce stories with the clarity of an essay regardless of audience, then set that expectation. Even if you are allowing a good deal of leeway for their stories, it's reasonable to expect students to be able to explain their choices and defend their work. Media choices need to be accessible, effective and, above all, support the story rather than detract from it. Chapter 14 should be helpful in this regard.

Assess student understanding and presentation of content. This recalls a number of the traits of digital stories discussed earlier, including "story versus report," "teaching about myself versus myself teaching about something," and "passive versus active viewing." Did students demonstrate that they understood the material? Did they critically assess the material, draw original conclusions from it, and complete the other objectives that were set out in the goals of the project? In the end, if students are creating academic stories, then they need to demonstrate an understanding of content.

Assess student teamwork and use of resources. Digital stories are very adaptable to individual as well as group projects. If students are doing group projects, then assess their involvement and contribution to the project. It may require—or specifically not require—that students involve others such as community resources and media experts. Make sure that it's part of the assessment plan that is clearly understood by students.

Assess their performance. DST performances provide an important opportunity for public participation in the assessment process. Ultimately, students need to know if their piece worked. Showing them or performing them before an audience is a good way to find out. Begin by having students show their stories in your school, then perhaps somewhere else in the community. Part III contains a section that describes a number of ways to perform digital stories.

I recommend that you promise students a performance or publication venue at the outset, largely because the quality of student work improves when they know that people beyond their classrooms will see it. Opportunities to publish on the Web are abundant these days and allow everyone from distant family members to local businesses to see their work without much trouble.

Have students self-assess their projects. Having students reflect at the end of the media creation process is critical. In effect, the process of creating a digital story is itself a story. What were the problems they encountered, and how did they transform in order to solve them? What did they learn? Knowing what they know now, how would they have improved their work? How would they do things differently next time? Part III addresses this in some depth as well.

🏮 A Proposed Set of Traits

Table 4.1 is a list of traits distilled from a number of rubrics I've used over the years. I never use every trait for every project—each project is different and demands a fair amount of rubric customization. Typically I select four to six traits, often combining and rewording some traits as required. In terms of a grading system, suffice it to say that any approach that teachers feel comfortable using will work.

Before we leave the area of assessment, here are two important points to consider:

1. *Rubric length.* Because digital stories are so complex, an assessment rubric used for their evaluation could be many pages long and still be incomplete. The reality is that if my rubric doesn't capture what is truly important about a class assignment in a page or two, then it becomes useless. Elementary teachers with 35 students doing multiple assignments every day, and middle and high school teachers with 100 to 200 different students each day, simply won't have time to use it. Thus, my approach is simple but includes a good deal of latitude.

2. *Rubric evolution.* While my writing rubric can become somewhat static for periods of time, my DST rubric, as well as rubrics I develop for Web sites and other new media projects, are in a constant state of evolution. This reflects the evolving nature of the area as well as my evolving understanding of it.

New media assessment will be part of our futures, either by default or by design. The more enthusiastically our education systems accept the need for new media assessment, the better prepared our children will be for the world beyond school.

Table 4.1   Digital Story Assessment Traits

Master List of Digital Story Evaluation Traits

Story	How well did the story work? This trait can address structure, engagement, character transformation, or any of the other qualities of story discussed in Part II. In fact, an entire rubric can be devoted to evaluating the quality of the story.
Project planning	Is there evidence of solid planning, in the form of story maps, scripts, storyboards, etc.?
Media development process	How well did the student follow the media development process covered in Part III?
Research	Was the student's project well researched and documented?
Content understanding	How well did the student meet the academic goals of the assignment and convey an understanding of the material addressed?
Assignment criteria	Did you require stories to be under two minutes, use no more than 10 images and 30 seconds of music, and provide citations in MLA format? Whatever your criteria, be clear and stick to them.
Writing	What was the quality of the student's written work exhibited in the planning documents, research, etc.?
Originality, voice, creativity	How creative was the production? Did the student exhibit an original sense of voice and a fresh perspective?
Economy	Was the information presented through the story sifted, prioritized, and told without gaps or detours?
Flow, organization, and pacing	Was the story well organized? Did it flow well, moving from part to part without bumps or disorientation?
Presentation and performance	How effective was the student's actual presentation or performance? This includes burning a DVD, posting the story on the Web site effectively, performing it before an audience—whatever the assignment required.
Sense of audience	How well did the story respect the needs of the audience?
Media application	Was the use of media appropriate, supportive of the story, balanced, and well considered?
Media grammar	How bumpy was the story? Media grammar and its relation to "bumps and squints" are described in Part III. There are many facets of media grammar, and you may want to choose a few to focus on.
Citations, permission	Has everything that is not original been credited? Have permissions been obtained where necessary? Do citations appear in the format required by the project?

SOURCE: Ohler, 2004.

Part II

The Art and Practice of Storytelling

5

Thinking About Story

The Story Core, Story Mapping, Story Types

Honoring the Storytelling Covenant

Storytelling is an ancient social dynamic that is built upon an unspoken covenant of trust between speakers and listeners. Tellers trust that they will receive the attention of the listeners and not be distracted during their delivery. In return, listeners trust that the speaker will honor their time and attention by telling a story that is interesting and engaging and that creates and resolves a state of expectation. In addition, tellers trust that they will be granted a good deal of latitude in telling their stories. They don't like to be questioned during story delivery or told to hurry along. On the other hand, listeners trust that the speaker's story will follow a path that makes sense. If it is too unbelievable, or wanders too much, either skepticism or impatience will kill the story.

The storytelling covenant is alive and well today. Successful stories, including traditional oral stories, jokes, books, movies, and digital stories, honor the covenant. From a practical, experiential perspective, the covenant consists of the following traits:

- Listeners can't wait to hear what will happen next, and when they do, they aren't disappointed.
- Listeners feel that what happened next made sense but wasn't predictable (McKee, 1997). This keeps listeners' "willing suspension of disbelief" (Coleridge, 1817) engaged and their skepticism at bay.

- Tellers stayed on message and didn't "bird walk." That is, they didn't include information or events that didn't support the story.
- Tellers feel they commanded the listeners' attention from beginning to end and delivered according to listeners' expectations. Listeners were motivated to listen without interruption.
- The story wasn't too long, and the payoff at the end was in proportion to the listeners' investment of time, trust, and attention.

Sounds simple enough. So how do you do it?

No Formulas for Success, but There Are Guidelines

If, as we saw in Part I, story covers such a vast expanse of human activity and can be expressed in so many different ways, are there any rules we can teach to help students understand and create stories of their own?

Most who tell stories for a living—whether through movies, oral presentations, or lesson plans—will tell you that there is no formula for a successful story. But as McKee (1997) points out, while there are no formulas, there are guidelines. When the guidelines are applied effectively to original, interesting material, the story has a much better chance of succeeding. The primary guidelines I use when working with students are embodied in what I call the story core.

The Story Core

Joseph Campbell (1973) is well known for his book *The Hero With a Thousand Faces,* in which he distills a number of myths and stories from throughout the world to find what he believes to be a universal story form he calls "the hero's journey." According to his theory, the journey that the hero takes consists of particular stages, including being called to adventure, denying the call, accepting a guide to help navigate the journey, passing tests, transformation, and return. I discuss Campbell's work later in the book when I look at story mapping, but suffice it to say for now that the world of Western storytelling relies heavily on his work. The media stories that students are bathed in these days—from movies to TV programming to Internet animations—often use Campbell's approach to story in some form.

Other approaches to story. However, it's important to note that not everyone uses Campbell's monomythic story line as a basis for the stories they tell. Native American authors such as Momaday and Silko, as well as postmodern writers from the Western European tradition such as Faulkner and Joyce, are just a few. Campbell's story form also doesn't adapt well to new media art projects or more abstract forms of expression. Later in this book I will look at some alternative approaches to storying in a bit more detail so that teachers can consider using them with their students in digital story projects. But for now, we use the Western story core because it directly relates to much of the Western storytelling that students experience in the infosphere.

Story core components. The story core I use with teachers and students is a vastly simplified version of the hero's journey. I like to think of it as Campbell's quest in concentrated form that focuses on primarily one thing: how people change, learn, and grow because of the challenges and opportunities in their lives. In the world of education, this translates very directly into how students are transformed by their learning. In the context of a digital storytelling (DST) project, the story core is a planning tool that students use to identify the following key components of their story that compose the essence of their narrative:

- *The central challenge that creates the story's tension and forward momentum.* This can be a question, a problem, an obstacle, an opportunity, or a goal that needs to be addressed by the main character in the story. The challenge creates tension that gives the story its forward momentum, which in turn produces listener involvement. Note: The main character can be anything from a rock to a group of animals to a student to, in some cases, the audience itself.
- *Character transformation that facilitates the response to the challenge.* Difficult and often resisted, this is the essential change that the character needs to undergo to address the challenge, obstacle, or opportunity. Sometimes the transformation occurs at the end, and rarely, at the beginning. But it's usually most powerful when it occurs in the middle and facilitates the response to the challenge. Typically, change is a struggle. Either life or "the old you" pushes back as new circumstances or "a new you" struggles to emerge. If change comes too easily in a story, the audience disengages.
- *The response to and resolution of the challenge that resolves the tension and leads to story closure.* Facilitated by transformation, the character addresses the challenge. This can mean solving a mystery, slaying a dragon, reaching a goal, applying new academic knowledge or learning processes, overcoming an obstacle—anything that addresses the challenge, resolves the tension, and leads to closure. Closure by no means implies a happy ending, just a resolution of events.

Figure 5.1 is one way I like to depict the dynamics of the story core. In this figure you see two versions of the main character or life—the old version and the new version that emerges owing to the transformation in the story. The old version faces a problem or challenge and either (a) tries to resist changing or (b) is challenged by circumstances to keep from changing. The new version needs to push itself past the tipping point in order to transform, resolve the story, and reestablish the balance that existed before the challenge came along. Without this tension-resolution dynamic, there is no forward motion or internal rhythm, making it difficult for listeners to relate their stories to the ones they are listening to.

Figure 5.1　The Story Core

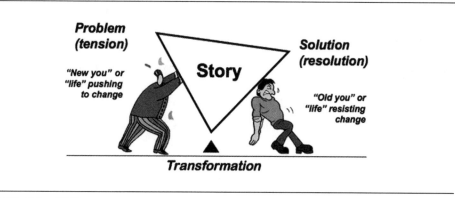

SOURCE: Ohler, 2003.

Introducing the story core at the beginning of a DST project helps students to focus at the outset on the power of their stories, and helps them see their own experiences as a great source of story material. While the story core can be used to help students understand the essence of stories in their lives, including books, movies, and advertisements, it can also be used to help them understand many of life's challenges in very simple but essential terms. I've had many interesting, probing conversations with students about the struggle between their old and new selves using the story core.

A few points about the story core before we continue:

- This is not nearly as serious as it sounds. Stories can be fun and humorous. Some of our favorite comedies have story cores at their centers.
- Keep in mind that the story core addresses Campbell's (1973) quest story, the heart and soul of most drama we watch. Other kinds of new media, like documentaries, use a variety of story approaches. I will address this a bit later.
- Transformation doesn't have to push the change. Fate, luck, or persistence can bring about events that help characters realize things in

hindsight. However, when story characters evolve through growth and learning, they more closely model the learning process we hope our students undergo.

▓ Seeing Stories Through the Story Core

To see how the story core works, let's look at the story cores of three of the digital stories described in Part I.

In *Making a Ball Roll,* students are given the task of showing how to animate a rolling ball. In their first attempt, they encounter a problem: the ball skids rather than rolls. In terms of the story core, life pushed back and created a challenge for them to overcome. Their transformation is twofold: they realize that they didn't consider all aspects of the task, and then, through research, they gain a more complete understanding of the mathematics associated with the task. They resolve their problem by applying their improved mathematical understanding in a successful way. It's important to note that we, the audience, got to transform with the students because we experienced their learning process. Had the ball rolled the first time, this piece would have been a report, not a story, because there would have been no challenge or transformation.

In *Creative Awakening,* a student details her problems as she struggles to get in touch with the artist within. In story core terms, her story is very much about the battle between her old and new self and the struggle she undergoes in order for her new self to emerge victorious. Her transformation comes as she realizes that she needs to slay her inner insecurity demons if she is ever going to be successful. She decides to face her demons by signing up for an artist's meditation retreat. This pivotal event in her life helps her to find "the stillness to begin again," which in turn helps her resolve many of her issues. In the end she's reunited with her inner artist.

In *Fox Becomes a Better Person*, Fox realizes he has a problem: he's lonely because he's mean to everyone. He wants to have friends, but realizes that in order to do this, he'll need help to become a friendly person. This transformative insight leads him to seek out Dove, who helps him become "a nice person"—the new version of himself. In story core terms, Fox pushes against his old self by reeducating himself. Fox is a good student, works hard, and, in the end, resolves his problem by becoming pleasant to others and enjoyable to be around.

▓ Using the Story Core in Education

From a pedagogical perspective, the story core is an apt metaphor for a unit of instruction and can therefore provide a transition mechanism for teachers wanting to explore moving from unit to story-form planning. The two approaches are compared in Table 5.1.

Table 5.1 Comparing Heroes and Students

Story core	Unit of instruction
Hero's problem or challenge	Inquiry assignment, academic challenge
Hero's transformation	Learning and growth through research and analysis
Hero's resolution	Discovery, applied learning

SOURCE: Ohler, 2005.

The student learning story is one in which a student traverses from inquiry to discovery and achieves closure by applying what he or she has learned. The emergent self is one who pushes back against his or her lack of knowledge or understanding and in the end comes to understand new things about himself or herself and the world. In other words, transformation is learning that enables completion of an assignment (see Table 5.1). The similarities between a story core and an interesting, effective unit of instruction provide teachers with a departure point for casting academic material in story form. The value of story as a pedagogy is addressed later. But suffice it to say for now that stories use rhythm and anticipation to emotionally involve learners in ways that other approaches to learning often do not. Students come to school already understanding the story form and expect to find it in use (Egan, 1989). It makes sense that we would consider it as a methodology.

> In education, a quest story becomes a question story.

Using the Story Core as a Media Literacy Tool

Earlier I defined media literacy as the ability to recognize, evaluate, and apply the methods of media persuasion. While media literacy usually focuses on media technique, it's also concerned with how media are structured as an aspect of persuasion. The story core is often employed as a way to structure many forms of media, including advertisements, documentaries, and entertainment. Because it's subtle, it can easily pierce the neocortex and engage audience members emotionally, without causing them to question too much of what they're experiencing. Specific media techniques are then used to present details in a highly convincing manner. Having students recognize how the story core is used in various forms of media can be an effective beginning point for the study of media.

Applying the Story Core

How do teachers and students use the story core for story planning? Here are a number of issues to consider:

Do students draw or write the story core? Either or both. I described the story cores above in words because I wanted to make sure I was being clear about the process. But I could have sketched them using Figure 5.1 as a template, describing each core aspect with a short phrase. In fact, as we shall see later, when students transition to the story map, having the story core in diagram format might be a good idea. For now, teachers should let their curricular goals as well as the age and skills of their students determine what approach to use.

Can students begin by creating a story core? Yes, especially if students know where their stories need to end up. They can then work backward through the kinds of transformation the characters would need to undergo to get there—Wiggins and McTighe (2001) meets Joseph Campbell (1973).

Do students need to begin a story by creating a story core from their essential story idea? Emphatically no. Many times, stories emerge through a process of discovery rather than by thinking in terms of a particular process, a topic I address throughout this book. However, after students have conceived their stories, they can apply a story core check to gain perspective about their stories. The truly important point here is that the story core—or whatever approach teachers use for story planning—must pass muster *before* students begin committing their work to the digital domain. Once the media production process is rolling, it's difficult to significantly change directions.

How can teachers teach about the story core? One way is to have students analyze stories—whether from books, movies, or memory—in terms of the story core. Once they see it in the stories they listen to, they will be better able to use it in the stories they tell. Also, see my comments above about using the story core as a media literacy tool.

Does the story core have applications outside education? Absolutely. If you need to make a pitch to the school board for a budget item, are trying to sell an idea to others, or simply want to be understood on a point, think in story core terms. Who are the audience members? What do they need to understand— that is, what transformation do they need to undergo—and what is keeping them from doing so? In others words, who are the old and new selves in this situation, and why is the old self resisting transformation? Think in terms of telling a story *first* and presenting statistics and charts afterwards.

Is a story core present in documentaries and personal stories? Great question. To me the answer is yes, but in varying degrees and often in very interesting ways. Here are three:

1. By employing a narrator who functions as a protagonist. The narrator investigates a situation by trying to answer a question that is stated or

implied. The process yields discovery and transformation as the truth is revealed.

2. By casting those being studied in the role of protagonist. During the documentary, they come to understand their situation more clearly and are moved to transformation and perhaps action.

3. By being so compelling that audience members become protagonists because they're transformed by what they learn. News briefs do not achieve this effect, but personal stories and documentaries often do. When they don't, they tend to be episodic and boring.

Can I use the story core as the basis for an assessment rubric? Bingo. Earlier I pointed out that a number of DST rubrics I had looked at didn't assess the quality of the story! Assessing the presence and quality of the story core is one simple, powerful way to go about this. As always, let the kind of assessment artifacts you would like to evaluate guide the kind of work you want students to produce. A story core narrative? A diagram? Up to you.

▓ From Story Core to Story Map

It's not unusual in a media development class for students to learn to go directly from story idea to storyboarding. From my perspective, this skips a few steps that can provide students an opportunity to focus on the development of the story itself.

One of these steps is the development of a story core, which I've already addressed. If the stories are short and simple, students can go directly from the story core to the next steps of the

> **Story planning and development steps:**
>
> Get idea
> Create story core
> Create story map
> Write the narrative, story, and/or script
> Create storyboard, if warranted

process, which are covered in some detail in Part III of this book. But typically, students are well served by creating a story map before doing so. With a story map in hand, students have an effective road map for how to proceed.

What is a story map? Think of a story map as simply a story core that reflects more plot information and a deeper consideration of story core elements. By the time the story map is complete, the basic emotional flow, as well as the overarching action of the story, is complete. Like a story core, a story map is a simple diagram that can fit on one piece of paper. In fact, story map information can merely be added to a story core that has already been sketched out. If enough information is added, it can also serve as a storyboard for shorter media pieces.

> Storyboards show the flow of story motion, while story maps show the flow of story emotion.

But before we head into story mapping, let's take a short detour and look at storyboarding. I do this because readers usually have some familiarity with it but typically have very little with story mapping. Comparing the two can illuminate their essential difference: storyboards ensure that the sequence of events of a story makes sense, while story maps ensure that the sequence of events supports a story that is compelling and memorable. In a sentence: story boards show the flow of story motion, while story maps show the flow of story emotion. So, let's review how storyboarding works so we can understand why it's not necessarily the best next step to take in the development of a story.

▦ Storyboarding Versus Story Mapping

Probably the closest thing to a formal storyboard for the average reader is a PowerPoint presentation, which consists of a series of slides that create a visual outline of the sequential flow of events in a presentation. When I deliver a presentation that is accompanied by a PowerPoint slide show, I use each slide as a cue card to help me stay on track and keep my story flowing. When I want to see a visual outline of my entire presentation to get an overall sense of flow and continuity, I can look at all of my slides at once by using PowerPoint's slide sorter tool.

Similarly, movie directors, computer game developers, and others in the creative content business use storyboards that resemble PowerPoint presentations to describe the different scenes in their projects so they can check the overall flow of events. Although every developer handles storyboarding differently, storyboards typically consist of event panels. Each panel has a sketch of the action in the event as well as information about camera angles, music, and so on (see Figure 5.2). Taken together, the panels serve as an outline of the flow of events in the project.

Storyboards are important planning tools in media-based projects because the inclusion of media in the storytelling process greatly increases the complexity of the project. The larger a media project is, the more important the storyboard becomes. Owing to the shorter, more compact nature of digital stories, a number of approaches to storyboarding digital stories have evolved that don't require the preparation of formal panels. These approaches are discussed in Part III, when storyboarding is addressed in more depth.

But regardless of the form of storyboarding used, the important point here is this: storyboards are primarily concerned with story events, not story essence. While a storyboard can help ensure a story stays on track, it's less helpful in ensuring that it's engaging and memorable. For this we began with the story core and now turn to story maps.

Figure 5.2   Simplified Storyboard

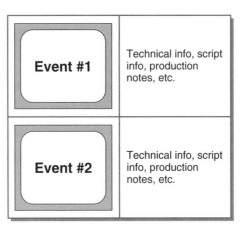

⚘ Story Mapping

Recall that a story map is simply a more fleshed-out version of a story core. As we shall see, a story map evolves naturally from a story core and, in essence, embodies and extends the story core by providing new information about the plot and more in-depth consideration of elements of the story core: problem, transformation, and resolution. If you elect to use story mapping with your students, then you will find that it's the tool they will use to do their most important work in terms of articulating the essential elements of their stories. As a bonus, story mapping is easy to do and costs almost nothing to use.

What do story maps look like? They can take many forms. In Chapter 9 we look at a variety of them, one of which goes all the way back to Aristotle! I should also note that over the years I've encouraged students to create their own story maps, and they have produced many creative approaches that are original and effective. As with all things in storytelling, there are guidelines but no formulas.

But for now, we'll use an approach to story mapping developed by Brett Dillingham (2001, 2005) called the "visual portrait of a story" (VPS), which I've expanded for my purpose to include transformation and a few other elements. It's one of my favorites, and it's where I usually start story mapping with students.

The map presented in Figure 5.3 is annotated to describe the nature of the story elements. However, when students create their own maps they begin with a "blank map," and effectively replace the annotation with information about their own stories.

Take a good look at the VPS story map presented here in Figure 5.3. You can see the story core clearly labeled within the map: problem, transformation, solution. Walk through the map in your mind a few times, following the solid

Figure 5.3   Annotated Visual Portrait of a Story (VPS)

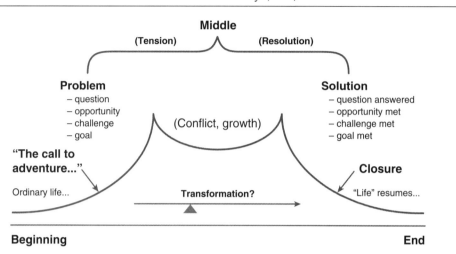

SOURCE: Adapted by Ohler (2001), from Dillingham, B. (2001). *Visual portrait of a story: Teaching storytelling* [School handout]. Juneau, AK.

black line as though you were following a path into new yet somehow familiar territory.

Starting at the left we begin on flat land until we receive a "call to adventure," which takes us up the first slope headlong into a problem, question, opportunity, challenge, or goal that needs to be addressed. This provides the forward momentum in the story. We are now in a state of expectancy, which is labeled "tension." In the center part of the map, the story unfolds and transformation comes into play, which moves the story forward to the solution of the problem, resolving our state of expectation. We leave by going down the right-hand slope into closure, resuming "life," which I've put in quotation marks on the VPS because life is now somehow different because of the experience. That is, "the hero" returns but is changed by his or her experience.

Next let's take a closer look at the story elements, including those within the story core, and observe how they're accommodated by the VPS. Keep in mind that no matter what kind of story map you use, either these elements should be present in some way or there needs to be a good reason for their absence. Also keep in mind that being able to draw the VPS as smoothly as you see here is hardly the point. A rough approximation will do. The only reason this story map looks as good as it does is because I used a computer to draw it so that you could read it. Normally, I would just use pencil and paper. Typically, I discourage students from using computers to create story maps, because I find that technology just gets in the way at this point in the story development process.

> Don't have students use computers to create the VPS. They just get in the way at this point. Just have them use paper and pencil.

☷ Story Elements

Well-meaning people have probably told you since childhood that a story consists of three parts: a beginning, a middle, and an end. While you can see from the VPS that this is more or less true, each part needs to have certain elements in order to be effective. These elements compose the components of the VPS and are explained below. Note how they are present in simplified form in the story core.

Elements of a beginning. The story begins with a call to adventure (Campbell, 1973) by moving out of the flat, ordinary events of life to new heights of experience. The upward movement of the curve suggests that characters are going to need to climb to get to where they're going. The key characteristics of the beginning are as follows:

- Information is presented or implied that grounds the listener in the ordinary life of a character, setting the scene from which adventure emerges.
- A main character, which, as I mentioned earlier, can be anything from a rock to a group of forest animals to a student to the audience itself, is called to adventure; the ordinary routine of life is interrupted. A quest or process of inquiry has begun. It's because of the suspension of ordinary events that a story emerges. If the story does not emerge from ordinary events, doing so is implied, perhaps because the opening events contrast sharply with listeners' expectations of normal life.
- A quest of some kind is described, implied, or begun. The listener understands that the main character, sometimes with help from others, needs to accomplish something, understand something, or go somewhere. This establishes the beginning of a problem that must be solved, which can be a question, obstacle, opportunity, goal, or other challenge that needs to be fully addressed.

Elements of a middle. Look at the VPS. What does it suggest? To me, it looks like a tension bridge, held together by cables that keep it from falling apart. It also looks like a high-wire that characters are going to need to cross in order to get to the other side: resolution. It's slumped rather than straight, suggesting that things might become more challenging before they resolve; that is, the characters may falter on their way to the other side, but they will get there eventually. On top of that, the VPS looks like a circus tent, a great place for stories. In fact, it's within this tent that the real drama of the story unfolds.

On the left side of the middle is the "problem," which, as I noted earlier, can be a number of things, including an obstacle to overcome, an issue to resolve, a question to answer, a goal to meet, a mystery to solve, an opportunity to realize—anything that challenges the characters in the story. Regardless of what it is, it creates the expectation of future events, which in turn creates the tension that gives the story its forward motion. Thus, tension is the primary heading on the left-hand side and exists to create within the listener a sense of expectation for something to happen next. "Resolution" is the primary heading on the right. The solution can be overcoming the obstacle, resolution of an issue, solving a mystery, fulfillment of an opportunity, and so on. Tension/resolution is the heartbeat of so many great stories.

Characteristics of the middle are as follows:

- The full extent of the tension, problem, or conflict is made apparent. The story includes a series of adventures that are related to solving the problem and relieving the tension. Adventures can be physical, mental, emotional, spiritual, or any combination of these. They can consist of anything from hacking your way through a jungle forest to digging through your past in order to understand it. The character could just as easily be sitting quietly in a chair as riding in a caravan going across the desert. The world of adventure is vast, and much of it occurs personally and without special effects.
- Tension is increased through the use of situations that beg for some kind of resolution; readers subconsciously want to know what's going to happen next. Failure to answer that question (by providing extraneous detail, gratuitous special effects, etc.) dilutes the story. There can be a series of such situations in which the characters, through failure, persistence, luck, or personal growth, finally achieve a goal. As McKee (1997) points out, it's often most effective for these events to seesaw between advancing the quest and hindering it.
- In the process of traversing the path from problem to solution, the character learns, grows, and becomes a new person in some significant respect. Ideally, the listeners vicariously do too. Typically, transformation occurs in such a way as to make the resolution possible. Transformation is addressed next.

Transformation (middle, continued). Let's consider the transformation component of the middle separately for a moment, as it is the heart of both the story core and the story map.

Note that it is represented in Figure 5.3 as an arrow moving toward the resolution, which is set on an off-center fulcrum. Visually, it makes the arrow tip, implying motion. That is, things will move but only after a tipping point is reached, a concept introduced in the story core. The key to transformation is that the central character cannot solve the problem of the story easily or simply; he or she needs to change in order to solve it. In story core terms, as characters push forward, their own inertia and fears, as well as circumstances within the story, push back. They have to be pushed and tested by the situation to grow and learn something new.

If the central character does not undergo some sort of transformation on the way to solving the problem, then the story is your average B-grade action film: Problem: bad people. Solution: shoot them. Listeners are dissatisfied because there is no struggle and personal transformation to relate to. The bottom line is that the central character must be a different person at the end of the journey. And in the best of all possible stories, so are you—the reader, listener, or viewer—because the story resonated with your own life.

Elements and characteristics of transformation are as follows:

- The main character needs to transform in order to solve the problem or achieve resolution. He or she needs to become stronger, smarter, wiser, more mature, or some combination of these. Different kinds of transformation are covered in some detail in Chapter 8.
- Transformation runs the gamut from the allegorical (Luke Skywalker needing to become a Jedi to defeat the Dark Side) to the banal (a character in an advertisement realizing he needs a more effective deodorant to be successful in life); from the very external (Popeye eating spinach and growing muscles) to the very internal (the narrator of *Creative Awakening* realizing that she is an artist who needs to reconnect with her artistic self).
- Transformation often involves slaying some personal, internal dragon, such as fear, insecurity, misunderstanding, ignorance, cowardice, close-mindedness, or some other character flaw. Coupled with slaying an external dragon, transformation becomes a very powerful story force.
- In a phrase, internal transformation can be summed up as the slaying of an internal dragon through an attitude adjustment based on realization. This is an oversimplification, to be sure, because not all of the focus of transformation is internal. But stories with inner transformation tend to be more memorable than stories without it.

> Internal transformation in a sentence: slaying internal dragons through attitude adjustment based on learning and realization.

- Personal transformation is often a metaphor for universal transformation. That is, we see our own transformation in the changes of the character. The character reminds of us where we have been or what we need to do in order to resolve something in our own lives. In so doing, the story makes us think of our own story.
- Sometimes there is a transformative moment—a tipping point, as described in the story core—when the character shifts and makes a quantum leap in development. Other times transformation can be more gradual. For example, students involved in inquiry-based research to understand the causes of global warming could proceed slowly through

smaller steps of realization, perhaps punctuated by a Eureka! moment about their contribution to the situation. No formulas, just guidelines.

- Sometimes using themes, morals, or values is also a good way to approach transformation. If students are required to tell a story that shows a particular theme or value, the transformation is often implied. For example, I worked with a group of elementary students who were studying cultural values. As part of their project, they created stories that needed to demonstrate one of the cultural values they were studying. This drove the story and in the process nearly always involved someone who changed by learning something and realizing the importance of a cultural value.

In fact, transformation is so key that I will go so far as to say that the rest of a story basically exists to support it. Without it, you can have story for story's sake. Such stories can be entertaining and even interesting and valuable, but they don't tend to be memorable or powerful. That's why I recommend that instead of asking yourself what you could do in your story that would be surprising, or even interesting, ask yourself who is changing and how are their changes pushing the story forward.

Elements of an end. After the story's problem is solved, there needs to be closure that doesn't leave the listener feeling like the storyteller "has simply run out of material" (Egan, 1989). By no means does this require a triumphant or a they-lived-happy-ever-after ending. It simply means that audience members need to feel as though a goal has been reached, an issue has been resolved, or events have been concluded, even if it involves the realization that a goal is unreachable or an issue is unresolvable. Do you know how disappointed you feel when a movie you are watching ends with "to be continued"? Or do you remember that art film you saw that deliberately left things up in the air? This can work, but I recommend you use it sparingly and with great finesse.

Essential elements and characteristics of an end are as follows:

- Closure. Stories need to have endings that allow listeners to feel as though their personal investment in listening has been honored. Typically, this means that by the end of closure, all questions have been answered. Not answering questions is a violation of the unspoken storyteller–story listener covenant. This doesn't mean you shouldn't do it; but it does mean that if you are going to do it, do so deliberately, with intent and purpose. Keep in mind that a question can be fully addressed by making it clear that it can't, shouldn't, or no longer needs to be answered. The key here is closure, not the answer.
- The essential transformation, and what is learned from it, is somehow put into play. Life goes forward differently because people have been

transformed. Ideally, you, the listener, also feel changed. You feel that you understand or have experienced something that you would not have otherwise. This includes rediscovering something you already knew but had forgotten or been avoiding. Also, further transformations and realizations can come at the end, often building on previous transformations.

> "We will begin our descent into the airport shortly and I will need to pick up the DVD players in about 15 minutes. Now would be a good time to fast forward whatever movie you are watching so you can see how it ends." —Flight attendant aboard a flight I took recently

- Stories can conclude in an obvious way, such as stating what has been learned in the form of a moral or personal revelation. Or the story can move forward with some action or narrative that shows changes have been internalized by the characters. This is what is often called "showing rather than telling" in the world of fiction writing.

※ Facilitating the VPS

Typically I don't use a VPS handout. I simply put a copy of it on the board or on a display screen using my computer. How much annotation I include depends on the audience. I show almost none for elementary students, but I show all of it for teachers. Students draw the VPS shape themselves, without the annotation, filling in the details of their stories. Having students draw a story map themselves is their first step in making it their own, personalized tool.

Earlier I mentioned that I don't like having students use computers at this point because they just get in the way. I want to emphasize this. You want students to go from idea to story core to story map with as little technological distraction as possible. Have them scribble all over the VPS. The point is for their story maps to make sense to them.

Once the VPS is done and reviewed (either by peers, the teacher, or both), students should keep it handy. It's the blueprint of their story. Story development as part of the media development process is covered in Part III.

※ Impact of Story Mapping on Digital Storytelling

Story mapping can be used for any kind of storytelling, from no-tech traditional storytelling to high-tech media extravaganzas. It's particularly important in DST for a number of reasons:

- When teachers use story mapping with their students, an amazing thing happens: students talk about their stories rather than their technology. And because story mapping happens at the very beginning of the process, using pencil and paper, students aren't distracted by technology as they develop their stories.
- One of story mapping's greatest values is that it helps dissuade students from writing episodic stories in which one thing happens after another, after another, without any sense of internal rhythm. There is nothing inherent in the structure of storyboarding that suggests rhythm; in fact, it looks like a good way to capture episodic information. On the other hand, a story map compels storytellers to create a story experience with rhythm and forward motion that has a beginning, a middle, and an end, and the tension/resolution and transformation necessary to keep it moving. A story map gives storytellers a place to express their story core.
- Essentially, a story map is a portal into a student's mind, allowing teachers to see what students see and to talk to them about their vision for their story. It provides a way for teachers to interact with student work in an easy, low-tech way at the beginning of the process, when their input can actually impact what students produce.
- The story map provides teachers a way to quickly ascertain the potential of a student's story. It provides a clear visual aid that teachers, students, and peers can refer to as they discuss the power, quality, and value of their stories.
- Changing a digital story that is already in production is very difficult to do. Having a story mapping review process at the beginning of digital story development helps minimize changes after production begins.
- On a practical level, a story map is a simple diagram that anyone can sketch. It fits on one piece of paper, allowing teachers or peer reviewers to grasp the story line and story core quickly. I've used student story maps many times as a basis for encouraging students to strengthen their stories. I would like to think that I saved them hours of taking pictures, shooting video, and recording music and narration that they wouldn't have needed. Conversely, I hope I helped them identify the media they did need.

Typically, digital stories are short (two to four minutes), for which a VPS is ideally suited. Incidentally, the VPS can be adapted for longer stories and, in fact, a series of them can be used to articulate subplots as well as a main plot. However, this isn't a topic we'll address in this book.

Let's map a few stories. That's next.

6

Applying Story Maps

Seeing the Core, Mapping the Story

Let's begin by mapping the same three stories for which we previously created story core narratives: *Making a Ball Roll, Creative Awakening,* and *Fox Becomes a Better Person.*

Making a Ball Roll is a great example of something that is half report, half story. In it, you will recall, students are presenting the mathematics behind a rolling ball. However, their first attempt makes the ball skid rather than roll. They research, explain, and apply the math to make it roll, and in the end, we watch as they succeed. Figure 6.1 shows how I would story map this story:

The students' transformation comes as a response to "Oops—what should we do now?" They realize that they hadn't seen the full extent of the task in all of its complexity, which caused them to learn and apply more math. When I show this story to teachers, they see its value in terms of assessment opportunities. Students who take on a problem, and demonstrate their learning process, provide a much richer data set for teacher assessment than students who simply provide answers to questions on a right or wrong basis.

Let's map something more personal, like *Creative Awakening.* The student who created this produced a story map that is more detailed than what I offer in Figure 6.2. I've taken the liberty of summarizing some parts of it while hopefully preserving the essence of it.

The call to adventure begins with the decision to reconnect with the artist within. After a promising start, she begins to doubt her abilities. Her realization that she needs to do something drastic if she's going to succeed is the transformation that pushes her toward her solution: attending a meditation retreat that provides the stillness she needs to begin as an artist again. If we're astute, we realize that her struggle to connect with something deeper

Figure 6.1 VPS of *Making a Ball Roll*

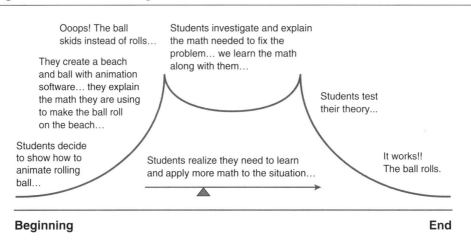

SOURCE: Adapted by Ohler (2001), from Dillingham, B. (2001). *Visual portrait of a story: Teaching storytelling* [School handout]. Juneau, AK.

Figure 6.2 VPS of *Creative Awakening*

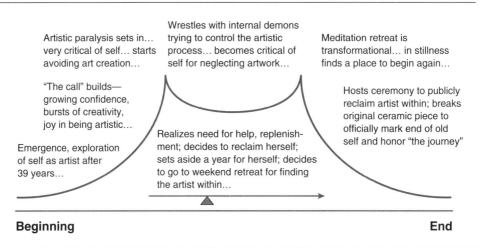

SOURCE: Adapted by Ohler (2001), from Dillingham, B. (2001). *Visual portrait of a story: Teaching storytelling* [School handout]. Juneau, AK.

within herself is also our struggle. Hopefully, we also realize, as she did, that making this kind of connection often requires conscious fearlessness. Incidentally, in her digital story she uses no music, no fancy transitions; her story consists mostly of pictures of her immediate surroundings and artwork and a well-developed script that she reads. I would call it a media-minimalist piece of new media that is extremely effective. At the end of it, I feel I really understand something essential about her and her relationship with her creative side.

Figure 6.3 VPS of *Fox Becomes a Better Person*

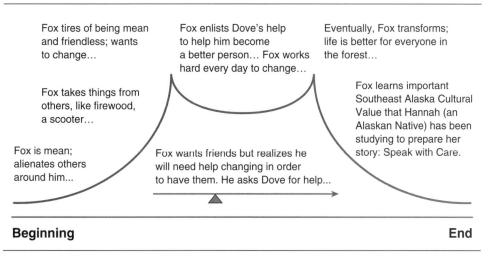

Fox tires of being mean and friendless; wants to change...

Fox enlists Dove's help to help him become a better person... Fox works hard every day to change...

Eventually, Fox transforms; life is better for everyone in the forest...

Fox takes things from others, like firewood, a scooter...

Fox learns important Southeast Alaska Cultural Value that Hannah (an Alaskan Native) has been studying to prepare her story: Speak with Care.

Fox is mean; alienates others around him...

Fox wants friends but realizes he will need help changing in order to have them. He asks Dove for help...

Beginning   **End**

SOURCE: Adapted by Ohler (2001), from Dillingham, B. (2001). *Visual portrait of a story: Teaching storytelling* [School handout]. Juneau, AK.

Let's map Hannah's *Fox Becomes a Better Person*. Unfortunately, I don't have the original, so I've re-created in Figure 6.3 what I believe to be a reasonable facsimile. In that story, we meet a mean, lonely Fox who realizes he needs Dove's help to become a likable person. In the end, Fox becomes a better person, returns things he took from others, apologizes to those he has offended, and becomes someone that the rest of the animals in his life enjoy having as a friend.

Note that the primary transformation for Fox isn't so much his eventual change into a better person. Rather, it's his realization that he needs help that blossoms into his changed personality. Hannah ends her story by citing a tenet of the *Southeast Alaska Cultural Values* (Southeast Native Elders, 2004) that she studied to prepare for developing her story: speak with care.

Our involvement in the story occurs because we want to know what happens and if Fox is successful. If we're astute listeners, we learn something more universal: sometimes you need help to change.

⚵ Mapping a Longer, More Detailed Story

Finally, let's look at something a little longer. This is an actual story that I tell during my workshops in traditional oral fashion. Afterward, I lead participants through the process of mapping this as a group exercise. The story comes from my novel, *Then What? Everyone's Guide to Living, Learning, and Having Fun in the Digital Age* (2003). I am going to tell it in stages with commentary, changing it deliberately to show what works and what doesn't in terms of the elements of a story we considered earlier. Then we will story map it.

William Tell and the Young Girl Who Could Fix Computers

Once upon a time, there was a director of information technology for a large company named William Tell. He was shy, skinny, and only 22 years old. It was his job to make sure everyone's computer worked just right and that everyone's Web page looked and acted wonderfully well. There were over 500 people in the company, so that was quite a job.

One day, William's boss phoned him. "I'm calling to remind you that this Saturday is Company Family Day," he told him in a gruff, no-nonsense bosslike voice. William knew all about Company Family Day. It happened every third Saturday of every February. Husbands and wives and kids and moms and dads and aunts and uncles of all the employees got a tour of company headquarters. They listened to boring PowerPoint presentations by self-important people who were trying to be funny (but weren't). In between presentations they ate free hot dogs on mushy white buns. Even though William didn't like crowds, he always went to Company Family Day in case someone needed technical help.

"This year we're going to do something different," his boss continued. "I want you to show everyone the new company Web page you have been working on. Set everything up in the auditorium and be ready to go at 10 a.m." Before William could beg him to let someone else show the Web page who actually wanted to stand up and talk in front of a bunch of people, his boss hung up. William suddenly felt that someone with a hand the size of a bowling ball had socked him in the gut.

That Saturday William went to the auditorium early to make sure all the connections were connected, the microphone didn't squeal, and the Web page didn't look too fuzzy on the vast projection screen that filled the wall behind him. At 10 a.m., William walked onto the stage, hit a button, and his Web page lit up the auditorium. The audience oohed and aahed as he explained the need for the bold new colors, nifty icons, and persuasive animations. He showed 3-D rotating pictures of members of the board of directors and explained how to get weather forecasts of anywhere the company did business. He was afraid he used too many acronyms and technical terms. But the audience oohed and aahed so loudly and long that William's boss gave him a raise. And everyone lived happily ever after.

Actually, this isn't how the story goes at all. I deliberately left out the tension-transformation-resolution that would have made it more engaging in order to show what a story needs. So far, it's a good example of a story that has a beginning, a middle, and an end and works from a functional perspective, but is not powerful, memorable, or useful. There's some tension, caused by the fact that William doesn't want to be on stage. But we have no sense of him struggling to overcome the issue. In a sentence, the problem with this story is that William is the same guy at the end of the story as he was in the beginning—he doesn't change at all. So far, this is basically flat and forgettable. Let's pick up the story halfway through and make some changes to improve it:

> But as people started filing into the auditorium, something went woefully wrong. William could see the Web page on his computer screen, but it had suddenly disappeared from the big screen behind him. Where once appeared the company's new Web page was now a vast gaping screen full of fuzzy nothing. He began frantically checking all his cords and connections.

Better. There's a rise in the story because of the presence of a problem that needs to be solved. We have a glimpse of a memorable story. So let's solve the problem:

> Whew! The cord from his computer was disconnected. He reconnected it and everything was fine.

Oops. The story just fell and became eminently forgettable. Why? Two reasons. First, the problem was solved too easily, without conflict or tension. William's experience sounds like something that could have happened to us on a normal day—and stories aren't usually told about ordinary people on normal days. (If they are, it's with the intent of showing how extraordinary the ordinary can be if we alter our perception—but that's another story entirely.) And second, our hero, William, wasn't required to transform. If William is going to be an engaging character, then the situation needs to force him to grow somehow in order to solve the problem. Here he wasn't required to slay any inner dragons or to change, learn, or grow in order to fix the situation. Let's create a situation in which he has to change. But first, let's raise the stakes, making the tension a bit more tense:

> As the auditorium filled with buzzing, expectant people waiting to see the new Web page, William frantically checked his cords and clacked away on his keyboard. But no matter what he did, nothing appeared on the big screen behind him. William could hear heckling erupt throughout the room. A woman in the front row said, "It's no wonder my husband didn't get a bonus last year with bozos like this driving the bus." In the third row sat a group of young boys with their baseball hats on sideways who began to chant, "Loser, loser, loser . . ." So much perspiration rolled down William's body and into his shoes that they made a sloshing sound when he walked.

Better. We've ratcheted things up. The situation is more dire. The greater the tension, the greater your emotional involvement in wanting to see it resolved. Now, whatever transformation William undergoes will seem more important, memorable. Imagine ending the story right here. You'd have me arrested for lack of resolution! So let's get back to the story before you get too ornery:

> Just then, a young girl with coke bottle glasses and long blond pigtails walked up to the stage and called out to him. "Mr. Tell, Mr. Tell! I had the same problem with my computer. If you hold down the Shift key and press the F12 key, the image will come up just fine." William did just that, and indeed, the big screen behind him filled with the company's new Web page. He thanked her and delivered his presentation, and everyone lived happily ever after.

Too weak. The introduction of the girl presents the possibility of the need for William to change. In a sense, he does: he learns a few keystrokes. But he didn't have to work for his transformation. He simply accepted her advice, no questions asked. The resolution is much too weak for the tension that exists. So let's try the ending again.

> William tried not to be gruff with the young girl as he told her that he was very busy. But she insisted on helping. "But Mr. Tell, just hold down the Shift and press F12," she chimed in a friendly singsong. "That's all you need to do." William smiled a fake, nasty smile as he was thinking, I'm the adult. I am the director of information technology. I'm not going to be embarrassed in front of this crowd by some young girl telling me how to fix my computer! Not in a gazillion years!

Hear William wrestle? He's in the throes of an internal conflict. An inner dragon rears its head. He feels the young girl is causing him to lose face in public, yet he needs to solve his problem. On top of all of this, he's shy and doesn't even want to be there! What's he going to do?

> Everyone in the back row got up to leave, talking loudly about going to get a drink to take their minds off the stupid Web page demonstration that never happened. The boys with their baseball hats on sideways chanted a little more loudly, "Loser, loser, loser..." The young girl tugged on William's sweaty shirt, which made his perspiration-filled shoes slosh. "Mr. Tell, why don't you just press Shift, F12?" she asked. "Don't you know where the F12 key is?" William turned beet red. The veins in his forehead started to twitch. "Yes, I know where it is!" he shrieked. "Then why don't you press it, Mr. Tell?" she insisted. "We're all waiting." But William didn't move a muscle.

The dragon looms. William's sword is drawn. He's at the tipping point.

> William looked up at the crowd that was growing impatient as entire rows got up to leave. He turned and looked up at the blank screen behind him, then down at the young girl tugging on his shirt, then at the crowd that seemed filled with nothing but disgusted parents with unruly kids who were using PDAs, no doubt instant messaging each other about what a loser he was. He looked up at the blank screen, down at the young girl, up at the screen, down at the girl,

> and then, in one fluid motion during which he could feel something within his psyche shift with the power of tectonic plates grinding away in an earthquake zone, he held down the Shift key and pressed F12. WHAM! The screen filled with the company's new Web page. Everyone applauded. The people who were leaving to get a drink sat back down. The mean kids wearing sideways baseball hats stopped chanting. William walked up to the microphone in his sloshing shoes and publicly thanked the young girl for making it all possible.

Sometimes a moral helps sum up the hero's transformation and provide a sense of ending. In this case, it's useful:

> Years later, when William was a technology teacher in an elementary school, he often recalled that Company Family Day. Now, whenever a young girl tries to give him advice about how to run his computer, he listens.

In order to solve the problem of the computer image not appearing on the projection screen, William needed to overcome his prejudice about listening to someone much younger than himself. He had to develop the courage to swallow his pride, let go of his ageism and perhaps his sexism, and accept a world in which adults not only can learn from children but shouldn't feel threatened when they do so. As a result, he was a new person. In the very end, he reflects on how he has changed and how he uses what he learned. By the way, William should consider himself lucky, because we could have turned the young girl into someone who reminded him of his little sister whom he never liked. Then he would've had to face a slew of personal issues from his childhood too. But we cut him some slack . . . this time.

Let's story map this:

The story core, basic plot, and emotional flow were fleshed out with notes that are attached to each major story element. The VPS incorporates big-picture action as well as details that flavor the action. We understand why William is different at the end. That is, we understand the transformation that has caused him to become different.

It's important to note that William's experience resonates with us because we can imagine similar situations in our own lives. After all, who isn't surrounded by kids who know a lot more about technology than adults? This kind of resonance allows the moral at the end (listen to young girls who can help fix your computer) to transcend the immediate situation. If we're astute, we understand that it's a metaphor for many situations that might require us to learn from those whom we never expected to be our teachers.

Figure 6.4   VPS of *William Tell and the Young Girl Who Could Fix Computers*

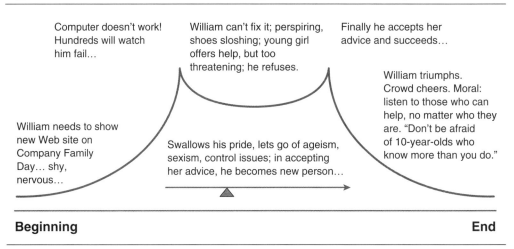

Computer doesn't work! Hundreds will watch him fail...

William can't fix it; perspiring, shoes sloshing; young girl offers help, but too threatening; he refuses.

Finally he accepts her advice and succeeds...

William triumphs. Crowd cheers. Moral: listen to those who can help, no matter who they are. "Don't be afraid of 10-year-olds who know more than you do."

William needs to show new Web site on Company Family Day... shy, nervous...

Swallows his pride, lets go of ageism, sexism, control issues; in accepting her advice, he becomes new person...

Beginning   **End**

SOURCE: Adapted by Ohler (2001), from Dillingham, B. (2001). *Visual portrait of a story: Teaching storytelling* [School handout]. Juneau, AK.

For teachers, William's realization translates into a particularly poignant and useful moral: don't be afraid of students who know more than you do. In fact, deputize them and integrate their skills into your classroom. Teachers who don't mine the talent of their students, particularly when it comes to using digital technology, are going to be less effective and have less fun than those who do. Besides, if teachers let the kids remember the tricks and clicks that come and go in the technology world, then they get to concentrate on what is truly gratifying as a teacher: managing learning and helping kids develop the interpersonal skills they need to become better teachers themselves.

Keep in mind that if you had heard a lecture that cited the findings of 10 great studies conducted by 10 famous scholars that proved the effectiveness of kids helping adults with technological problems in 10 different ways, you probably would have forgotten it by next week. But there's a good chance you'll remember this story. In fact, there's a good chance that a month from now you could tell it yourself.

> We forget lectures, but we remember stories.

7

Story Planning Considerations

Tips, Techniques, Lessons Learned

This chapter contains lessons I've learned over the years about the story planning process. I pass them on to you, one storyteller to another. Incidentally, I'd like to hear what you've learned as well. Please drop me an e-line through www.jasonohler.com.

Teaching Story Planning

Introduce the Story Core and Story Mapping

I introduce the concepts covered in Part II, including story cores, maps, and elements. I address thinking of stories in terms of problems, challenges, and opportunities that have solutions or responses, because characters change in order or respond to them.

I Tell a Story, Then the Group Helps Me Find the Story Core and Map the Story

Following the introduction of story structure, I tell a story or show stories created by others and then involve the participants in helping me identify the elements of the story core in the stories they watch. They then help me map the stories. It's always instructive and fun during this process to suggest changes to the story, in particular "bad" changes, to see how they would impact the strength of the story.

I Lead a Story-Storming Session

Story storming is simply brainstorming about stories. The goal of the story-storming process is to tease story cores out of my participants so they can begin to see stories take shape that are based on events in their own lives or are products of their own imaginations.

There are many ways to do story storming. Typically, I lead a discussion at the board (or use a computer hooked to a display) that uses a table consisting of three columns that compose the story core: Problem, Solution, Transformation. The table should look a bit like a tic-tac-toe grid (see Table 7.1). For younger students, transformation becomes change, learning, realization, theme—whatever is appropriate.

Table 7.1   The Story-Storming Grid

Problem	Solution	Transformation

I keep going until I get at least three good problems and then three good solutions for one of the problems. We then discuss the kinds of transformations that are implied in the solutions. Once the transformations are fleshed out a bit, the solutions with depth and salience become obvious. The stronger the transformation, the stronger the story.

The next steps in the story development process are detailed in Chapter 11, in which I discuss adapting story planning to media production.

❖ Story Planning Adaptations

Do I teach story planning the same way every time?

Never. Every group I work with is its own unique subculture with its own needs. In addition, each student is a unique storyteller looking for the most effective way to get in touch with the story within.

When I'm conducting a workshop, the nature and goals of the group, as well as the time and resources that are available, always determine some aspects of my approach. That's why I like to talk to

> When it comes to digital storytelling planning, one size does not fit all...

organizers prior to a storytelling event to determine how to best meet the unique needs of their participants, regardless of whether I'm working in a classroom, a workshop, or at a conference.

Here's an example of an adaptation of the story planning process described earlier. Recently I conducted a workshop with at-risk youth who were using the digital storytelling (DST) process therapeutically. In reality, storytelling is usually therapeutic for everyone, just in different ways. But in this case, therapy was the stated objective. Many of the participants were working through personal trauma and had turned to the process of DST to help them in their process of self-discovery.

The approach their counselors and I had agreed to use was to have participants create two personal stories. The first would address the question, Who am I and how did I get here? and the second would address the question, Where do I want to be three to five years from now, and what changes in my life do I need to make in order to get there?

After talking to the group, I decided that the story map would be overkill. Instead, the participants and I watched some digital stories and talked about them with the help of their counselors. Then we talked about the three points of the story core and discussed how to frame their story question in ways that would help lead them to a sense of personal discovery. This was all the formal story planning they needed for the first story. The rest of their planning was done individually with their counselors and largely focused on developing a narrative script. However, their second digital story project involved them projecting where they want to be in the future and determining how they

> **Story blocked?**
>
> Try creating a story about not being able to create a story. These have been some of my favorites to listen to over the years...

have to transform in order to get there. In effect, in their second story they became heroes of their own future lives. Story mapping was an ideal tool to use for this.

Finding Stories

I've yet to meet someone without a story to tell. But every now and again I do meet a workshop participant who gets story blocked, even after watching several digital stories created by others. I find the best way to help them discover their stories is simply to walk them through a series of questions.

If I'm working with a teacher who is trying to create an educational story, I might ask, "What's an important concept you teach that you feel students have a hard time grasping?" Students searching for a story often need to do so within the context of a unit of instruction. In that case I might ask, "What concept from your homework do you find either particularly interesting or perplexing?" If a participant is creating a more personal story, I might ask, "When is the last time you cried or got really excited?" If I'm trying to help an organization tell its story, I might ask, "What's the most important thing you think people need to understand about the value you bring to their lives, and can you remember a time with a client that exemplifies that value?" I find that it doesn't take much for the ideas to begin to flow. If participants are having trouble committing their stories to paper, even after the ideas start to flow, then I also offer to sit with them and collaboratively map what I hear as a rough sketch, whether as a core, a map, or simply a list of bullets.

The story discovery and articulation process is so personal that participants will sometimes develop their own ways to plan their stories on the spot. In my workshops, students have used a number of different approaches to this, including creating traditional outlines, writing copious amounts of narrative, fashioning their own maps, bouncing ideas off colleagues until a series of bullets emerge, arranging objects on a table in a particular way to re-create an event, drawing a series of sketches, and just sitting and staring at a wall until the story emerges in a writing frenzy, to name a few. Regardless of the approach that students use, teachers can always help storytellers look for story criteria, like a story core, to help them determine whether a story will effectively convey what they want to say.

✸ Containing Stories

While finding a story is usually not a problem for students, containing it can be. Part of the art of writing a good story is limiting what is included so that a focused, coherent narrative emerges that doesn't wander. To help those who are experiencing story wander create a story that's manageable, I will sometimes use what I call the research box (see Figure 7.1). On a sheet of paper, students draw a box of any shape or size. Inside the box, they write everything they're going to include in their stories. Outside the box, they write items that are related to their stories but are not going to be directly addressed. This encourages storytellers to brainstorm and not throw anything away, while also encouraging them to limit their stories in terms of the time frame covered, the places it involves, relationships, events, or whatever else seems appropriate. As storytellers' thinking progresses, some things get moved to the inside of the box and others to the outside. However, nothing gets discarded. Even those things that are outside the box are still present and can be referred to; they just can't be directly addressed in the story. The research box enables teachers to quickly ascertain what students are trying to include in their stories. In turn, this helps them talk to students about limiting or expanding the scope of their stories in order to make them more coherent and manageable.

For example, after listening to participants, I might recommend confining a story to just their relationship with a particular family member while they were living in a particular town, perhaps because that relationship seemed to capture the essence of the personal question they were trying to address. These end up inside the box. Other relationships and places were outside the box but still visible as reference points.

Incidentally, I use the research box whenever I teach the research process in a more formal sense. It's a handy tool for students to use to develop a research design that doesn't leak into so many variables and possible areas of inquiry that the project becomes undoable.

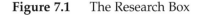

Figure 7.1   The Research Box

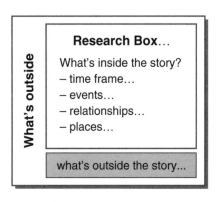

SOURCE: (Ohler, 2000).

▨ Mapping Short Stories Versus Long Stories

As listeners, we consume stories of every imaginable length, from 10-second advertisements to two-hour movies. But as tellers, we tend to tell stories that are fairly short. The stories we bring home from work about what happened to us during the day are short; when they're not, we can see everyone roll their eyes. Teachers require students to create short stories rather than novels because that's what fits into a curriculum. When businesses tell their stories, they do so within the context of a 10- to 30-second advertisement or a PowerPoint presentation that mustn't go on too long for fear of losing the audience. Most of the digital stories I've experienced are usually in the two- to four-minute range. This length is driven by a number of things, including the amount of work it takes to create a technologically based piece, as well as the time constraints of the average curriculum. Fortunately, story mapping is ideally suited for story projects that are short.

However, rest assured that story mapping can be adapted to longer stories. At the heart of most movies is a story core and a central map surrounded by subplots and submaps. Recall my earlier discussion about students telling the story of their future selves, in which they become heroes of the lives they want to live. The starting point for that map could be today and the other end could be next week, five years from now, or longer. Between now and then, there are problems to solve, things to learn, and transformations to undergo.

The Downside of Short

There is a potential downside to creating stories that are short: an audience can tolerate anything for a short period of time, including underdeveloped stories. To an audience, pain rises exponentially with time when listening to a story that doesn't work. The difference between a two-minute and a four-minute story that is not working is excruciating. The solution is not to create longer pieces but rather to pay close attention to the short pieces we develop. Story mapping is an extremely good tool to use in this regard.

Special Tips for Working With Younger Kids

Story planning needs to be developmentally appropriate and suited to the age and skill level of the students. Here are some points to consider in this regard:

- Concepts like problem/solution and tension/resolution can be heady ideas for younger students. Try using "getting into trouble and getting out of trouble." They almost always know what you're talking about.
- The concept of transformation can also be too advanced for some. Try asking questions such as "How did the character change?" or "What's different in the character's life at the end?" My favorite question to ask is simply, "What did he or she learn or figure out?" Also, try leaving out transformation altogether to see if students address it anyway, either explicitly or implicitly. When they do, you can use this as a teachable moment to talk about transformation in stories if it suits your goals. When they don't, you can ask questions that help them address it.

Fellow storyteller Brett Dillingham reports great success with requiring students to draw a picture that reminds them of something in the story. It helps students focus on the story and the journey described by the story map. He also reports great success with having young, first-time storytellers develop stories about animals. Doing so provides distance between the reality of their lives and the story they want to tell while at the same time offering a vantage point to talk about personal events and issues. Animals are a safe yet creative and revealing point of view to use. I call it "third-person magical."

If oral storytelling is part of your project, most students will need at least some training in how to do this effectively. See Resource A for details about my approach to oral storytelling training. Also see Brett's Web site for great materials in this area: www.brettdillingham.com.

Special Tips for Team Members

The concept of story map as a portal into the mind of the teller is especially important for team-based projects for the following reasons:

1. You've heard the saying "Let's make sure we're all playing from the same sheet of music." The story core and story map provide the sheet music for your project. Team members should converge on them, brainstorm about them, and finalize them as a group. These planning tools allow everyone to discuss the essence of the story in shorthand, without forcing anyone to commit to specific narrative. The clearer the core and the map are, the easier it's going to be to storyboard and script the story.

> **A story map is a portal into the storyteller's thinking.**
>
> It's a plan that teachers can respond to, team members can refer to, and storytellers can easily carry around in their pockets and in their minds.

2. A story map is a great tool for a team (or an individual) to use to pitch a story idea because it concisely captures the essential elements of a story. Have students practice pitching using "peer pitching" (Theodosakis, 2001).

Telling Stories From the End and the Middle

Stories don't need to be conceived from the beginning. In fact, I rarely begin developing stories by settling on an opening event. Instead, through a process of discovery, I come across something that may be a beginning, a middle, or an end. The story evolves from there. Here are some thoughts about not starting at the beginning.

⚙ Beginning at the End

It actually makes good sense to start at the end if you already have a goal in mind or a point you want to make with your story. Here are a few scenarios that can make use of the beginning at the end approach:

- You're a teacher who is going to use storytelling in a content area. No doubt your lesson plan already spells out learning objectives. Use these objectives as the end of your learning story and design backward (Wiggins & McTighe, 2001) to create stories through lesson plans.
- You want your school board to understand the importance of DST in the curriculum. In the same way you might construct an essay around a central thesis, create a presentation to show the board with that in mind.
- You've learned something important over the years that you want to convey to others, such as "Beware of pain you get used to" or "Don't pet a burning dog." Create a story that will allow you to deliver that moral. Although it doesn't matter how you get to the moral, in order to be effective you'll want to use relevant references that are tailored to your audience.
- You have a product or idea that you're trying to sell to customers or clients whose transformation will consist of their going from a state of not realizing they need what you offer to believing they need it. Create relevant problem/resolutions that focus on experiences common to them that would naturally lead them to this conclusion.

⚙ Telling From the Middle

If you can start from the end, can you start from the middle? Sure you can. In fact, most people find themselves in the middle of a story map in everyday life, unsure of how they got there and where to go. Even more important, they're not sure what success would look like to them and therefore haven't written the ending to the story.

Seeing life as a story that can be written by each of us is a powerful and pragmatic metaphor. If we start from the point that today is the day that we're called to adventure to address a problem, question, opportunity, challenge, or goal, then we place ourselves squarely in the center of our own personal story maps. It's up to each of us to resolve our issues and finish our stories. This much is clear to me: if we don't write the stories of our lives, someone else will do it for us. The stories they write are rarely what we need or want.

> If we don't create our own stories, someone else will do it for us.

Figure 7.2   Start Your Story Anywhere

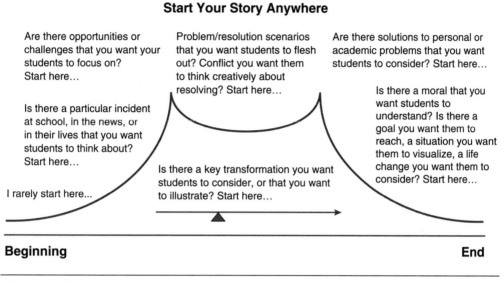

SOURCE: Ohler, 2003.

▓ Telling via Transformation

Part of the method I use for teaching storytelling involves having students brainstorm problems as well as a number of potential ways to solve each problem. These problem/resolution scenarios then serve as the basis for story development. As a way to assess the power or "storyability" of the solutions, participants and I talk about the kinds of transformation each solution could compel the character(s) to undergo. It quickly becomes clear which transformations are more powerful than others. If the point of a story is to explore or model how and why people change, a storyteller may be better off conceptualizing a story in terms of the story's character transformation rather than in terms of the problem.

Specifics about how I conduct this part of the workshop are addressed in Part III. For more about different kinds of character transformation, see Chapter 8.

▓ Telling Personal and Universal Stories

Earlier, I noted that part of the definition of a memorable story is that it's universal. What about more personal stories? Can these be universal? Most of the good ones are. And when they are, they have *resonance*, one of the story qualities that intrigued teachers who watched the digital stories I showed them (see Part I of this book). Let's flesh out the concept a little more here.

Let me direct your attention to country-western music for a moment. It seems that many of the songs belted out by the twangy crooners of C&W are telling a tale of woe that happened to them personally (or to their truck or dog). Yet even if you aren't a C&W fan, you can often relate to the stories in the songs because they contain elements of universality. For our purposes, a story is universal if the experiences of the main character connect with your life and your experiences. Because of the connection, we can learn and be transformed as a story listener. As with most things in life, if it involves us, there's a greater likelihood that we'll care about it and remember it.

Universality is a particularly important concept in the world of DST, in which an amazing thing happens when first-time digital storytellers fully comprehend the tools available to them: they realize they have a chance to be heard. For this reason students often gravitate toward telling first-person narrative stories of self-exploration. If teachers want students' stories to resonate, then I suggest they require students to consider questions that facilitate resonance, such

> "Every storyteller collects and arranges vital inner pictures; behind these live universal ordering principles."
>
> —Nancy Mellon
> *The Art of Storytelling*

as, "How are you different having developed this project? What do you realize now about your life or about life in general that you didn't before? How does what you have learned relate to others in similar situations?"

Here's an example. The students in the master of arts in teaching degree program at my institution had the chance to teach in a remote area of Alaska for two weeks. Many took advantage of the opportunity. As their educational technology teacher, I asked them to document their experience and produce a digital presentation about it. The projects they produced varied widely. A number of them basically chronicled the details of the experience; these tended to be episodic and somewhat forgettable, like a slide show of someone else's vacation. However, there were also projects in which students explored what they had learned within the broader social context of the multicultural situation of rural Alaska. These were much more powerful and memorable. They resonated because most people have experienced cultural disorientation, either when traveling or simply from living in a multicultural society. What my students learned about handling those situations could be transferred to the situations of the listeners.

> Powerful experiences become powerful stories when we reflect on how the experiences changed us.

How you approach the stories you tell has to do with your goals. Determining whether your goal is personal or professional, or public or private, will also determine the best approach to use. If you want to create a story that is memorable and useful for listeners, then connect your experiences to theirs through universal appeal. It's often quite simple to do, because your story is often everyone's story. Powerful experiences become powerful stories if authors reflect on how the experiences have transformed them. The question for storytellers is not just "What happened?" but also "How has what happened changed me?"

❊ Documentaries Versus Fictional Stories

I've addressed documentaries in a few places in this book thus far. I address them here so that readers can see how story mapping can be used in a nonfiction context.

There is no question that documentaries and fiction are very different. According to www.dictionary.com (2007), a documentary consists of "presenting facts objectively without editorializing or inserting fictional matter," while a work of fiction is a work "whose content is produced by the imagination and is not necessarily based on fact." But recall from my earlier discussion about documentaries that they are like stories because they contain story cores. In a good documentary, the narrator, the study subject, the audience, or some combination of these assumes the role of protagonist by learning and transforming.

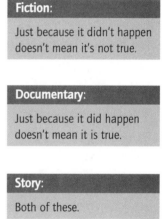

Fiction:
Just because it didn't happen doesn't mean it's not true.

Documentary:
Just because it did happen doesn't mean it is true.

Story:
Both of these.

The student's documentary of teaching in rural Alaska was, in essence, a documentary. The student assumed the role not just of narrator but also of protagonist, who reflected on her journey of understanding as she chronicled actual events involving actual people. Because the questions she asked at the outset became mine, I transformed with her.

The point here is this. In addition to using story maps to help understand and plan fictional stories, students can also use them to understand and plan documentary stories, including personal stories, traditional documentaries, and academic stories. Story—it's big.

❊ Breaking the Rules

I'll never forget something that happened in a photography class many years ago, long before digital photos were available, when my favorite piece of

> Learn the rules, break the rules, then make the rules.

photography gear was a fully manual Olympus camera. My teacher had just spent an entire class period explaining the rules of composition for shooting a good picture. To drive the rules home, he showed us numerous examples of photos that consisted of well-composed subjects. Then he showed us one of his favorite photographs, which just happened to break all the rules. "Break the rules after you understand them and can use them effectively," he coached us.

I think these are wise words. My suggestion to you is that you begin by building and telling stories using the story core and story-mapping techniques. Then feel free to begin pushing the envelope and breaking the rules. Your new adventures will benefit tremendously from an understanding of what has made stories work for many years. And when you feel that you have something to say that simply can't be contained by established processes, go for it. But beware—you might be creating art.

8

Transformation Formations

How We, and the Characters in Our Stories, Change

I've mentioned and modeled transformation throughout this book without fully exploring what it means. This chapter explores it in more depth.

Transformation is like change on steroids. It is important to note that big changes are not necessarily significant changes. Significance is a measure of depth, transformation, and resonance. It is the transformation of characters in a story that gives the audience a chance to transform as well.

How do people change? And more specifically, how do characters in stories change in ways that work for the listener?

The catch-all definition I use for transformation is "slaying internal dragons through attitude adjustment based on learning and realization." The adjustment is necessary because of what is often referred to as "the hero's flaw" that identifies a hero's imperfection and how he or she needs to transform to address it. The flaw also tends to define the nature of the challenges that the hero will face during the course of the story. While this definition works in a general sense, let's get specific. Let's look at a few ways of understanding transformation so that you have more control of what you can do with your story and so you can help students have more control of what they do with theirs.

❖ The Eight Levels of Transformation

From my reading, creating, and listening to stories, I have identified eight basic levels of transformation (shown in Table 8.1). The levels are not mutually exclusive by any means; therefore, characters often transform at more than one level at the same time.

Let's look at how the characters transformed in the stories we mapped earlier:

- In *Making a Ball Roll,* the students transformed through learning, intellectual development, and the application of creative thinking (Table 8.1, level 7).
- In *Creative Awakening*, the storyteller finds the inner strength to face her insecurities about her artwork. Through a blend of emotional, psychological, and spiritual insight, she begins her life anew as an artist (Table 8.1, levels 2, 5, 7).
- In *Fox Becomes a Better Person*, Fox develops the insight and inner strength to seek help in becoming someone more mature and socially responsible (Table 8.1, levels, 2, 3, 5, 6).
- In *William Tell and the Young Girl Who Could Fix Computers*, William physically and intellectually learns some new keystrokes (Table 8.1, level 1). But he also gains courage and maturity (Table 8.1, levels 2, 3) in order to accept advice from a young girl in order to solve his problem. Ultimately, he changes a number of his attitudes about society, particularly with respect to how teaching and learning happens (Table 8.1, levels 5, 6).

Consider B-grade action movies again for a moment and why they tend not to stick with you. While they usually contain a lot of conflict and resolution in the form of endless fighting, there is very little internal conflict; very few inner dragons are slain. The good guys tend to be good, the bad guys tend to bad, and no one is transformed. Just a lot of fighting. Boring. And what does boring really boil down to? Unmemorable. Effective transformation creates the potential for memorability.

❖ Bloom's Cognitive Taxonomy and Levels of Transformation

It's difficult to graduate from a teacher education program without studying Bloom's (1964) taxonomy of cognitive processes. Although it was developed

Table 8.1 The Eight Levels of Character Transformation

Level	Kind	Explanation
1	Physical/ kinesthetic	Character develops strength or dexterity. Popeye eats spinach and grows muscles; Baby (Jennifer Grey in *Dirty Dancing*) learns how to dance and wins the contest.
2	Inner strength	Character develops courage, overcomes fear. Lucilla and Proximo (Connie Neilson and Oliver Reed in *Gladiator*) help Maximus (Russell Crowe) in his effort to restore the republic of Rome.
3	Emotional	Character matures, thinks beyond his or her own needs; Han Solo returns to fight the good fight in *Star Wars*.
4	Moral	Character develops a conscience; Schindler develops his list.
5	Psychological	Character develops insight, self-awareness. Neo (Keanu Reeves in *The Matrix*) understands who he is in relation to the Matrix.
6	Social	Character accepts new responsibility with respect to family, community, or a group; Max (Mel Gibson in *Road Warrior*) sticks around to help the small community defend itself against terrorist bike gangs.
7	Intellectual/ creative	Character advances his or her intellectual/creative ability in order to learn or do something new; this allows him or her to solve a problem, puzzle, or mystery, leading to new understandings about a situation (Neo in *The Matrix*). This level captures the essence of making students heroes of their own learning stories.
8	Spiritual	Character has an awakening, which changes his or her entire perspective. With the help of a spiritual mentor, Larry Darrell (Bill Murray in *Razor's Edge*) achieves a sense of enlightenment that alters his perspective about what is important in life.

SOURCE: Ohler, 2005.

as a way to classify how we learn, it also works well as a system for classifying how we change. Essentially, what Bloom developed is a hierarchy of transformation. As with the last hierarchy we looked at, transformation usually happens on more than one level at a time. But any one of the levels by itself could be used to cause a transformation of some kind (see Table 8.2).

Let's apply this hierarchy to *William Tell and the Young Girl Who Could Fix a Computer*. On the most basic level, William gained new knowledge that he

Table 8.2 Bloom's Taxonomy of Cognitive "Transformation"

Level	Kind	Explanation
1	Knowledge	Character knows, remembers, or describes something.
2	Comprehension	Character explains, interprets, predicts something.
3	Application	Character discovers, constructs, or changes something; applies understanding to a new situation.
4	Analysis	Character deconstructs a situation, distinguishes between options, plans or organizes something, compares and contrasts different things.
5	Synthesis	Character pieces together parts to form a new understanding of a situation.
6	Evaluation	Character assesses a situation, critiques and/or defends an idea, person; evaluates a situation in order to respond to it.

SOURCE: Bloom, 1964. Reprinted with permission.

applied to the situation: the young girl taught him a new set of keystrokes that helped him out of a jam (Table 8.2, levels 1, 3). But on a more visceral level, he also discovered a number of new things that he was forced to synthesize and apply on the spot (Table 8.2, level 5). In addition, years later, when he evaluates what happened, he vows to always listen to a young girl with computer advice.

▓ Bloom's Affective Taxonomy and Levels of Transformation

Bloom also created a taxonomy about the affective domain: the world of emotions and feelings. It appears below in Table 8.3.

How does William fare according to this transformation hierarchy? At first, not so well. After all, he certainly didn't start out listening to the young girl respectfully (Table 8.3, level 1). But by the end of the story, he promises to always listen to any young girl with computer advice, showing that he had come to value a new belief system (Table 8.3, level 3). I don't want to give away the rest of *Then What?* (Ohler, 2003), from which this story was taken, but I can tell you that as the story progresses, William gradually does make his way through Bloom's affective levels. I can also tell you that the butler didn't do it and no one dies in the end.

Table 8.3   Bloom's Taxonomy of Affective "Transformation"

Level	Kind	Explanation
1	Receiving phenomena	Character listens to others respectfully.
2	Responding to phenomena	Character participates in solutions, works with a team, helps others.
3	Valuing	Character demonstrates belief in a value system that manifests itself in solving problems for others and in valuing cultural and individual differences.
4	Organization	Character prioritizes values, resolves conflicts, develops personalized value system; balances freedom and responsibility and accepts standards of moral behavior.
5	Internalizing values	Character acts on value systems as an individual, rather than in response to group expectations; uses teamwork effectively, values others for their intrinsic merit rather than external qualities.

SOURCE: Bloom, Krathwohl, & Masia, 1964. Reprinted with permission.

▓ Using Transformation

There are a number of ways to use the transformation taxonomies presented in this chapter in your digital storytelling (DST) adventures. Here are a few:

To help students tell more effective stories. You can use the taxonomies to facilitate a conversation with students about how the characters change in their stories and, in particular, how different changes at different levels might make their stories more powerful and effective. This doesn't necessarily mean engaging students directly in a discussion of Bloom's taxonomy. Rather, it means using the taxonomy as your pedagogical agenda to facilitate growth and improvement. For example, you could ask students questions about their stories as you review their story cores and maps. Prompting questions might include the following: What else does she need to figure out in order to solve the mystery (Table 8.1, level 7)? What did she finally understand about being from a different culture (Table 8.3, level 3)? What's another way the character might get off the island (Table 8.2, levels 3, 4)?

Are some changes better than others? Perhaps. But most important, story characters need to change in ways that make sense within the context of the story. As always, what you're really doing here is challenging students to understand something in greater depth. After all, this is what teachers do. You're just using their stories as the vehicle to do so.

To understand students through their stories. Bloom's work was originally created as a means to view and evaluate student work. It remains in wide use today because of its enduring utility. Stories are an important place to look for student progress in a number of areas. By studying how characters in students' stories behave and progress, teachers can get a sense of how students look at the world as well as what areas of their lives have potential for growth.

To help students grow through their stories. Character transformation represents personal growth, in many cases the kind of growth you want your students to experience. While there is no linear pathway through any of the taxonomies I've presented, characters often move between levels in stories in ways that most of us would identify as a kind of positive progress, whether social, intellectual, or emotional. You can facilitate the same growth in your students by asking them to write a story in which characters exhibit particular kinds of transformation. For example, you might ask students to create a story in which a character realizes the importance of his or her family (Table 8.1, level 6), one in which a character applies his or her understanding of a scientific principle to a new situation, perhaps to solve a mystery (Table 8.2, level 3), or one in which a character develops an understanding of the value of working with a team (Table 8.3, level 4). It's interesting to think about using this approach to develop an Individualized Education Plan (IEP) with each student.

Teacher idea:

If you haven't had enough educational theory for one day, try using Kohlberg's "Stages of moral development" (1984) as a way to view character transformation. Kohlberg's work tracks moral development, beginning with looking out for number one, to the more advanced stages of valuing justice and morality. Characters who mature in stories often move through his stages.

9

More Story Maps

From Aristotle to Present Day

Story mapping is not new; it's just underutilized. In this chapter, we are going to look at more approaches to story mapping. My hope is that if the visual portrait of a story (VPS) doesn't work for you, something else will. Here are a few more story map models to consider.

Aristotle's Dramatic Diagram

Long, long ago, in an English classroom on the campus of the University of Toronto, one of my professors sketched out the diagram in Figure 9.1 to depict the nature and flow of what Aristotle considered to be one approach to creating effective drama, or in our terms, telling a good story.

It's derived from Aristotle's famous treatise about art and drama (among other things), called *The Poetics*. While *The Poetics* isn't what I would call a page turner, it's amazing how well it describes the essential elements of a good story even today. The basic shape is a hill or mountain, which represents the journey the protagonist must make. Aristotle referred to conflict/resolution in terms of tying and untying a knot. Transformation is brought about through a reversal of fortune of the hero at the top of the mountain.

I have actually used Aristotle's story map with video production students with great success. To me, Aristotle's story map has a useful kinesthetic quality to it, as I recall trying to untie a knot in my shoelace or untangle an electrical extension cord I'm trying to use. This diagram is easy to

Figure 9.1 Aristotle Story Map—Simplified

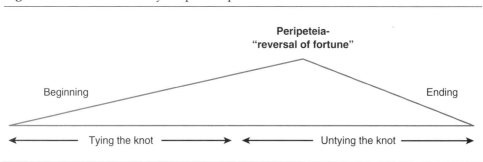

relate to, and for that reason it has a special utility for younger students for whom a detailed VPS might be too much to grasp. It shows the rising and falling of the story in very simple terms; it's basic yet powerful.

If you find the historical aspect of story theory interesting, then I recommend looking at Freytag's Pyramid, which appears in Resource D. It was developed by Dr. L. Kip Wheeler (2004) as a synthesis of the work of another important story theorist, Gustav Freytag, whose book *Technik des Dramas* was published in 1868. It looks a good deal like Aristotle's story diagram above but with much more detail.

❖ Simplified Joseph Campbell Map

Earlier I mentioned Joseph Campbell's work and how I viewed my story core as an adaptation of his hero's journey in highly concentrated form. Campbell's influence on developing the Western perspective of storytelling can't be underestimated. He spent his lifetime finding similarities in myths and stories throughout the world and presenting a coherent view of the kinds of universal emotional, psychological, and social needs that stories meet. Here in Figure 9.2 I present a modified version of a diagram he created that is, to me, essentially a story map. The original, which appears in Resource G, is more complex than we need for our purposes. Besides, parts of it would make sense only if you had read the book from which it's taken, *The Hero with a Thousand Faces* (Campbell, 1973). If you compare the simplified version in Figure 9.2 with the original in Resource G, you will see that Campbell has used some different names and included a good deal more detail. But the basic journey—or story—is the same.

The basic shape is the circle, which conjures up a number of useful metaphors, in particular the never-ending story and the journey home. Campbell believed that heroes ended up where they began, though they were changed by their experience. At the end of their journeys they live in two worlds—the one they left and the new one from which they emerged, both of which are present at the top of the circle. In *William Tell and the Young Girl Who Could Fix Computers*, William comes full circle. That is, he starts and ends on stage in the auditorium, though he ends as a changed man. He essentially now lives in two worlds: the one in which he began and the new one that has been informed by his experience. If you squint at the modified Campbell map, you can see the VPS in circular form. All the components, including the story core, are there.

Figure 9.2 Campbell Adventure Diagram— Simplified

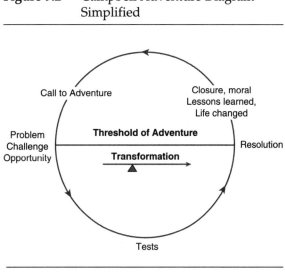

▓ Treasure Maps

Between the bridgelike structure of the VPS and the circular map of Campbell lies a more free-form approach to story mapping that I call "the treasure map" because it reminds me of the treasure maps I used to see in comic books as a kid. I use the letter X to mark both the treasure and the transformation. It's probably easiest to think of the treasure map as a VPS that can be significantly modified in that you can create the hills, valleys, and paths for your story rather than have them provided for you, as the VPS does. The example I use here in Figure 9.3 demonstrates how to apply this technique to the William Tell story.

Let's walk through this. It begins like the VPS—with a rise to denote a call from the flatline of ordinary life. But in this map the rise is very sharp. This is because William doesn't ease into his situation—he is suddenly and thoroughly confronted by it. Then there are two dips at specific points, signifying low points for William. One occurs when people start to heckle him and another when the young girl approaches him. Note that at the end of each of these, the line moves higher on the page—the tension is building.

Now he really needs to work to solve his problem. When the story finishes, the end of the map is higher on the page than at the beginning. The difference between the two is denoted by X. Visually, the X denotes not only the presence of a transformation (the treasure we seek) but also the difference between who William was at the beginning of the story and who he is at the end.

Figure 9.3 Treasure Map Story Map

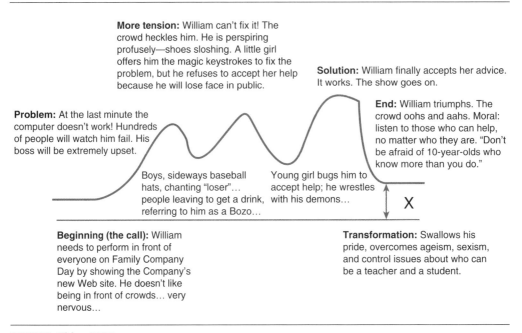

More tension: William can't fix it! The crowd heckles him. He is perspiring profusely—shoes sloshing. A little girl offers him the magic keystrokes to fix the problem, but he refuses to accept her help because he will lose face in public.

Solution: William finally accepts her advice. It works. The show goes on.

Problem: At the last minute the computer doesn't work! Hundreds of people will watch him fail. His boss will be extremely upset.

End: William triumphs. The crowd oohs and aahs. Moral: listen to those who can help, no matter who they are. "Don't be afraid of 10-year-olds who know more than you do."

Boys, sideways baseball hats, chanting "loser"... people leaving to get a drink, referring to him as a Bozo...

Young girl bugs him to accept help; he wrestles with his demons...

Beginning (the call): William needs to perform in front of everyone on Family Company Day by showing the Company's new Web site. He doesn't like being in front of crowds... very nervous...

Transformation: Swallows his pride, overcomes ageism, sexism, and control issues about who can be a teacher and a student.

SOURCE: Ohler, 2003.

The treasure map allows flexible customization of a story map. You can have as many peaks or valleys as you like, which can help to more accurately represent the action in your story. In addition to multiple peaks and valleys, you can add other annotations that are helpful to you. In my media literacy class I have students story map commercials. In the example I show here in Figure 9.4, a student found three challenges, denoted by the three sharp peaks, and two "reversals" in the action, denoted by the two small circles. This example shows how adaptable story mapping can be. Perhaps you can use arrows to denote an attack or jagged lines to denote a rough trail. How about musical notes to show where music supports the emotional content? Play with it and make it work for you. No formulas, just guidelines.

McKee's story schematic. While feature film development is far beyond the scope of this book, McKee's (1997) story schematics depicting the flow of emotional energy in a movie are very instructive. While he offers a number of them in his book *Story,* I find the quest diagram shown here in Figure 9.5 particularly helpful. Bear in mind that to McKee, nearly all good movies are quest movies.

There's a good deal to look at here. The objects of desire—the material, emotional, and spiritual goals of the quest—are sought on conscious and unconscious levels. In fact, they're often in conflict, adding substantial tension to the story. For example, in *William Tell and the Young Girl Who Could Fix Computers,* William wrestles with his conscious desire to get his computer to

Figure 9.4   Adapted Story Map

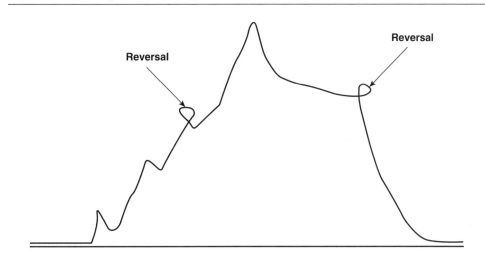

SOURCE: Christenson, 2005.

Figure 9.5   McKee's Quest Diagram

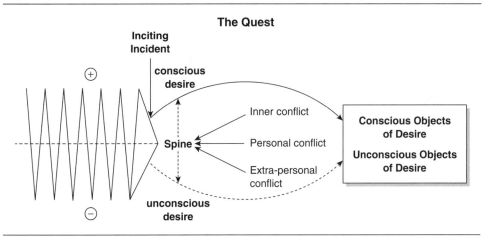

SOURCE: McKee, 1997. Reprinted with permission.

work, which is at odds with his less conscious desire not to lose face by letting a young girl tell him how to fix his computer in public.

What I find particularly interesting in McKee's diagram are the sharp teethlike lines at the beginning, which represent taking the audience alternately in positive and negative directions with the action. To McKee, a story is most engaging when it moves in the direction of resolution, then away from it, then toward it, and so on. In practical terms, something happens that moves characters toward their goal, then something happens to undermine this—playing Ping Pong with the audience's emotions, so to speak. It's the seesawing that maintains a constant edge of tension/resolution that keeps listeners wanting to know what will happen next. I wrote *William Tell and the Young Girl Who Could Fix Computers* before I had read McKee's book, and now see that I should have considered having William seesaw, perhaps by finding a cord that was unplugged, only to have that not be the problem, or by restarting the computer, only to have the same problem reappear, or even better, *get worse*. Next time. To McKee, characters' lives are thrown so out of balance that they spend the story struggling to regain it. Doing so becomes a question of how to go about it and for what purpose. McKee's book contains a wealth of information for anyone who wants to understand storytelling, and I highly recommend it to anyone, no matter what kind of storytelling project they're developing.

✿ Kieran Egan's Story Form in Education

Kieran Egan (1989) is well known in education circles for his commitment to leveraging children's most underutilized resource—their imaginations. At the time he wrote *Teaching as Story Telling*, Egan's theories disagreed with conventional teaching wisdom in many profound ways, two of which are of primary concern to us here. First, the predominant belief at the time was that children learned new material only in terms of previously mastered material, while Egan believed that children could learn new material based on what they were capable of imagining. Second, while many professionals believed that children possess limited capability to understand complex topics, Egan believed that children's ability to understand emotionally complex stories proved otherwise.

To capitalize on children's imaginative abilities in learning situations, he recommended that teachers develop lesson plans based on the story form rather than the typical task-subtask lesson plan structure that was (and still is) in such prevalent use. To him, there was little that was inherently meaningful to the young mind in a logically constructed sequence of tasks. On the other hand, the story form provided an effective context for content instruction because it was affectively engaging and took advantage of children's understanding of how stories work. In fact, since reading *Teaching as Story Telling*, I have come to appreciate that quite often when students say, "This is too hard" or "This doesn't make sense," what they're really saying is "Where's the story?"

The crux of the story form is what Egan (1989) calls a set of "binary opposites," a structural device that establishes a central conflict that can be described in broad terms but that plays out in very concrete ways.

The conflict created by the binary opposites determines the selection and organization of the story content, as well as helps guide the structure and flow of the story. In short, it provides the force behind the story that defines what happens, how people change, and what we learn as participants and listeners.

Children are accustomed to binary opposites from the stories they hear. To use Egan's example, consider the story of Cinderella. The heart of the story consists of the binary opposites of good versus bad, embodied by Cinderella and the wicked stepmother respectively. Most children's stories embody some form of binary opposites like this, whether it's "good vs. bad, courage vs. cowardice, fear vs. security" (Egan, 1989, p. 14). Subconsciously, children expect to encounter binary opposites to guide a story and to create the expectation of and basis for resolution.

To Egan, lesson plans—as well as news stories, dramatic works, and a number of other human activities—are most meaningful if they're built upon or understood in terms of a set of binary opposites. Thus, a unit on the Vikings can be cast in terms of barbarism versus civilization, rather than in terms of dates and conquests. A unit of science studying steam generation can be cast in terms of heat as helper versus heat as destroyer, rather than as a list of facts or a progression of physical events.

In essence, binary opposites form the conflict that is resolved in a learning story. What Egan adds to our discussion about story conflict is that beneath the problem/resolution dynamic that provides a story's forward momentum is a thematic tension created by two opposing forces of human nature or of nature itself. Children, either intuitively or through exposure to stories, understand this, so why not use it as a teaching tool?

Because Egan is an educator, his book focuses on classroom uses of the story form, specifically lesson plan development, using the series of questions that appear in the story form model in Figure 9.6. But his notion of binary opposites is relevant to general considerations of stories as well. How the opposites are mediated—that is, what occurs in the story to resolve the conflict at hand—typically describes the nature of the transformation the main character must undergo during the process of conflict resolution. It's easy to view many forms of story, including personal stories, advertisements, and movies, in terms of the resolution of some overriding set of binary opposites that provide the emotional schema for the story.

Although Egan's work is impossible to summarize in a few pages, hopefully I have provided a glimpse into its value as an approach to organizing a learning experience. Before moving on, here are some important points that emerge from Egan's work comparing traditional and story form–based education that can benefit any teacher or storyteller:

Figure 9.6 The Story Form Model

1. Identifying importance:
   - What is most important about this topic?
   - Why should it matter to children?
   - What is affectively engaging about it?

2. Finding binary opposites:
   - What powerful binary opposites best catch the importance of the topic?

3. Organizing content into story form:
   - What content most dramatically embodies the binary opposites, in order to provide access to the topic?
   - What content best articulates the topic into a developing story form?

4. Conclusion:
   - What is the best way of resolving the dramatic conflict inherent in the binary opposites?
   - What degree of mediation of those opposites is it appropriate to seek?

5. Evaluation:
   - How can one know whether the topic has been understood, its importance grasped, and the content learned?

SOURCE: Egan, 1989. Reprinted with permission.

- Story form content is inherently memorable, while lists of tasks and subtasks are not. We make lists because we forget things; we tell stories to help us remember them.
- Story form content is emotionally engaging, while the same content set within a logical task-oriented context is emotionally disengaging. Stories involve a sense of what's next and how things end that keep us listening and engaged; logical lists do not.
- Story form content is inherently contextualizing, while logical lists are not. Lists exist in an open-ended and often disconnected mental environment, while stories create a closed system, allowing for considerations of consistency, relatedness, and meaning.

▓ *The Story Spine* by Kenn Adams

The Story Spine is another step-by-step approach to providing story structure that was developed by the playwright Kenn Adams (1990). In it, Adams provides the skeleton—that is, "the spine"—of a traditional story by providing "sentence starters" that introduce important segments of a story. By following the steps in sequence, one can't help but tell a story.

Look at the "spine list" in Figure 9.7. If you squint, you can see all the major story core and story map elements. The Platform items describe ordinary life, while the Catalyst—"But one day"—functions as a call to adventure. The Consequences—"Because of that"—imply that life, as well as the characters in the story, begins to change as the adventure unfolds. "Until finally" tells us something has changed in a significant way. In the hands of a skilled teacher, this can easily be played as a transformation. The Climax and Resolution imply that consequences created problems or situations that needed to be resolved. The moral at the end brings closure to the adventure for the characters as well as the readers.

Figure 9.7   The Story Spine

The Platform	– Once upon a time…
	– Every day…
The Catalyst	– But one day…
The Consequences	– Because of that…
	– Because of that…
	– Because of that…
The Climax	– Until finally…
The Resolution	– Ever since then…
	– And the moral of the story is…

SOURCE: Adams, 1990. Reprinted with permission.

The first time I was introduced to the story spine, the facilitator asked audience members to work in pairs to create a story together. It was a very powerful experience as my partner and I created a situation "with consequences," that is, a situation that naturally sought some kind of resolution. What we found was that we were exploring what we were learning at the conference, the problems and opportunities of using our new knowledge, and how we were going to change some of our processes at work.

I use *The Story Spine* often as a warm-up activity when working with a group, large or small. Typically, I call on people in the audience and together we build a story as we go. It's always great fun and a great way to get people in the storytelling frame of mind.

Bottom line: Whatever story planning approach you decide to use, remember that while storyboarding will help you keep story events in order, it does little to help you determine whether your story will be engaging, memorable, or effective. That's the job of the story core and story mapping. Introducing the story core and story mapping at the beginning of your unit involving digital storytelling (DST) helps students determine the power of their story before they begin using all of that marvelously empowering yet distracting technology. If you don't have them plan their stories first, then there's a risk that you and your students won't be able to determine the power of their stories until students have invested many hours in technical production. At that point, it's usually too late to do anything about it. DST = story first, digital second.

❖ Homework

Ask your grandparents. If the opportunity avails itself, ask your parents, relatives, friends—but particularly your grandparents—to tell you a story about when they were growing up. Sit back and listen. When it's all over, see if you can find the reason the story stuck with them all those years. No doubt you will find a call to adventure, events that changed them, and other elements of story I have been discussing.

Watch TV. Whether you love TV, hate it, tolerate it for the few good shows it brings you, or secretly like it more than you would care to admit, I am going to ask you to watch it. Pick a drama or a sitcom—it doesn't matter— and try to map it. To facilitate this, record it so you can watch it twice, back to back. Why twice in immediate succession? Because the first time you are so involved with the story that you can't see anything else. But if you watch it again right afterward, you haven't had a chance to forget the story, which has been resolved and now is boring to you. That frees you up to watch for the story core, story elements, media persuasion techniques, use of music to manipulate the emotions, and all those other things you missed the first time. For this reason, watching things twice can be an effective approach to teaching media literacy in your classroom.

Watch things twice to develop media literacy: the first time to watch the story, the second time to watch everything else.

Watch commercials. And while you're at it, find the story core in a few commercials and then story map them. In most cases, they're trying to convince you that you have a problem they can solve. Your transformation? You become an enlightened consumer when you realize you need their product. Of course, true resolution doesn't occur until you have actually purchased what they're trying to sell you. Ads may be very superficial stories in content but not in technique. They're often highly sophisticated, highly concentrated story nuggets that are using the story form to maintain your focus for the very short amount of time they have your attention.

The important point here is that most things you watch in Western media can be story mapped in some way. You will find a central conflict (and some auxiliary ones), problems that get solved, characters that realize new things or evolve in some way, and endings that wrap things up.

Story is like air. It's big, it's everywhere, and we need it to stay alive.

10

Other Kinds of Stories

*Other Story Forms
and Story Perspectives*

I began this book with what is perhaps the only rule of digital storytelling (DST): stories without digital work, digital without stories doesn't. Of course, it's a trick statement, because "story" is a human construct of great depth and dimension that means many things to many people. Because people and cultures are different, stories are different.

The information I've presented thus far about story form applies primarily to Western stories that employ the Joseph Campbell (1973) worldview—story as hero quest. Even though Campbell drew upon myths and stories from many cultures throughout the world to formulate his theories, scholars have questioned the universality of his monomythic worldview. I've used Campbell's approach to explicating story, because today's youth are immersed in a story culture largely built upon that worldview. But quest stories are not the only kinds of stories in existence, and thus my material, and Joseph Campbell's outlook, aren't always relevant and can be limiting and unintentionally prejudicial. Let's consider some other kinds of stories to see what they offer teachers and students as storytellers.

Stories Told by Indigenous Storytellers

I wade into this area with great respect and reluctance, compelled by my belief that mentioning this area ineptly, as I most certainly will do despite my best efforts, is better than not mentioning it all. As a small consolation, I promise to be brief. My reluctance is due to the fact that none of us knows what we don't know, a reality that Thomas King (2005) compassionately considers as he illuminates the vast world of Native culture and story largely unknown to most in his book *The Truth About Stories—A Native Narrative.* As it turns out, what most of us don't know is quite substantial.

> We don't know what we don't know, a fact that ensures we all have a lot to learn.

In brief, King deftly shows through story and explication how media stereotyping over the decades has produced a mythic, romanticized, composite "Indian" that bears very little resemblance to Native Americans as they actually exist. Because the media presents the composite view so consistently, we believe we are rediscovering the same truths about Native Americans when they are referenced in news, books, movies, and other media forms when, in fact, all we are really doing is finding consistency within a closed system that was built upon false assumptions and information to begin with. It's the same composite mentality that has given birth to a construct called "native storytelling," a genre that is impossible to consider as a monolithic entity. Within it there is so much variation, both in North America and throughout the world, that attempts to do so are disrespectful as well as highly inaccurate.

In practical terms, the composite approach makes it difficult to know important things about stories, such as to whom stories belong, as well as how, when, and why they are told. This in turn makes it impossible to distinguish authentic from inauthentic stories or to understand that authenticity is even an issue in play. After all, authenticity is not typically an issue that Western story culture concerns itself with. When a movie is produced that takes liberties with the book it's based on, any protesting that does occur is usually minor and short-lived.

All of this produces a situation that is at least confusing if not dangerous if, as King tells us, "stories are all we are."

So here is the little bit I do know. I've had the pleasure of hearing and reading stories told and created by indigenous tellers as well as hearing secondhand about indigenous stories that have survived throughout the ages. Some stories feel familiar in content and form if I wear my "Western audience" hat. Others do not, and it's through them that I experience dimensions of story that I wouldn't otherwise. For example, some stories are mostly dreams or are set in environments that use dream sequences and logic. Some stories include problems without resolutions and very little suspense. Some have heroes who vanish before they finish their journeys; others involve people who change from human to nature form for what appears, from the Western perspective, to be no particular reason. Some use nonlinear, associative story lines that would be best mapped using a bubble diagram rather than anything I have shown in this book, if they could be mapped at all. Some take days to tell; some even take weeks. Some have been around for so long they are ageless, and yet they change each time they are told.

In the parlance of modern storytelling, they all "work" as stories, and have for centuries, perhaps millennia. We don't see these kinds of stories very often because they don't fit well within the modern mediascape. When we do see them, we realize that they bring to storytelling a breadth and depth that seems, despite the many years they have been in existence, quite new.

For those wanting to consider this area further, I suggest the following. First, take advantage of the scholarship that does exist. Writers like King are invaluable in this regard. Also, consult local resources. Some communities have Native scholars or groups who can help teachers who are looking for authentic approaches to traditional storytelling. Your state's department of education may have good resources, but it's always a good idea to check with local Native scholars about their authenticity and utility.

> Involve Native scholars and local storytellers in the study of story with your students.

Second, explore the area in which you live for live storytelling events and for Native storytellers who will visit your school. Consider doing a unit about this topic in your classroom and perhaps having students capture what they learn using the storytelling tools described in this book. If time and resources allow, involve local Native scholars in helping students understand issues of respect and authenticity related to their projects.

Third, if you're involved with helping members of the Native community tell stories, then invite elders, scholars, and other interested people to be part of it. Again, authenticity and respect are key.

And last, it's a good idea to officially recognize the differences in storytelling approaches when involving Native themes or community members in a storytelling project. For example, in Alaska, a number of groups concerned with Native education developed *Guidelines for Respecting Cultural Knowledge* (Assembly of Alaska Native Educators, 2000), which describe, among other things, specific ways to use and cite the use of Native artwork and story material. These guidelines include being "as explicit as possible in identifying the background experience and personal reference points on which the interpretation of cultural meaning is based" (p. 14). In retrospect, *Fox Becomes a Better Person* should not only have cited the elders and the song origination and permission in the credits (which it does) but should also have somehow acknowledged the approach we used to build and tell stories. Next time.

⚞ The Story Edge of the Western Tradition

Some of the 20th century's greatest storytellers are noted for their departure from traditional storytelling. Joyce, Faulkner, and others experimented with stream-of-consciousness storytelling, in which much of the characters' experience appears immediate and unfiltered by the process of formal writing. In fact, it is well-crafted narrative intended to explore the medium of writing and story while at the same time redefining the edge of plot and narrative. Story mapping Joyce's (1957) *Finnegan's Wake* or Faulkner's (1956) *The Sound and the Fury* would prove challenging indeed. Yet their contribution to the world of story is indisputable.

Other authors, such as Samuel Beckett and Franz Kafka, experimented with the notion of story form by melding medium and message, producing stories based not so much on dependent events as on interconnected emotional experiences. Beckett's (1954) *Waiting for Godot* is a story about two characters who wait for someone who never shows up; they neither understand why they are being kept waiting nor seem all that interested in finding out. In the end, they decide to leave, but they don't move—they are Campbellian antiheroes to the extreme.

Kafka (1964) often casts characters in situations that are intentionally never fully revealed and in which the details are rendered irrelevant. In *The Trial*, for example, the main character is abruptly arrested and subjected to a lengthy judicial process for a crime that is never identified. Instead of focusing on the details of the crime itself, Kafka focuses on the impact of the process on everyone involved. Without plot details, it's an antistory and is an entirely different experience from a John Grisham legal drama. Yet it has all the emotional involvement of a conventional story.

Both authors make the story listener a part of the emotional process of the characters. *Waiting for Godot* is not so much *about* waiting as it *is* waiting. Because *The Trial* focuses on the experience of the trial rather than the details of the crime, readers keep reading not to find out who did what but to ride the

> Antiheroes, antiplots, stream of consciousness, telling with texture, and other forms of narrative all stretch our concept of story in interesting and useful ways.

roller coaster of the judicial process as copassengers with the characters in the book. With both authors, the end result is tension without traditional resolution. Story mapping anything by Beckett or Kafka would be challenging, to say the least.

McKee (1997), a firm believer in the quest story as a successful story model, is very articulate about nonquest stories that have been made into movies, many of which have achieved success in some way. Some highly regarded directors, such as Robert Altman, use what McKee calls "multiplots" that are half plot, half texture. What might seem to be a thin or scattered story line is held together by a well-crafted texture of the lives of the characters. Altman's (2006) recent movie, *A Prairie Home Companion,* is a good example of this. McKee also discusses antiplots, miniplots, arch-plots, and other story approaches, none of which are quest stories in the classical sense. Yet he cites successful examples of each genre.

❖ Art Stories and Music Videos

I've seen "unconventional" digital stories that look like everything from visual poetry to the antiplots described by McKee. There is no question that pursuing DST as an experimental form of art and story resonates with a young audience. As always, it's up to teachers to describe the goals of a DST project and evaluate the results accordingly. Recalling earlier discussion in this book, it's up to teachers to decide whether they expect students to create an essay or a poem, or something in between.

Music videos are a great place to look for inspiration in this area. They are perhaps one of the most prevalent forms of short media known to students, lasting about as long as a digital story that teachers might assign. Story is not a requirement of a successful music video; many are pure texture. Some music videos tell a story through a pictorial collage that moves in concert with the song lyrics of the music, setting up tension, resolution, and an expectation of events. But many simply paint with sound and images, largely because the song lyrics don't tell a story. The 2005 winner of the MTV Video Music Award, Green Day's "Boulevard of Broken Dreams," is a good example of this. It consisted of the band members walking along a surreal boulevard among debris that one imagines represents the wreckage of broken dreams. There's no explicit plot or story core, which is to be expected, since the song lyrics are more poetry and texture than story. Given that rock videos are music set to videos, rather than videos set to music, we should expect images to serve the music rather than vice versa.

Recalling earlier concerns about students using the emotional impact of music to overwhelm their digital stories, we shouldn't be surprised that music videos are so popular. Music video artists masterfully repackage songs that already make deep emotional connections with young people by adding powerful visual imagery that intensifies the connection. Coincidentally, these are the same young people who will be creating digital stories in your classroom of about the same length using tools similar to those used by music video artists.

School Train. In Chapter 2, I described a piece of new media created by Glen Bledsoe's elementary students called *School Train.* It's consistently one of the most eye-opening pieces of new media that I show teachers. This is partly because the graphics and editing are so overwhelming. But it's also because it's not a story in the conventional sense. There is no real core or tension-resolution within the story. Like a powerful documentary, the story core plays out within the minds of the viewers, who transform as a result of watching it. *School Train* is part music video, part documentary, part stream of consciousness, part very successful academic assignment. It defies the Western concept of story. Yet it works.

Bottom line: Story structure is culturally dependent, not universal. While much of the storytelling that Western students experience is based in some way on the principles of the story core, the quest story is not the only approach to story development. Having your students experiment with creating digital stories using non-Western story forms can help them develop a multicultural appreciation of story. Also, having them create music videos and more experimental kinds of narrative will help them appreciate the wide range of options open to them as new media narrators.

Part III

Going Digital

11

The Media Production Process, Phase I

Developing the Story

Everyone Can Tell Digital Stories

Does the term "digital technology" make you cringe in fear, like you might if you got a registered letter from the IRS?

Let me put your mind at ease by telling you that I've never met a teacher who couldn't create a digital story. Not one. With a little training, particularly within a collaborative workshop setting, every teacher can develop a story and tell it in words, pictures, sounds, performance, and/or music. If you haven't had a lot of experience using a computer, then here's the good news: you get to skip the last 20 years, when producing new media with desktop digital technology was exasperating and expensive! Most of the work I do with teachers involves using hardware they already have on hand and software that's free and easy to use. Now is a great time to enter the world of digital storytelling (DST).

And don't forget this one very important fact: your students don't expect you to be a digital wizard. Digital technology is just intelligent furniture to them, and they're quite comfortable with it. When it comes to the technical end of DST, the teacher's job is to help manage their skills and talents by helping them do the following:

> Be the guide on the side, not the technician magician.

132

- Tell a story that is strengthened rather than weakened by the media they use
- Form a learning community so they can share their ideas and talents
- Meet the educational goals of the project
- Leverage their imagination and creativity

The last thing you need to be is a digital whiz.

🔲 The Media Production Process in Five Phases

The use of media in storytelling adds a layer to the production process, which is known to most in the media production world as, predictably, the media production process. Although this process varies from producer to producer, it's used in some form for most media production, including movies, cartoons, documentaries, and newscasts. It turns out to be an effective process to use with DST as well. As you'll see, the process used to produce media is conceptually as easy to understand as the process used to make a cake.

The phases of the production process are outlined in Figure 11.1 and briefly described below in general terms. Following that, I describe each phase in depth in terms of how it's applied to DST projects in the classroom. I've split my discussion of this process into two chapters, simply because of the amount of material that needs to be addressed. In this chapter I address Phase I, Story Planning, as well as what I call Prephase I, Getting Ready. In the next chapter we'll look at Phases II through V: Preproduction, Production, Postproduction, and Performance, Posting, Showing, and Distribution.

🔲 Phase I. Story Planning

This phase involves finalizing the story as well as the planning documents you'll be using, including story maps, scripts, and storyboards.

🔲 Phase II. Preproduction

In this phase you generate the list of media elements you'll need for your digital story, such as pictures and music. You then collect media, often in raw form, and begin the process of editing them so they can be used in your project. Typically this involves activities such as scanning the pictures you collect and extracting the portion of the music you'll use. Also, you begin creating new media components you'll use in your story, signaling the transition from preproduction to production.

Figure 11.1

MEDIA PRODUCTION PROCESS				
Story Planning	Pre-production	Production	Post-production	Performance, distribution
• ideas • story storming • story map • peer pitching • scripting, writing • story-boarding • telling/re-telling	• make media list • gather raw media components • begin editing raw media components & creating new ones	• finish creating, editing media components (voice-over, music, pics, video, scans, etc.) • assemble media into final product • formative review	• mix, add transitions, titles • add credits & citations • final review • final editing • export final product into readable format	• showing in class, community • Web posting • local TV • local festival? • DVD? • notifying others

❧ Phase III. Production

Phase III involves two major tasks: finishing the media components that compose the story and assembling them into a rough draft using a media editor, typically iMovie on the Mac or Movie Maker on the PC. By the end of the production phase, your piece should be in draft form and ready to show to others for purposes of critique.

❧ Phase IV. Postproduction

In Phase IV you finalize your project. Typically, this involves the following tasks: addressing any last-minute media component needs that emerged during the critique, finishing the audio and image mix, and adding titles, transitions, and credits. It also entails saving your work in such a way that it can be viewed via the technological means of the day. As of 2007, this means via the Web or DVD. However the ways we view new media will most certainly continue to evolve.

A built-in assessment schedule.

Note how the media production process provides a built-in formative assessment schedule. Simply develop a checklist or rubric based on each phase to help your students stay on track and to help you provide helpful and timely assessment of all phases of their work.

▩ Phase V. Performance, Posting, Showing, and Distribution

Your final product is shown, performed, posted, and/or duplicated and distributed. I describe a number of performance and distribution options when we look at Phase V in detail in the next chapter.

▩ Demystifying the Media Production Process: Making Media Is as Easy as Making a Cake

It's been my experience that the media production process often mystifies people. The reality is that it's a fancy name for a creative problem-solving process we use frequently for many of life's challenges. For example, Figure 11.2 shows how this process can be adapted for making a cake. Notice how similar it is to making new media.

Basically, whenever you're engaged in a project that requires planning, successive iterations of development, and sharing your results with others, you're using the five-phase production process. This process could be called the "how to do just about anything process" and consists of the following five basic activities:

- Phase I: Planning
- Phase II: Identifying and gathering materials, expertise
- Phase III: Development and implementation
- Phase IV: Honing, editing, and finalizing
- Phase V: Sharing with others

If your students are having difficulty understanding the five-phase media development process, I recommend having them translate something they already know how to do into this process, such as mastering a skateboard maneuver, building an address book on a cell phone, or conducting an experiment for science class. Translation is a great way to test for comprehension. Students can translate something only if they understand it.

With this overview of the media production process in mind, let's take a more detailed look at how it's used in DST projects in the classroom.

Figure 11.2

MAKING A CAKE, BASIC PROCESS				
Cake planning	Pre-production	Production	Post-production	Performance, distribution
• ideas • brainstorm • decide on cake • get recipe, directions	• make ingredients list • gather, buy ingredients • begin making cake components	• finish components (dough, frosting, etc.) • taste test • assemble cake into final product • bake, let cool	• frost • decorate • add candles • credits, citations for those who helped	• cut the cake • distribute, share • seconds anyone? • take leftovers to work • share recipe

❧ Using the Media Production Process With Digital Storytelling

Keep in mind that what I present here is a fairly generic treatment of this process. Which steps I include or emphasize depends on the nature of the activity, the time allotted for the project, the available resources, and the needs of the participants. I find that no two situations are the same, and thus no two projects, workshops, or units of instruction follow the same path. Thus, feel free to adapt this process to your own needs.

❧ Prephase I: Getting Ready

What's this? Another phase? Sort of. Before explaining the details of Phase I, there are a few big picture issues to consider that can make or break a project. They fall under the following basic headings: technology training, interest and support, parent permission, curriculum alignment and assessment, infrastructure and gear, copyright and artist permission, and storytelling training.

Getty ready. Do you have:

1. Training scheduled?

2. Administrative and teacher buy-in?

3. Tech access and support?

4. Parent permission?

5. Assessment strategies?

6. Permission to use media?

❧ Technology Training

There's nothing worse than being in the story development mood and having to pause to figure out a new piece of hardware or software. That's why

I recommend that students begin learning their digital tools before they need to use them to create a story. Doing so allows for a much smoother transition from development to preproduction.

If you're a teacher planning to use DST in a unit of instruction, then find a way for students to play with the hardware and software before the project begins. To help students prepare for a DST project, I'll sometimes give them less demanding assignments, like introducing themselves in 60 seconds using nothing but voice narration and a few photographs. Doing this using either iMovie or Movie Maker will help students develop many of the hardware and software skills they need to create a more demanding digital story. Above all, encourage students to simply play with the digital tools they'll use outside of class. Even a little bit of familiarity is helpful.

▓ Interest and Support

Interest in a DST project makes it possible; support makes it successful. I find the following kinds of interest and support necessary in order for a DST project to succeed:

Teachers

Every project needs a classroom teacher who is keen on being involved—passive interest won't suffice. The teacher needs to have the interest and passion in the project, as well as the time in his or her curriculum to devote to it. I always talk to teachers who are considering a DST project ahead of time to make sure they understand what is involved. Time is one of the most important issues in this regard. Time requirements are discussed in detail a little later, but suffice it to say for now that teachers will need to find one to two hours every day for a week for students to produce a computer-based digital story and about double that time to produce performance-based digital stories. These time estimates assume that technology and expertise are available and the project is carried out in a supportive environment.

Tech Support Staff

Earlier I talked about how both teachers and students can often provide the in-class tech support necessary to complete a DST project. However, tech support is still necessary to do out-of-class things such as locating and maintaining equipment, buying and installing software, and burning multiple copies of DVDs. That's why I always try to involve any formal tech support that exists in the building. I just completed a DST project in which I worked side-by-side with both the teacher and the technology teacher in the school. It was an ideal situation.

Administration

I always contact administrators during the planning stages of a storytelling project to let them know what it involves. Principals understandably want to know the projects going on in their schools. Once they do, they're usually very happy to let the public know they're doing something so interesting and beneficial to students. In fact, I've never worked with an administrator who wasn't supportive of my DST efforts. But in order to be supportive, they need to know what's going on.

▓ Parent Permission

A special kind of interest and support is parent permission. Because digital stories often involve showing not only students' work but also the students themselves via photographs or recorded performances, teachers must get express written permission from parents for their child's involvement. In Chapter 3 I provided a sample letter to send home to parents announcing a DST project; this is also available through my Web site (www.jasonohler.com/storytelling). Teachers use it as a template, modifying it to fit their particular projects.

I then encourage teachers to follow up by sending a permission slip to parents that asks specifically for permission to record, show, and distribute their child's work. What permission slip should you use? My strong advice is to use the standard media release form adopted by your district. Your administration should be able to help you locate this. Don't forget: if a parent doesn't sign a permission slip, then a student's work cannot be recorded and distributed. Case in point: if a DVD has been created that contains a number of student stories and you've obtained parent permission for all students except one, then the DVD can't be distributed.

▓ Curriculum Alignment and Assessment

I encourage teachers to think about how they want their digital story projects to support and align with their curriculum well in advance of the DST project. Ideally, they should flow from a classroom unit of instruction as seamlessly as possible. I also encourage teachers to determine ahead of time how they want to assess DST projects—as literacy projects? art projects? performance projects? content-area projects? some combination of these? It's important that teachers consider the important issue of assessment before they get started so they can steer the project toward their educational goals. To help teachers focus on this issue, I ask them, "Suppose a parent asks you why you're doing this. What would you say?" Part I provides a rubric as well as a good deal of material about how to assess new media.

Infrastructure and Gear

I know this sounds like something Captain Obvious would say, but no gear = no DST project. Make sure you have what you need, that it works, and that it hasn't already been reserved for the time you'll need it. The kind of equipment you need is listed in the Preface and explained in greater detail in Chapter 13. The good news is that new media production doesn't require expensive or fancy equipment anymore. Teachers can do a great deal using common computers and free software. But if there simply is not any equipment, then I recommend you do a traditional storytelling project rather than give up on storytelling entirely. Part II of this book explains how to help students create stories, and the resources at the end of the book give tips on how to tell them in traditional fashion.

Copyright and Artist Permission

I address the issue of copyright and fair use in some detail in Chapter 15. For now, it's important to point out that teachers should try to anticipate and address any issues in this area that might arise during their project before the project begins. Otherwise, an entire project can be held up while students chase down permissions. And should they not attain them, an entire project can be put at risk.

While students use a number of information sources in digital stories, two of them are particularly problematic with regard to copyright and permission: (1) interviews and live recordings of others and (2) media that students download from the Internet, CDs, music players, and other sources. As I point out in Chapter 15, there are a number of strategies open to teachers for dealing with this kind of material, from requiring students to use nothing but original media to requiring students to cite and obtain permission for everything they use. Whatever strategy teachers elect to use needs to be in place and communicated clearly to students before the project begins.

Storytelling Training

While telling stories seems like the most natural thing in the world, when students do it within the context of performance or media production, they often require training. I provide a good deal of information about how to teach storytelling in Part II, particularly Chapter 7. Also, I've included information in the resources that should be helpful in this regard.

▓ Phase I. Story Planning and Development

Phase I of the media production process is often called story planning and development, or simply, development. In Phase I you finalize your story and complete all the planning documents needed before going into production. Story development and media production are never completely separate. In fact, they have the same kind of symbiotic relationship that medium and message have (McLuhan, 1964): your production capabilities will always dictate some aspects of your story and vice versa. However, separating story and media at the outset will help your DST project be a storytelling event, rather than a technical exercise. This is why development is a distinct phase.

▓ Two Kinds of Digital Storytelling

While there are many approaches to DST, recall that earlier I described two that I'm typically involved with. They are worth describing in a bit more detail here before looking at the story development process used to create them:

Computer-Based DST

Even though DST is relatively new, it has developed a sense of tradition. To many, a digital story is built on a voice-over narration, to which is added images, music, and other media. Images can be original, scanned, or downloaded. Video is rarely used, largely because it's comparatively expensive and complex, but that's destined to change quickly. The end result is reminiscent of a Ken Burns documentary. Most of the digital stories I described in Part I were in this form.

The heart of this kind of digital story is the spoken narrative. Most of the storyteller's efforts should be focused on developing narrative that speaks their "story truth" as clearly as possible. Pictures, music, transitions, and so on are then used to support the narrative.

Performance-Based Green Screen Storytelling

Green screen performance-based storytelling: Harry Potter production techniques meets traditional storytelling performance.

I described this earlier as students performing their stories in traditional fashion in front of a green surface—usually a painted wall—and then either finding or creating artwork that they add behind themselves using the computer and chroma-key editing software. Besides allowing students to stand and deliver their stories—an immensely powerful and beneficial experience for the confidence building it develops—this approach also gives them a peek into one of the most persuasive media techniques used in their mediascape: chroma-key editing. The software needed to perform chroma-key editing is inexpensive (typically less than $50 plug-in for the Mac) and in my opinion will soon become a standard feature with some movie editing software packages. You can find software recommendations at www.jasonohler.com/storytelling.

There is nothing mystifying about green screen editing for kids. One time I was doing a green screen storytelling project with a group of fourth graders and asked how many knew that Harry Potter wasn't actually flying around on a broom in a stadium during the Quidditch match. Every hand went up. I called on a student who was eager to share his understanding of it, and he explained that Harry was in a green room and that everything else was added by computer later because the walls were green. All the kids agreed— one even said "Duh!" Every adult in the room asked me, "What's a green room?" This is the norm.

The Basic Process

The basic process I use for story development combines my work with that of others, most notably Dillingham (2005) and Theodosakis (2001). I've attempted to capture the basic process used for both kinds of DST in the flowchart presented in Figure 11.3. Keep in mind that this represents a generic process and that every DST activity modifies this process in some way. Each of the steps in the flowchart is explained below.

Map

Students create a story map. This was covered in great detail in Part II of this book. I should add here that students are encouraged to take their maps home and share them with their families. Besides helping students fine-tune their stories, it keeps friends and family in the loop.

Peer Pitch

Peer pitching is an approach to student peer review that involves students pitching their ideas to each other as a form of critique (Theodosakis, 2001). The metaphor for peer pitching is the Hollywood "sell session," in which would-be movie developers pitch their movie ideas to potential financial backers. In my adaptation of this process, students pitch their stories to peers, using their story map as a basis. I usually put students into groups of two to four and allow each person five minutes to pitch his or her idea to the rest of the group.

Figure 11.3 Story Development Process

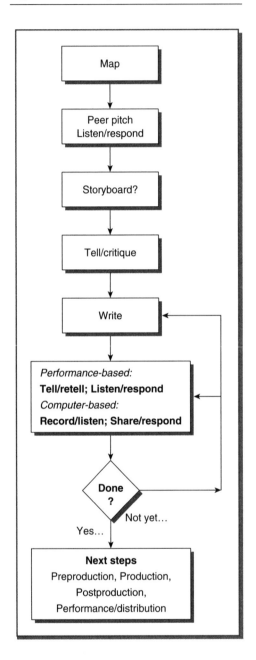

Participants are instructed to give feedback in terms of how well the components of the story core were articulated and whether the story was engaging enough to sustain their interest. Teachers should stress the fact that the purpose of peer pitching is for students to help each other clarify, not criticize, each other's stories. Comments can focus on the following:

- Were the elements of the story core clear and well connected?
- Was the character's transformation clear and compelling?
- Did listeners want to know what was going to happen next? Did the story progress in a way that made sense but wasn't predictable? In other words, would the story have a good chance of honoring "the storytelling covenant" that I described earlier? Always be on the lookout for extraneous material. Two-minute stories don't have time for subplots.
- Did the conclusion work? Was closure reached? Was anything left hanging?

If I have time, I also have students explain their stories to each other. That is, after students pitch a story, someone in the review group will pitch it back to the students. Hearing someone else summarize and tell your story idea to you has an amazingly clarifying effect.

Storyboard?

Note that this appears in the flowchart as a question. That's because shorter digital stories don't always require the kind of formal storyboarding usually associated with media production.

Recall that earlier I compared story mapping with storyboarding in the following way: a story map shows the flow of emotion in a story, while a storyboard shows the flow of motion. That is, a storyboard is used to make sure that the story flows logically and sequentially, without holes or detours. While a formal storyboard might not be necessary for shorter media pieces, some method of capturing the flow of events in a planning document is. If students are limiting their stories to around two minutes (which I recommend) and have created either a detailed story map or a completed written narrative, then I don't require them to make a formal storyboard. Instead, I use less formal approaches to storyboarding, such as the following:

- *Annotate the story map.* Usually there's enough room on the story map students are using to sketch details for scene changes, visual images, music, and so on. This is the approach I almost always use with performance-based green screen storytelling.
- *Annotate the written narrative.* If students print out their written narrative double-spaced and with wide margins, they can add enough direction and annotation to it to create a useful story planning document. Typically, I use this approach with computer-based storytelling, though annotating the story map is also quite useful.
- *Use a media assembly program, such as iMovie or Movie Maker.* Digital storytellers can use the same media programs they'll use to assemble their stories (e.g., iMovie or Movie Maker) as a storyboarding tool. Students can load pictures into the program as placeholders and use the program's titling tool to create words to describe the action or pictures that will appear. However, I need to caution teachers. Using this approach tends to give students the feeling of being already in production, when in fact they're still in the planning stage. It will be up to teachers to make sure that students complete their media lists and narratives before actually trying to enter the production phase.

If you want students to create something more formal, here are two suggestions:

1. *Use PowerPoint.* Typically, a storyboard looks something like a PowerPoint presentation, so why not use PowerPoint? A professional storyboard usually consists of a series of panels, each with a picture and text explaining the action and production requirements of the scene. A new slide or panel is created whenever there is a significant change in the story, such as a change in image, location, or character. PowerPoint is ideal for creating such a document.

2. *Use my DST storyboard template.* I adapted the standard formal storyboard template to accommodate some of the specific needs of DST projects. (See www.jasonohler.com/storytelling.)

Keep in mind that whatever storyboarding approach you elect to use must lead directly into generating a media list (discussed later), which is part of Preproduction, the next step in the media development process.

Tell/Critique

This step pertains more to performance-based than computer-based storytelling. At this point in the story development process, students tell their stories to the whole group. The focus is on the students' telling, rather than their stories, though the process usually compels students to also consider story changes as well. Comments are usually in the form of what made it an effective telling and what could make it stronger. Typically, there is time for three to five students to tell their stories. At this point, I'm just trying to model the tell/retell peer review process that they'll use during tell/retell.

For computer-based storytelling, I do something similar. Students are encouraged to describe their stories to the whole group, whether through storytelling or simply by explaining their stories in an animated way. Even though performance is not a goal, the process of telling their stories helps students hear what is important, what needs emphasis, how their stories can best be supported through media, and so on. Students then critique each other's stories and are encouraged to brainstorm about what kind of media could be used to most effectively support the narrative of their stories.

Write

Students write the narrative they'll record. When students write, they think. When they think, they create better stories.

The role of writing for computer-based versus performance-based DST differs in one important respect. With computer-based DST, students are often creating something that is read and recorded verbatim. Therefore, teachers may want students to spend extra time polishing what they write. In the case of performance-based DST, students don't write and memorize a script. Rather, they write out their stories to be used as a guide for their telling. We expect students' stories to change at least a little every time they tell them.

When we write, we think.

How much should students write at this point? That depends in part on the grade level. For younger kids, perhaps one short paragraph for each major section of the story. In the case of older students, let your language arts curriculum goals guide you. Don't forget: DST can be used to develop writing skills. If this is the goal of your project, then have students write and rewrite as often as you feel is appropriate.

Performance-Based Stories: Tell/Retell; Listen/Respond

In the case of performance-based stories, students tell and retell their stories in pairs and small groups. They listen, respond, and provide feedback about improving their storytelling, including what worked and what could be improved. In addition, I recommend you experiment with having students tell each other's stories to them. It's an effective way for students to hear their own stories with fresh ears and get ideas about how they might be improved.

Computer-Based Stories: Record/Listen; Share/Respond

For computer-based stories, students record themselves speaking their narratives and then listen to their narratives for purposes of revision. Amazing things happen when students listen to rather than just reread their writing. Unlike the standard writing process, the "write-record-listen" renarration process forces students' writing outside the confines of their own minds. This creates a certain distance and objectivity that facilitates self-evaluation that might not be possible with the writing process. It's up to the teacher to decide at this point whether there is time to have students share their narration for purposes of peer response.

Done?

Do students need more work telling? Narrating? Listening? Writing? Literacy objectives will drive this decision. Keep in mind that sometimes technical issues will also drive this. For example, a narration might need to be rerecorded because it was too weak or because of ambient noise. A tech tip: record a few sentences, listen, and adjust the volume before recording your entire narrative.

Next Steps

Students now proceed with the media production process, adding images, music, and so on, as well as editing. This is covered in Chapter 12.

▓ Adapting the Story Development Process

Do I follow this approach every time? Absolutely not. Every group has different needs. Besides, time constraints often won't allow it. Here are some common adaptations. Bear in mind that the time estimates provided cover only my initial presentation, not any follow-up with participants.

If the Emphasis Is on Storytelling Performance

Acting out becomes a good thing.

An interesting benefit of storytelling in your classroom is that it provides an opportunity for students to "act out" in positive ways. While normally it is rude for students to bring attention to themselves in class, this is expected during storytelling. Using storytelling teaches students when it is and is not acceptable to be the center of attention, as well as how to show respect for others when it is their turn to have the attention focused on them. Instead of telling students to be quiet, you can tell them, "save it for storytelling."

I introduce story concepts, the story core, and story mapping. I tell a story, then we identify the core and map the story. Following that, we story-storm. Students then develop their own stories, peer pitch them, adjust them, and write them out in a page. If there's time, students tell and retell, as well as write and rewrite, their stories. I provide oral storytelling training (see Resource A). Students perform their stories. *Time required:* Two hours is great, but I've done this in one hour with limited performance time. To complete the entire project requires about one to two hours a day for one week.

If the Emphasis Is on Digital Story Preparation

I show a few digital stories and introduce the story core and story map. I then lead a group discussion in which we map the stories we've watched. I tell a story and the class helps me map it. If time permits, we story-storm. Students develop their own story ideas, map them, peer pitch them, write them in a few paragraphs, and tell them informally. *Time required:* one to two hours.

If the Emphasis Is on Academic Stories

Same as above, but make sure that the examples are academic and that the content is academic during story-storming. Teachers should be involved at all points to make sure that curriculum objectives are receiving the appropriate focus.

If the Emphasis Is on Evaluating Digital Stories

I use the process described in Chapter 2. I show a series of digital stories, after which participants do a quick write and discuss their thoughts, particularly as they relate to assessment. I slowly introduce story concepts as

I straddle the line between wanting to say enough to be helpful and not limiting their perceptions of what they see. The viewing and discussion process usually happens at the beginning of a DST workshop. The emphasis is not so much on creating polished digital stories as on understanding how to evaluate what their students will create. *Time required:* variable, but usually no more than three hours.

▓ If the Emphasis Is on Introducing the Audience to Storytelling

I use Kenn Adams's (1990) *The Story Spine*, explained in Chapter 9, in order to get rolling. I use it to first create one story by myself and then to have the audience create a few with me. *The Story Spine* works well whether I'm using it with 3 people or with 300. Next, I tell a story, explain the story core and story elements, and then map the story. If there's time, I show and explain a few digital stories. *Time required:* as short as 15 minutes, as long as two hours.

▓ If the Emphasis Is on Using Storytelling to Persuade

While all storytelling persuades, what I'm referring to here is the use of storytelling to specifically sell an idea, perspective, or course of action. For example, I've helped organizations tell their stories so the public better understands what they do. In this case, I tell a story and ask participants to help me find the core and map the story. Then we story-storm about the issues they want their audience to understand. The kind of follow-up I do is determined by whether they will be delivering their stories orally or via digital media. *Time required:* 30 to 60 minutes.

▓ If the Emphasis Is on Telling Personal Stories

I show examples of personal digital stories, then talk about the story core and story elements, emphasizing the three kinds of transformation that can be present in a documentary that I discussed in Chapter 5. Briefly, transformation can occur through the experience of the tellers, those in the story, and/or the audience. From here it depends entirely on the group. Some participants want to talk about their stories, while others don't. I've actually used individualized approaches to story discovery planning in these cases. *Time required:* less than an hour.

▓ If the Emphasis Is on Developing Research Abilities

I show a few stories and then deconstruct these with help from the audience in terms of the research they probably required. I typically frame this in terms of the research process I use with students: question, methodology, data collection and analysis, presentation of results, and call for further study. This works surprisingly well for personal as well as academic stories.

With media, as with report writing, much of the value of research can't be separated from the distillation and synthesis process required to produce something concise and coherent for an audience. An important point for teachers to consider is that DST can be a carrot at the end of such a process for students who might be more enthusiastic about media production than report writing. As always, what teachers elect to do needs be driven by a blend of academic goals, skill development goals, and student interest. *Time required:* variable; from 15 minutes to 2 hours.

▓ If the Emphasis Is on Media Literacy

I provide an overview of the story core, story elements, and media grammar (topic of Chapter 14). We watch digital stories, advertisements, and a variety of media snippets in "active viewing mode," observing Rule #1 of media literacy viewing: watch something twice—once for the story, the second time to see persuasion techniques. In addition, I present tools and resources to be used in a media literacy program. If there is time, I have participants create a story core about a product they want to sell, then develop that into a map. We might transition from here to actually creating a 30-second ad. *Time required:* variable; from 15 minutes to 2 hours. This doesn't include the time needed to create an ad.

▓ If the Emphasis Is on the DAOW of Literacy

Feel free to emphasize whatever literacies represented by the DAOW of literacy (digital, art, oral, writing) that are important to you and the goals of your project. If you see DST as a way to improve digital skills, then emphasize production. If art literacy is most important to you, then insist that students create rather than find the artwork they use in their stories. If one of your primary goals for the project is for students to improve their presentation and speaking abilities, simply include oral presentation or performance at several points throughout the process. Writing skills can be emphasized easily in a DST project by simply adding reflective writing to any of the processes involved in DST creation. The bottom line is this: DST is a tremendously flexible and rich experience that can be used to support a number of educational goals. *Time required:* variable, depending on the degree of emphasis given to each area.

12

The Media Production Process, Phases II–V

From Preproduction to Performance

Continuing With the Media Production Process

Recall that the media production process is in five phases, and that in the previous chapter I covered Phase I, Story Planning. In this chapter we pick up where we left off and begin with Phase II, Preproduction.

Preproduction in a nutshell.

1. Finalize story planning (story map, storyboard, script)

2. Create media list

3. Get the media

Phase II. Preproduction: Preparing Your Story

Preproduction involves the steps that students need to take before they begin formal production. As described earlier, this involves generating a media list, collecting media to be used in their stories, editing the media they collected, and beginning the creation of new media they will need. Each is described below.

149

- *Develop a Media List.* Developing a media list is analogous to making a list of everything you need to make a cake before you go shopping for ingredients. There are no shortcuts for this step. Once your digital story is planned, you need to develop a list of all of the media that it requires, including music, narration, sounds, graphics, pictures, video clips, and other elements. Typically, students use their story map, narrative, or storyboard to create a list of the images, sounds, and other media they will need. I model this by walking through a story map and identifying places where media would be useful to support the narrative. If students use the Digital Storytelling Storyboard Template (see www.jasonohler.com/storytelling), then this is already done. Different kinds of media that students can use are addressed later on in this chapter.

> **Teacher tip:**
>
> Find out who the software and hardware experts are in your classroom or workshop and feel free to call on them. You may be sheriff in your classroom, but you can use all the deputies you can get. Kids make GREAT technology deputies.

  Don't be surprised when students don't want to spend a lot of time with this step. Often they're in a hurry to get on the computer and translate their ideas into media. But the reality is that creating the list will save them a good deal of time while helping them develop good planning habits.

- *Get the media!* Students gather all of raw the materials they have identified in their media list. This usually means gathering materials that already exist in some form (music on CDs, photos, movie footage on a VHS, images on the Internet, etc.).
- *Edit and begin creating media.* With most of the media in hand, students now begin to edit what they have, and create what they don't. Typical activities here include scanning collected photos and objects, digitally editing photos, extracting the snippet of music needed from a song, and so on.

Video recording a storytelling performance as part of a green screen storytelling project represents a special case of media preparation. Usually a final storytelling performance would fall under Phase V, Performance and distribution. However, with the case of performance-based green screen storytelling, it's more appropriately considered here because the recorded performance is needed as a media element during the production phase. That is, as you enter the production phase, students should have recorded their final performance in front of a green screen so they can edit it.

Once the raw material is gathered and edited, students begin creating anything new they need. Actually creating media components signals the transition to the next phase, Production.

Phase III. Production: Assembling Your Story

Students sit at the computer with their completed story, narrative, and media and assemble the story. Generally this involves the following steps:

- *Learn the basics of iMovie or Movie Maker.* If you've managed to find time to do the training component of Prephase I, then this is not an issue. Otherwise, students will need to learn how to use the hardware and software. While they are generally comfortable with technology, learning how to use it still requires

> **Production in a nutshell:**
>
> Create rest of media
>
> Pay particular attention to writing and speaking the narration
>
> Add media and assemble story in movie/media program to produce rough draft

time. Even though many software programs can be used to assemble a digital story, I recommend iMovie and Movie Maker because they are free, easy to learn and use, and generally are powerful enough to accommodate most classroom-based DST projects.
- *Finish media—focus on the narrative.* Students finish the process of media development begun in preproduction. They edit and finalize all media pieces so they're ready to be added to the story. This includes creating their audio narrative or recording their performance.
- *Add the narrative or recorded performance to the story.* Students open a file in their media editing program and add their recorded narrative or performance first. If they're doing computer-based storytelling and have used iMovie or Movie Maker to create the narrative, then they've already completed this step.
- *Add visual media to the narrative.* Students doing computer-based storytelling add pictures, scanned images, and so on to support the narrative. They could also add animation and/or video, but doing so typically adds a level of cost and complexity that is hard to accommodate in an average K–12 classroom. This will most certainly change in the near future. Students doing performance-based green screen storytelling add their artwork "behind" their performances using chroma-key editing. For information about specific software and training materials for this process, see my Web site (www.jasonohler.com/storytelling).
- *Add music, sounds, other voices.* Audio information is added to supplement the story. This is not required.
- *Rough mix.* Once all the media elements have been added to the story, students now mix the audio. They do a rough mix now and then do a final mix in postproduction. Of note: poorly mixed audio is a common problem in DST projects. Make sure that, above all, the narrative is

clear and that the music is not conflicting with the voice recording. Similarly, students need to make sure that visual information is mixed well with the narrative too. Images should appear at just the right moment and show for just the length of time necessary to support the narrative. More about this in Chapter 14: Media Grammar.

- *Peer/instructor review.* Having students show their work in progress can be very helpful. How teachers approach this depends on a number of factors, including class size, structure, and the purpose of the story-telling project.

▓ Phase IV. Postproduction: Finalizing Your Story

By this phase, the story is basically done but is still in rough form. Typically, at this point students do the following:

Postproduction in a nutshell:

Add titles, credits

Add music

Add transitions, effects

Do final mix, last pass

Export final story

- *Add titles.* Students add opening title information and maybe other titles that appear during the story. Titling within the story is in fact a hallmark of DST—it's something rarely seen in movies or TV programming yet appears frequently in DST projects. Most video editing programs, like iMovie and Movie Maker, have titling capabilities.

- *Add credits, citations, and copyright information.* A special application of titling is adding credits and citations at the end of story. Every digital story is incomplete until this is done. Period. Students must get into the routine of citing media sources, whether they're quotations from books, graphics found on the Internet, or music downloaded from a CD. To me, whether to use MLA versus APA format is not important until students are well into high school. It's simply important that students, regardless of grade level, show respect for the artists whose work they're

Teacher tip:

Use titling to show a word on the screen during a story when a picture is not appropriate or available. I recently saw a story in which a student displayed the word "confusion" while the narrative was talking about being emotionally and intellectually lost. It was an effective way to fill a blank screen without overfilling it or detracting from the narrative.

using. I provide fairly detailed information about copyright issues in Chapter 15.

- *Add background music during titles and credits.* It's up to you. It's often a nice touch.
- *Add music and audio effects elsewhere.* Are there other parts of your story that could be supported by music or other audio effects? Be sure it doesn't conflict with the narrative. In the best of all possible worlds, it's used very judicially to support the story in clear and compelling ways.
- *Add transitions.* Transitions provide ways to move from image to image, such as fading in and out, scrolling, and so on. Without transitions, the story displays one image, then abruptly displays the next. Often this works. Other times, transitions are required in order to make the story flow more effectively. Transition capabilities are built into iMovie, Movie Maker, even PowerPoint, and just about any software that might be used to assemble a digital story. Experiment with what the software offers. If you aren't sure what you like, watch a favorite movie or TV program and take notes about the kinds of transitions used to go from scene to scene. It's a great way to find ideas. It's also a great way to make this important point to students: generally speaking, professional media producers use transitions unobtrusively. Given that students can have a tendency to overuse or misuse transitions, this is good information for them to have.
- *Add effects.* Both iMovie and Movie Maker contain effects, which are like transitions except that they happen to a particular image or slide, rather than between two images or slides. They do many things, from adding the kind of graininess found in old films to providing jerky movements reminiscent of an earthquake. Newer software packages also provide sound effects, and zillions of them can be found on the Internet. They are just what you would expect: thunder, applause, chickens clucking, you name it. Again, experiment, and watch other media for ideas. And again, you do your students a favor by showing them that professional media producers don't misuse or overuse them.
- *Peer/instructor review.* Having an in-class showing can be a good way for students to get input before their final mix.
- *Final mix and polishing.* Students make any final modifications to their stories—the traditional "one last pass." By now, most students are tired of their projects. They're also so used to them that it has become very difficult to see the rough edges, just as it becomes nearly impossible to see typos in a writing project they've rewritten several times. However, this is the point at which students need to sit back and watch their story one last time in order to spot and smooth out any rough edges. This is

also a great time for one last peer review. Typically, digital stories are short enough that asking others to watch them isn't too imposing.

- *Export your story to a transportable format.* Exporting is different from saving. Saved files can only be viewed using the piece that was used to create them, whereas exported files can be seen independently of the original software using free, widely available media-viewing software. As of 2007, in iMovie the export command is either Share or Export; in Movie Maker, select Save Movie from the File menu. Transportable files created by iMovie on the Mac are usually QuickTime movie files. Movie Maker on the PC usually generates Windows Media Player movie files.

> **To export your story:**
>
> Use "Share" or "Export" in iMovie on the Mac to create QuickTime movies
>
> Use "Finish Movie" in Movie Maker on the PC to create Windows Media Player movies

A special note about file size, quality, and compression. When exporting files, you'll see a number of options to "compress" your movie, most of which have to do with file quality and file size. The higher the quality, the larger the file. If you have the room, save your story in the highest quality possible, which might be called "DVD" or "Full Quality." Typically, these need to be burned on a DVD because they're too large to fit on a CD. But the extra resolution makes it worth it. Using Movie Maker, you do something similar. The Movie Tasks list that usually appears in a column on the left-hand side of the movie construction screen has an option called "Finish Movie." Within that I typically choose "Save to Computer." As with iMovie, you're given options about quality.

> **What's an exported file?**
>
> If you embed a picture in a Word file and then send that file to someone via email, the file received on the other end has the picture in it. Not so when creating a story with iMovie or Movie Maker. Instead, both programs create a main source file that fetches the pictures and other media you use as the story plays. Keeping the media separate from the source file makes story development more manageable. Exporting your story embeds all the media in the story so that it can be played on nearly any reasonably up-to-date computer without special software.

- *Master a DVD.* Once a story is exported, it can simply be stored as a file on the computer (including computers on the Internet), or other storage device (e.g., an iPod), a CD (if it is small enough), or a DVD. CDs and DVDs can be used simply as storage media for backup. Used in this way, they won't self-launch like commercial CDs or DVDs. This means that watching a story requires finding the file and clicking on it. If students want to create self-launching DVDs like the kind played in home DVD players, then the DVD needs to be "mastered." There are a number of programs that can be used to master a DVD, like iDVD for the Macintosh.

▨ Phase V. Performance and Distribution

An untold story is an incomplete story. With your digital story completed, there are a number of ways to make sure student work is shared with others. Consider the following distribution and performance options.

> **Performance/ distribution in a nutshell:**
>
> Find venues
>
> Announce
>
> Perform
>
> Post
>
> Share movies

- *Within your class.* Students should always have a chance to share work with classmates. They are usually very proud of their work, as well as inspired by the work of others. In addition, sharing work within a class creates a much more meaningful context for assessment, including self-assessment.
- *Within your school.* This is a great way not only for students to share their work with others but also for teachers to introduce DST within their professional communities.
- *Within your department.* Showing students' digital stories at department meetings can be an effective way to stimulate thinking about new classroom practices. It's also a welcome relief from budget talk.
- *At a school board meeting or other public event.* The public loves to listen to kids tell stories. Featuring your students' work in public venues—from school board meetings to senior centers to more artistic venues—will generate support for both your classroom and your school. Our community has an organization dedicated to showing locally produced new media (see inset). Perhaps yours does too. If not, start one!

> **Teacher idea:**
>
> My community has an organization called JUMP (Juneau Underground Movie Project) that has provided an exciting venue for students to show their digital stories. No JUMP in your community? Start one. All you need is a room with a projector and a screen. Don't forget to let everyone know about it!

- *Via local television.* Many communities have cable companies that provide community service channels. Using them to air student work is a great way to show the community the digital stories that your students have created.
- *Via Webstreaming through your school district's Web site, You Tube or other Web sites.* Webstreaming allows playing video information on the Web in real time (vs. having to download an entire work before you can view it). In order to Webstream your students' digital stories, you need to save them in a specific way. This is not hard to figure out, especially

with a little help from one of your more technically oriented students, colleagues, or from tech support staff. Be sure to let parents know where they can view them.

- *Via podcasting.* Podcasting allows the public to subscribe to particular media events and be notified about new material that is available. Podcasting began primarily as an audio event and has often been compared to radio programming. It now includes video, images, and other media. Podcasting digital stories is a natural.

- *As burned CDs or DVDs.* There are a number of good reasons to burn your students' work to a CD or DVD. First, doing so provides a fairly permanent backup. Second, watching a DVD provides an easy viewing option that doesn't require the Web or even a computer; DVDs that your students burn usually play on most home entertainment systems. And third, there are still plenty of places in the world where Webstreaming doesn't work very well due to a lack of bandwidth. If possible, send a copy home with each student. Parents love to get them.

Teacher idea:

Always burn a DVD of students' digital stories. There is no guarantee that the stories your students created will remain on your server forever. Computers, and district directives for using them, come and go. Burn a DVD to be safe.

- *As part of a portfolio.* Whether your students are maintaining portfolios online or in a notebook, be sure to include their digital stories. If they're putting together more traditional kinds of portfolios, then they need to have a CD or DVD of their work. Digital stories are practically portfolios unto themselves, given the plethora of literacies, skills, and content they address. Don't forget to include the writing, planning documents and other work students created in the process of developing their stories as part of their portfolios.

- *Via contests.* More and more contests are cropping up that are looking for new media work created by students. A Google search should help you locate them.

- *At education and media conferences.* Are you thinking about attending a conference? If so, consider doing a session on DST in your classroom. It's how you can help the proliferation of new ideas among your colleagues.

- *What's next?* Look forward to watching digital stories on cell phones, e-textbooks and new mobile devices. We will also watch them via podcast, YouTube, and TV. We will also become part of them via games and immersive virtual environments and . . . much more. The future is just getting started, and digital stories are guaranteed to be an important part of it.

🐾 Postphase I. Final Assessment and Reflection

Yet another phase? Sort of. After the project is over, it's time to reflect on and evaluate the experience in order to glean what was learned so that the next adventure can be improved. This process is approached differently for the different groups of people involved:

- *For students:* What's the story of making your story? As a form of project closure, you may want your students to engage in a post-project assessment of what they've learned. An apt metaphor for their experience of creating new media narrative is "the story." During the process of addressing the opportunity to create a digital story and solving a number of problems along the way, students learned a great deal. What problems did they solve? How did the experience transform them? What would they do differently next time?

- *For teachers:* What does your rubric look like? When I conduct teacher workshops, I always try to return to the issue of assessment several times during the workshop. By the end of the workshop, participants have developed a tremendous amount of insight into what it means to create clear, effective, and successful digital stories, and often enjoy a chance to debrief. After a discussion of their experiences, I ask teachers to create a rubric of at least five traits and then share their rubrics with each other.

The rubrics that teachers create are as similar as they are dissimilar. Nearly all have a trait related to the story, as well as some aspect of technical production. However, some will highlight emotional engagement and originality while others will stress organization and thoroughness. It is important that teachers leave with a rubric, however preliminary. Creating a rubric for digital stories is often their first successful step in evaluating something that once seemed quite foreign to them.

In addition to rubric development, I always encourage teachers to reflect on how DST will impact their classrooms and communities of practice. DST is truly new for most teachers, and the impact of using it instructionally is potentially very great. Reflecting on what they experienced during a DST workshop, as well as the units of instruction they create that involve new media production, is key to their evolving sense of its use.

▓ Special Considerations for Performance-Based Green Screen Storytelling

For the most part, the media-production process is very similar for both computer-based and performance-based DST. However, here are some points that pertain only to performance-based green screen storytelling that are worth highlighting:

- *The color green.* There is nothing magic about a particular shade of green. What is important is that you use a solid, monochromatic color. In fact, students could perform in front of a black surface and theoretically produce the same results. However, if students are wearing black when they perform in front of a black screen, then their artwork shows up on their clothes! This is an interesting effect, as long as you plan for it. The industry has settled on a particular shade of green because people don't often wear it. I chose a particular shade of green from a green stickie—I call it "yuck green." I can then use the stickies to cover plugs, switches, and other imperfections in the background surface.
- *Don't wear green!* Tell students not to wear green on performance day. If you are sending a note home to parents about this, and are using "yuck green," then paste a stickie on the note.
- *The green surface.* Green sheets that work well are available for purchase. Just Google "green chroma sheet." You can also make green background sheets using bed sheets and green dye, though they don't tend to work as well. However, I much prefer painting a wall green to using sheets for a few reasons. A wall is smoother and therefore casts fewer shadows, creating a more monochromatic surface. Also, painting a wall creates a green space that invites other teachers to use it. To get the paint, I give the local hardware store a yuck green stickie and say, "A gallon of that, please."
- *Lighting and shadows.* Shadows are the enemy of chroma key editing because they make the green surface less monochromatic. Therefore, the goal is to have as much light as possible without casting shadows. While good lighting is always preferable, don't let bad lighting stop you. I have shot performances in low and variable light and the results are fine; they just don't look as vibrant or polished.
- *Background artwork.* Students can replace the chroma green with literally anything digital (video, animation, photos, images, etc.). However, I encourage elementary teachers to have students create original artwork using common materials (e.g., crayons and 8½ × 11-inch sheets of

paper) because it's inexpensive and fits into the overall flow of classroom events very easily. For a two-minute story, three to five pieces of artwork suffice. When students create their artwork, be sure they turn their papers sideways, because their work will better conform to the shape of a computer screen. Artwork is scanned using a common, inexpensive scanner (less than $100 these days). Ideally, students watch a recording of their performance and then determine what they need in terms of art. But there is rarely time for this. Keep in mind that original artwork has no copyright issues associated with it.

- *Record a dress rehearsal and have students study their performances.* Ideally, students would watch a recording of their performance for another reason: to learn from and improve upon their storytelling. Like dancers and athletes, storytellers can benefit tremendously from this approach to improvement.

- *Use a wireless mike.* Use a wireless lavalier-type mike rather than the mike built into the video camera. The sound is vastly superior. This will require you to use a video camera that has an external mike input. Technical information about buying and using video recording equipment is covered in Chapter 13.

- *Software, hardware.* This topic is covered in some detail in Chapter 13. But suffice it to say for now that in addition to the technology required for computer-based technology, green screen storytelling requires a wireless mike, a video camera with external mike and headphone inputs, and a software program that allows chroma-key editing. Fortunately, there are inexpensive plug-ins you can buy for iMovie for this purpose.

- *Students do everything.* Whenever possible, I have students do all the technical production themselves, including running the cameras, miking the performers, scanning their artwork, chroma editing their stories, and producing the DVDs. On the day of the shoot, each student has an opportunity to be videographer, floor manager (students love saying "Quiet on the set!"), and audio technician, making sure that performers have their mikes well placed.

How Much Time Does Digital Storytelling Take?

Teachers understandably want to know the time required to produce digital stories in their classrooms. I consider the issue of time in terms of research time and development/production time.

❈ Research Time

The role of research is no different for producing new media than it is for producing essays. Thus, if you would normally allow a week for conducting research for an essay or report, then you might think that allowing the same amount for digital stories should suffice. However, additional time requirements arise when students need to obtain research resources that are not normally included in an essay or report, such as an interview clip gathered in the field or an animation located on the Internet.

It's important to understand how the medium becomes the message in this case. Students think in terms of including a number of kinds of media in digital stories, because new media projects predictably encourage the inclusion of new media content. While it may well be your goal to have your students think in these terms, just remember to budget for it. A good rule of thumb is to begin by adding 25% to conventional research time and see how that works for you.

❈ Story Development and Media Production Time

Production time definitely increases when going from essay or report generation to new media production. Table 12.1 should be helpful in budgeting your time in terms of the kind of digital stories your students are doing. In addition, here are other factors that impact the time involved:

- *Producing original artwork versus using existing media.* Although it takes more time for students to produce original artwork, when they do so they develop fourth R art skills and sidestep entirely the issue of copyright infringement.
- *Including a media literacy component in your project.* As I explained earlier, new media production provides powerful media literacy learning

Table 12.1   Storytelling Time Requirements

Type of Storytelling	Time Requirements
Traditional storytelling	1 week, 2 hours/day, from beginning to final performance. Add time if you are going to video record the performances and produce a DVD.
Computer-based storytelling	1 week, 1-2 hours/day, assuming equipment is on hand and working
Performance-based green screen storytelling	2-3 weeks, 1-2 hours/day; 1 week for creating and performing stories, and 1-2 weeks for creating and scanning artwork, chroma-key editing, DVD production

opportunities. However, media literacy does not occur naturally. When students are focused on production, they find it difficult to zoom out to analyze the larger picture of media impact. Therefore, teachers who want to include a media literacy component in a DST project need to do so deliberately by building it into the unit of instruction. They also need to budget time for it and develop a means to evaluate student progress in that area.

- *Production values.* The level of production value you require of student projects will have an immense impact on the amount of time that projects require. Recall from my earlier discussion that production value refers to the degree of polish a piece of media has. A home video usually has low production values, while a Hollywood movie has very high production values. Also recall the rule of 80–20 from Chapter 2, which basically says that in a finished, high-quality media project, 80% of the time is spent on polish, rather than production. My suggestion? If you're crunched for time and you're teaching a content area course rather than a media production course, then forget the polish and save yourself a lot of time. Students will still produce quality projects, especially within the context of a classroom assignment. For the time being, close is good enough. Just as society has raised its expectations of writing over the years, they will raise their expectations of new media production as well. It is just a matter of time.

Media Elements

Throughout this chapter I've referred to "media elements" or "media components" that can be used in a digital story. What follows are descriptions of typical kinds of media and how and where to either find or produce them.

Standard digital story components:
digital photos
scanned objects, photos, artwork
music
voice-over narration
transitions and other effects
citation info
perhaps video, animation, interviews, sounds, performed music

Audio Media

This covers everything from an interview to sound effects. Here are some of the more common audio sources:

- *Voice-over narration.* This refers to the voice-over narration that I have described earlier as being the heart of computer-based DST. A common approach to recording narration is sitting and speaking into a desktop microphone or the microphone built into your computer. But the reality is that there are many ways to approach voice recording, including using a headset or a wireless mike, both of which allow students to actually perform as they record their voices, which in turn encourages them to inflect their narration. See Resource B for options in this area.

- *Interviews, and "found" sounds.* Students may want to include interviews or recorded sounds in their digital stories. Be sure to obtain permission to use interview material. Miking techniques for conducting interviews can be found in Resource C. Found sound gathered from the environment—including everything from the sound of traffic to the sound of a specific car starting up—is usually an interesting addition.

- *Sounds obtained from the Web.* Google "burp sound" and see what you find. It's amazing. Also, see the section in Chapter 15 on copyright and fair use that addresses using other people's material in digital stories. See my Web site for my latest list of Web sources for sounds (www .jasonohler.com/storytelling).

- *Downloaded music.* Typically, students creating digital stories include music that they download from a CD, iPod or the Web. There are also a number of sites that offer royalty-free music as well as music with some use restrictions; Creative Commons (www.creativecommons.org) is especially helpful in this regard. Also, read Chapter 15 carefully. Student use of music is one of the thornier fair-use issues teachers will have to address when students create digital stories. See my Web site for my latest list of Web sources for music, including copyright free music. (www.jasonohler.com/storytelling).

- *Original music, music borrowed from friends.* One way for students to avoid copyright issues regarding the use of music is to create their own. With programs like GarageBand, this has never been easier to do. GarageBand is described in Chapter 13.

The magic of GarageBand.

GarageBand is free software for the Macintosh computer that has brought music and sound composition within everyone's grasp. Have students use it to create music, rhythm tracks, or sound backgrounds for everything from poetry readings to rap songs to digital stories.

- Another way to avoid copyright issues is to get permission to use music created by friends and colleagues, as well as friends of friends and colleagues. At the beginning of a project, I often ask students if they have any original music to share. It's amazing how much friend-created music exists. And if your friends don't have music to share, their friends do. More about this in Chapter 15.

Pictures, Images

Typically, this refers to still images. Common kinds of still image sources include the following:

- *Digital photos taken with a digital camera and transferred to the computer.* This is a very common way to get images into a digital story. These days it's a very straightforward affair. See the section on digital cameras in Chapter 13 for more information.
- *Scanned objects, photos.* Scanners are cheap and easy to use. I recommend one scanner for every 5 to 10 participants at a workshop. Keep in mind you can scan three-dimensional things as well as flat objects like photos. See Resource F about finding scannable objects—you can scan much more than you might suspect.
- *Images downloaded from the Internet.* It's easy to find and download a world of images from the Internet. To get started, go to Google and click on the word "Images" above the search box. Now type what you're looking for in the search box and press Enter. Presto! What you're looking at are thumbnail images of many more pictures and graphics than you have time to wade through, let alone consider using. If you see an image you want to download, click on the image and then click on the words "See full-sized image." Usually the picture will appear on a Google page by itself in its original size. To download the image, simply click and hold down on the image until you see a menu that allows you to save the image on your computer. Some browsers require you to also hold down another key, such as the Control key, to invoke this menu. In some cases, you can simply click on the image and drag it to your desktop. Google is just the beginning. Flickr, Creative Commons, and a number of sites offer access to free, inexpensive, or limited-use images. There are also services that charge very reasonable fees for access to loads of images. There are very obvious copyright and fair-use issues related to using images downloaded from the Internet. These issues are addressed in Chapter 15.
- *Original art.* Like the world of music, the world of visual art has so much good, relatively easy-to-use software that creating original artwork has become very feasible. In addition, scanning original artwork created with traditional media (like pencil or crayon) is also very straightforward. Software options for creating artwork are addressed in Chapter 13.
- *Edited images.* Much of the time you'll want to edit your images and original artwork, either to correct some imperfections in the image or to help it blend better with your story. I do this regularly with images I purchase. Sometimes editing is basic, like cropping a picture or adjusting its brightness. Other times it can be more substantial. If you're concerned about your time budget, then the less image editing the better. However, image editing is an important aspect of "art the 4th R" (addressed in Part I) and is an excellent way to help students develop art literacy. For that reason, you may want to make sure there is sufficient time in the project to allow them to develop image editing skills.

▦ Video

Usually, this refers to anything shot with a video camera. Typical kinds of video sources include the following:

- *Original video.* Using video in digital stories has been rare, because it has been so expensive and difficult to use. However, in recent years video cameras have become so affordable, software so friendly, and the world of video information so vast that we can expect to see video-recorded information become more prevalent in DST. In this book I've addressed one kind of video material— performance-based green screen storytelling. However, anything shot with a video camera that can be downloaded to a computer can be included.
- *"Found video."* This is what you find when you start digging through all those videocassettes you have in a box in the closet. Or what your friends or family send you when you ask if they have footage of you that might be interesting. Found video might also be found on digital cameras, most of which can take short movies, or in files on hard drives, the modern equivalent of shoeboxes in closets.

  If Mom and Dad don't have old footage on VHS tape, Grandma and Grandpa might—on 8 mm, 16 mm, or perhaps Super 8. The reality is that most of us have been recorded numerous times, mostly informally and spontaneously. Much of it is great content, even though it may not be technically great video. The rest, well—it's at least fun. You can only pray that whatever footage people have kept all these years doesn't include you doing the disco duck in your favorite orange bell bottoms. But that's the chance you take when you rummage through old movies.

  How do you convert old movie information to digital information for your computer to use? There are services that will do this for you, if you can get over the jitters of sending your only copy of something old and precious to strangers. You can also show the movie on a regular movie screen and video record the showing. The results aren't bad. For more options, Google "converting movies to digital."
- *Downloaded video.* Is there prepackaged video that students can use on the Internet? Yes, but it's a gray area at the moment. A good deal of it is only downloadable in "viewing" form rather than in "source file" form, making it difficult for students to include in their own projects. But I expect a good deal will change in the world of Internet video in the not-too-distant future. As video becomes cheaper and easier to

produce, look for more and more of it to consist of everything from general interest video to artistic experiments to scientific demonstrations. Also, capturing video from TV is doable, with obvious copyright and fair use implications.

▨ Animation

Typical kinds of animation sources include the following:

- *Downloaded animation.* There are a few kinds of animation, from those pesky little moving objects that seem to bombard us wherever we go on the Internet to much more sophisticated animations normally created with a program like Flash. Typically, the lower-end animations look like cartoons with a little razzmatazz added to them. I just Googled "free balloon animations" and had my choice of dozens of little pictures of balloons doing all sorts of things—twirling, floating upward, bumping into each other—you name it. But there are also a number of very useful animations available on the Web that demonstrate academic concepts in the areas of math, measurement, science, and so on. Typically these are created with a program like Flash. Googling will locate them. If your students are doing an academic story, these could be very helpful. As always, they should ask for permission to use them.
- *Original low-end animations.* The lower-end animations are sometimes known as GIF animations (because they usually have a file type of .gif). There are a number of pieces of software you can use to create these, but you better have a healthy time budget. I used ImageReady (much like PhotoShop) to create a simple one, and it took forever. But it's doable.
- *Original high-end animations.* The industry standard for high-end animation software is Flash, though there are certainly other packages on the market. I find it takes a lot of time to create something I'm happy with, but students are beginning to use it as a matter of course. Besides, while animation may be time-consuming, it also offers something unique to the world of DST: the opportunity for students to show an activity or process the way they see it and understand it. This can include anything from how the planets revolve around the sun to the life cycle of a rock band to how Hamlet puzzles through his life. Animation allows for a much freer range of applied imagination than shooting video usually does. But animation takes a lot more time.

13

The Digital Storytelling Toolbox

The Tools Teachers and Students Need to Tell Digital Stories

Finding and Buying Stuff

Before diving into the specifics of hardware and software, let's talk about an obsession most digital storytellers have: locating and purchasing gear.

> **Disclaimer: I don't endorse brands!**
>
> I just describe experiences I've had with vendors and products. Ask lots of people and consult lots of sources about what to buy. Consider me just one source of nonexpert input on the subject. And by all means, let me know your experiences.

I'm frequently asked what equipment I use, where I got it, why I bought it, and other questions related to the acquisition of "stuff." My response often surprises people: I find hardware and software the way you do, by searching the Internet and talking to people. And, like you, I'm overwhelmed by what I find.

If I could clone myself, one of my clones would do nothing but try to stay on top of all the digital gear that's being developed and offered through the Internet (other clones would conduct the New York Philharmonic and model for *GQ*). However, for those of us without clones, here are some tips to help you get your bearings.

• *Start with what you have.* In my teacher workshops I like to use the equipment that teachers have on hand. Doing so makes it more likely that

166

teachers can and will transfer what they learn in the workshop to their classrooms. The good news is that there is a lot you can do with what seems like very little.

• *Find out what you've got.* Captain Obvious here, reminding you that before you can start with what you have—and before you can determine what you need to get—you have to find out what you've got. What isn't so obvious is that most teachers won't know what's available until they ask all the people who might know. This includes the tech-savvy teachers and students in their buildings, the IT folks, the district technology people, their department chair, and others who are in the technology loop. It seems that everyone has a piece of the puzzle, but no one has all the pieces. It's been my experience that schools have more gear than teachers realize, but it takes determination and tenacity to find out what's available.

• *Give yourself a "search time" budget.* Searching for the magic deal on the Internet is an endless process. So, make a deal with yourself: you will spend no more than X amount of time (e.g., two to four hours for major purchases, 15–30 minutes for less important ones) looking for something, after which you actually get to buy something. Positive reinforcement, like the promise of a new piece of equipment, is a good way to make it through the purchasing process. And don't forget to ask people who buy stuff. It may turn out that they can save you the two to four hours of search time because

My motto: one eye focused on today's classroom, the other looking down the road.

they've done the same search themselves. Note: I'm a member of many formal and informal online discussion groups about digital technology and learning. I find them invaluable when I'm looking for specific information about things like equipment.

• *Look for academic discounts.* I've purchased software with an academic discount from a number of companies. Check my Web site (www.jasonohler .com/storytelling) for information about where I shop. My advice is to simply Google "academic software purchase" to find companies that specialize in giving educators a good price break. Also, a number of companies offer educational discounts. Look into "teacher buy" programs when getting hardware or software.

• *Don't buy on the leading edge.* How about buying the latest and greatest stuff you read about online? I don't recommend it. Let someone else find all the bugs in Version 1.0 of something. My motto is one eye on today's classroom, one eye looking down the road. That is, we need to focus on using what we have now while anticipating what we might have in the near future.

> Fancy gear and software is not important. When it comes to effective digital storytelling, less is often more.

To help stimulate future think in workshops and presentations, I always try to find time to demo what's just around the corner by showing technology I've found on the Web and also by inviting students, teachers, and IT people to show some new piece of software or hardware they've discovered. Needless to say, much of the technology that's second nature to the students in your classroom—iPods, cell phones, game players, and so on—will become the digital storytelling (DST) tools of tomorrow, so we should start thinking about their role in DST today. But I want to emphasize again that leading-edge technology is not necessary to create successful digital stories. When it comes to creating effective stories with technology, less is often more.

❈ What's in My Digital Storytelling Toolbox?

What hardware and software are required to do all the things I described in the media development process? Here's my short list.

❈ Hardware

A Reasonably Recent Computer

In practical terms, as of 2007 this means a Mac running at least OS X.4 or later or a PC running Windows XP or later. In terms of RAM, one gigabyte is preferable, but I've used half that much very successfully. How much hard drive space is needed for a digital story? That's a bit like asking how big should a house be. But to give you an idea, the size of the stories created in my last DST class ranged from 5 to 55 megabytes. Don't forget that you'll need some overhead space to create and store the media components that compose your students' stories. Also, I recommend that you have storage media like jump drives handy so you can move stories from computer to computer and that you have at least one computer in your classroom that can burn CDs and DVDs in order to take the pressure off your students' hard drives. External fixed media like CDs and DVDs are great for distributing stories as well as for backing them up.

A Digital Camera

It's hard to remember life before digital cameras. There are zillions of them on the market these days and sorting among them is a thankless task. Hopefully, I can provide some helpful advice here.

One of the most important aspects of a camera is its megapixel capacity, which defines the clarity of the pictures it's capable of taking. This is particularly important when you use the zoom or enlarge your pictures. Basically, the more megapixel capacity your camera has, the better. The new low end (as of March 2007) is, depending upon whom you ask, 6 megapixels. However, I still use a 3.4 megapixel camera for many things quite successfully.

Bottom line: Know what your camera can and can't do, and use it within its capacity.

Most of us know as much about our digital cameras as we do about our word processors. That is, we know 10% of what they can do and don't even use most of that. I try to distinguish between "essential features" that I need and "bells and whistles" that I might use. To me, essential features include the following:

> **Your basic toolbox has**
>
> A fairly recent computer running at least OSX 10.4 on the Mac or Windows XP on the PC
>
> iMovie on the Mac or Movie Maker II on the PC
>
> A digital camera
>
> A scanner
>
> A mike—some computers have these built in
>
> A video camera and wireless mike, esp. if you are doing green screen storytelling
>
> Image-editing software
>
> DVD mastering software
>
> Perhaps music software, animation software

- Some zoom capacity
- A flash (to take pictures in low lighting)
- A view screen (so I don't always have to look through the viewfinder at what I'm shooting)
- Removable memory (so I always have the option of putting in a new memory card if the one I'm using fills up)
- The capability of plugging my camera into a computer through the USB port

What else can you get? Whatever bells and whistles are important to you. Personally, I love a swivel monitor. It allows me to hold the camera just about anywhere and still see what I'm shooting. Cool, but not essential.

What's a reasonable amount to spend on a good digital camera? Between $300 and $500, although if you're doing basic digital stories with mid-range production values, you can buy them for less. You can even buy inexpensive, disposable digital cameras these days. Don't forget, many of your friends— and your students' parents—have cameras at this point. In fact, many of them have last year's model they aren't using anymore. Consider asking them if they will loan or donate what they're not using to your DST project. They might also be a good source of information about what to buy.

How many cameras do you need for a DST project? If you're adept at managing classroom resources, you can get by with just a few per class of 25 students. A desirable ratio is one camera per every five students.

A Flatbed Scanner

A scanner works a lot like a photocopying machine: place something on the glass bed, press the button, and you get a picture. Typically, the photocopier produces a picture on paper (usually in black and white), while the scanner produces a picture file (usually in full color). You can then import this file into your digital story. You can put anything on a scanner that is more or less two-dimensional (keys, pictures, a toothbrush, your hand). You can even scan some three-dimensional things; I just scanned a spice bottle and it worked, sort of . . . (See Resource F for a suggested list of scannable objects.) You can buy a good scanner these days for under $100. See my Web site (www.jasonohler.com/storytelling) for my favorite scanners. And don't forget to ask at your next faculty meeting whether anyone has a scanner you can borrow for your project. There's a good chance someone does.

A Desktop Microphone

You can do a lot with the mike that comes built into most computers these days. If it just isn't good enough for your needs, then look into buying one of the many basic USB desktop mikes that cost about $20 these days. See my Web site for what I'm using. Also, recall my earlier comments about using headsets and wireless mikes to encourage expression. Resource B addresses this in detail.

A Wireless Microphone

As I mentioned at a few points in this book, if you're video recording student performances or interviews, don't rely on the video camera's built-in mike. The mike is part of the camera, which is usually at quite a distance from the speaker, and therefore it doesn't pick up voice well at all. What it picks up instead is the noise from your camera as you record. My very strong advice: get a wireless mike. The difference is night and day. You'll use a wireless once and never want to use the mike in your video camera again. Check my Web site for what I'm using these days.

> Audio is king. A clear voice, for computer- and performance-based digital stories, is an absolute must. DST gives students a voice. That voice must be clear.

For a little more money, you can buy units that allow you to record two people, which is very handy for interview situations. (See Resource C for interviewing techniques.) Also, recall my earlier comments about using a wireless mike to capture narration that's more expressive. For this reason I strongly recommend you have at least one wireless mike on hand whether you intend to shoot video or not.

Other Microphones

A wireless mike works well for one or two people, but how about a group? You might want to consider using one of these:

- **A boom mike**. If you want to professionally record groups (students acting? students in the act of learning?), then you might want to invest in *a boom mike*. This is the kind of microphone that you see professional crews holding just above a group of actors on the set or politicians speaking on the steps of the capitol. Downside: it requires separate people to run the video camera and to manage the boom mike. Low-budget boom mike suggestion: dangle a mike from the ceiling over the actors and out of view of the camera.
- **A shotgun mike**. Another approach to recording more than one person is a shotgun mike. Typically, it attaches directly to your camera and has the ability to pick up sound at a distance much better than the mike built into your camera. While it doesn't pick up a group that well, it does pick up whoever you're shooting at, thus allowing you to shift your focus among speakers. Downside: while only one person is required to record both the audio and video, the focus tends to be on one person at a time.
- **A flat "conference" mike.** You see these a lot at meetings lying in the middle of a table. They are typically about the size of an iPod and do a very reasonable job of picking up audio from a group of people.

Frankly, I rarely use any of these mikes, preferring to stay low end. I consider these serious microphones for the advanced digital storyteller with a bit of a budget. But if you're such a person, then go for it. I include this information in the book for one simple reason: clear audio is an essential part of DST. Without clear audio, the quality of digital stories drops dramatically.

A Video Camera

If you're doing green screen performance-based storytelling, or simply shooting video to include in your story, then you'll need a video camera and a wireless microphone. In either case, don't forget to use a tripod so your video is clear and nonjiggly. Also, make sure your video camera has the following features. They've become increasingly hard to find because amateur videographers, like most of us, mainly shoot things like family outings, scenery, and soccer games and typically don't need these features:

- **An input for an external mike.** Don't use the mike built into the camera unless you have no other options. It produces weak audio. It's much better to use a wireless mike clipped to a speaker.

- **An input for headphones**. You must be able to check to make sure you're picking up audio. You need headphones to do this. If you're using a wireless mike, check to see if the wireless receiver has a headphones input. This is usually the case.

Professional-quality video gear will always have these inputs but typically costs $1,500 and up. The reality is that most of us are buying consumer-quality gear, which is anything around $500 or less. The burden is on you to look (and look and look) until you find consumer gear that still has inputs for an internal mike and headphones. On my Web site, I've listed what I've found that works well and has the features mentioned above.

Also, make sure that whatever video camera you buy has DV (firewire) output, which allows you to download your video material easily to your computer. This output seems fairly standard these days. And make sure you're comfortable with whatever storage medium you elect to use: tape? minidisk? direct to memory? They all work. I still use my Sony Digital 8, a Hi8 tape-based machine, and I love it.

A Music Keyboard

If you're using only packaged music clips, as you might with GarageBand, then you don't need a keyboard. But if you want to include your own performed music (melodies, background chords, etc.)—something you can also do with GarageBand—then you'll need a keyboard as an input device. My advice: don't buy the keyboard with the most knobs! The keyboards I've used over the years have always had more knobs than I knew what to do with. Yet, not using them never slowed me down. Check my Web site for what I'm using these days. Incidentally, last year I bought an M-Audio Radium 61 keyboard that cost around $130 and weighed a few pounds. This replaced my Korg OMW1, which cost me $1,600 and weighed 25 pounds! Life is getting better . . . and lighter.

Other Hardware

There's a great deal of hardware available that can play a role in DST, including cells phones, iPods, joysticks, motion wand controllers, DVD duplicators—the list goes on. Some of these are moving firmly into the mainstream, while others are more specialized. What's important to remember is that while these are not necessary to create solid digital stories, students will understandably want to experiment with how to use them to do so. In my opinion, as long as students don't lose the story focus, as well as the goals of the assignment, they should be encouraged to experiment with the tools of the day. It's your opportunity as their teacher to help them use their technology effectively, creatively, and wisely.

Software

You'll use three basic kinds of software to create and edit your digital story: movie- or media-editing software, audio-editing software, and image-editing software. You might also use animation, music, and other kinds of software, which I touch on in this chapter. And you'll undoubtedly use more standard kinds of software, such as Word to prepare your narration, PowerPoint for storyboarding, Excel for putting together a budget, and an Internet browser to find sounds on the Internet. But here I'm focusing on the kinds of new media production software you'll need to actually create your digital story. They are the hammer, saw, and screwdriver of your DST software toolbox. Each is addressed in turn.

Note: I tend to emphasize what is free or cheap because I find that's what most teachers can afford. But if you have more money, another realm of quality and potential opens up to you.

Movie- or Media-Editing Software

Whether you're doing green screen chroma-key editing that's part of performance-based digital storytelling or simply combining still images, voice, and music to produce more conventional computer-based digital stories, you'll probably use what most people call movie-editing software to assemble your digital story. Let's look at this software category in terms of the two major platforms, Mac and PC.

- **Macintosh, using iMovie.** The premier piece of software for creating digital stories is iMovie. It's a jewel. It's free, easy to learn, and able to do just about everything you need it to do.
- **PC, using Movie Maker.** Movie Maker is like iMovie and comes free with Windows XP. Make sure you have the latest version of Movie Maker; free upgrades are available through the Microsoft Web site. The current version of Movie Maker has a frustrating shortcoming: it's difficult to create and mix two separate tracks of audio. This is significant because typically digital storytellers want to be able to create an audio track for narration and one for music and then mix the two. This is exactly what is hard to do with Movie Maker. So, if you have a PC, I urge you to download Audacity, a free, cross-platform audio-editing program. (Google "Audacity sound" to find it.) You master your audio using Audacity and then import that into Movie Maker.

To learn about other low-cost packages, Google the Web using simple phrases like "shareware Mac video" or "shareware PC video." The amount of free or low-cost software entering the market has increased each time I've looked.

Check my Web site for my software recommendations; check frequently because they change often: www .jasonohler.com/storytelling

Also keep in mind that if you have a budget, life changes. There's a great deal of mid-range software that is not very expensive and may add utility to your project. Adobe Premiere is a good example. As of this writing, it's available in a lite version for under $100. Unfortunately, it's only available for the PC these days.

As always, check my Web site for my latest list of software and software sites.

Audio-Editing Software

Both of the free video editors mentioned earlier (iMovie on the Mac and Movie Maker on the PC) have audio-editing capabilities. The capabilities of iMovie are usually sufficient for what I want to do, but Movie Maker's are not, owing to the audio-editing limitations I mentioned earlier. That's why I recommended obtaining Audacity, a free, feature-rich, cross-platform audio-editing software program. As mentioned above, if you're using a PC, then you would create your finished audio tracks first with Audacity, collapse them into a single track, then import that into Movie Maker. No doubt there are other free audio-editing software packages. I haven't explored this because Audacity does everything I need an audio-editing program to do.

Image Manipulation Software

Adobe PhotoShop is the industry standard in this category and, as of this writing, is available for both Mac and PC in a lite version for under $100. But in many cases the image manipulation you need to perform is simple enough to do in programs like iPhoto (for the Mac), PhotoPlus (for the PC), or GIMP (for both platforms), all of which are free or very low cost. But there are options these days, so keep Googling. Use search phrases like "free image manipulation software" and "alternative to Photoshop." New software is becoming available all the time. And, as always, keep checking my Web site for my latest discoveries, as well as those that people like you share with me.

Music Software

If you're going to use music software, then there is, in my opinion, one package that towers over the others: GarageBand. It's free, powerful, very easy to learn to use, and kids (like me) love it. As of Version 3.0, it even accommodates pictures and video, allowing you to create music while watching the images you want to accompany with your soundtrack. Wow.

GarageBand provides hundreds (thousands?) of music clips drawn from a wide variety of instruments and musical genres that are tonally and rhythmically in sync with each other. The result is that you can't create a combination of clips that doesn't work. I tried one evening but gave up after a few hours. I could certainly produce songs that sounded . . . different. But they still worked. The music clips include drum beats, bass lines, woodwind instruments, and so on and come from rock, jazz, world music, and many other genres. My unofficial estimate of the average time needed to learn GarageBand in order to be functional: under 10 minutes for most students.

GarageBand also allows students to compose and perform in more typical senses. It's easy to plug in a keyboard and add a melody to a song. It's equally easy to plug a mike or guitar directly into the audio port on the computer and add real performance tracks. After inputting a track, composers can add a number of effects. For example, after inputting a guitar melody, the input can be processed as Classic Rock, Creamy Shimmer, or New Nashville, each of which reflects a particular music genre. In addition, GarageBand can be used to lay down rhythm tracks and soundscapes for rap and poetry projects, as well as record a speech to be used in podcasting. It's immensely powerful and flexible.

The bottom line is this: GarageBand allows anyone to create music soundtracks. Not only does this allow your students to try their hand at becoming musicians and music producers, but it also solves the thorny issue of your students using copyright-protected music found on CDs and the Web. GarageBand is easy enough to use that students can usually produce sound tracks within the time and resource constraints associated with many classrooms.

Unfortunately, GarageBand exists only for the Mac platform. The PC world also has packages that function like GarageBand, such as ACID. I haven't had a lot of experience with it, but colleagues say it works well.

There are plenty of other packages that cost money for both the Mac and PC platform. Because I produce music, I use some of them. My favorite is Logic. However, if I try to use Logic after being away from it for awhile, I find that I need to relearn it. This doesn't happen with GarageBand. No matter how much time has passed since the last time I used it, I experience little or no learning curve. Its creators have found the perfect balance between power and ease of use.

Green Screen Software

Because I use iMovie a great deal, I use plug-ins that enable it to do green screen chroma-key editing. My PC-savvy friends tell me that similar plug-ins exist for Movie Maker as well. I describe green screen plug-ins on my Web site (www.jasonohler.com/storytelling). Keep in mind that higher-end packages, like Premier, will also do chroma-key editing. In fact, I haven't met a serious video editing software program that wouldn't. These tend to do a cleaner, more professional job than plug-ins do, but they're also more expensive and force students to learn an entirely new piece of software. I'm quite happy with what plug-ins can produce for most classrooms.

Some video cameras actually have built-in chroma-key capabilities. This approach can be a bit clumsy, but as long as you're not trying to create something for prime-time TV, then the results are fine. Your camera may have this capability, and you may not know it. This might be one of those rare times to actually read your video camera manual so you can see what your camera's capabilities are.

DVD Mastering Software

At a few points in this book I have stressed the importance of creating a CD or DVD of your final projects so that (a) you have a fairly secure backup source and (b) you can share your work with others. Being a Mac aficionado, I use Disk Utility to make storage disks or iDVD to make self-launching DVDs. Both are free and easy to learn and use. iDVD allows me to put a number of students' stories on one DVD, create a menu that allows selecting individual work (rather than having to play the DVD from beginning to end), and add graphics that can be printed on the DVD. This is all I really need my DVD mastering software to do at this point.

Also, a word about DVD duplicating hardware. If you're going to pay someone else to duplicate your class's final DST DVD more than a few times, then you're probably better off buying a machine for your school so everyone can use it. If several teachers are using it, then it's easy to recoup the cost of the machine in a reasonably short period of time.

Other Software

There's so much software available these days that could be used in DST that the possibilities are too numerous to mention here. As I type, another dozen pieces of software just became available that no doubt have great potential for DST. Such is life in the infosphere. The good news is that your students are often on top of the world of emerging software and would be happy to show you what's new if you provide them the forum to do so.

However, I'll repeat something I've already said a few times: you do not need fancy, expensive hardware or software to create effective, compelling stories. Your imagination will more than make up for a lack of high-end tools as long as you plan your story well and tell it clearly and with heart.

14

Media Grammar for Teachers

Assessing Media Expression

Becoming a Media Persuader

Earlier I defined media literacy as being able to recognize, evaluate, and apply the techniques of media persuasion. The reality is that the only way for students to become truly media literate is to become media persuaders themselves. Doing so forces them to lift the hood, so to speak, and see media's intricate workings that conspire to do one thing above all others: make the final media product appear smooth, effortless, and natural. Digital storytelling (DST) offers a very effective way to lift the hood.

Becoming a media persuader bothers many people. I understand why. Persuaders deliberately manipulate the audience—some for the sake of art, others for the sake of sales, but all because they want the audience to see something in a particular way, that is, their way.

However, we need to remember that media persuasion didn't begin with new media. For many years, in language arts classes throughout the world, children have been taught how to persuade with words. In fact, one of the hallmarks of literacy is being able to write a persuasive essay that convinces readers of a particular point of view using the techniques of effective writing. I suppose this is how lawyers get their early training. But while writing persuasive text is respectable, creating persuasive new media is suspect, largely, I think, because when students use new media to support a particular point of view, it looks too much like advertising.

I'll leave you to make your peace with this conundrum of new media authorship that often pits the desire to be honest against the desire to be effective. But rest assured that unless you actually create your own media, and do so paying particular attention to how to most effectively engage and convince your audience, then any appreciation you have of media's persuasive abilities will be shallow and theoretical at best.

❧ The Grammar of Media—Avoiding the Bumps

In this chapter, I address media technique and what I call "media grammar." Consider this Version 1.0 of this topic for the average content-area teacher who probably will never become a dedicated media developer and is simply looking for help in evaluating the new media his or her students will produce. My approach assumes that media production will happen in a classroom within a content area context, rather than in a professional media studio as part of a media production course. Thus, I don't spend any time on the details of fancy media-editing techniques or the latest, greatest editing gear. Instead, I address the "run-ons," "fragments," and other basic considerations of creating clear, effective new media. My goal is to help teachers begin to understand the grammar of effective media so that they can do two things: (1) develop the basic vocabulary and perspectives needed to discuss new media production with their students and (2) create assessment rubrics for new media production that are simple and useful.

According to McLuhan, every medium has its grammar.

What is grammar? Basically it's a set of guidelines for the use of any language or medium that facilitates effective communication. When I assess student written work, I'm hoping not to find "bumps"—those places in the writing that force me to stop, squint, reread, and puzzle over what the writer is trying to say. Besides being annoying, the bumps distract me from enjoying the writer's ideas. Typically, when I find bumps, it's because the writing has grammatical problems. That is, students didn't have a command of the language commensurate with what they were trying to say.

Looking for bumps. Thus, from a technical point of view, what teachers should be looking for in new media projects is where they "go bump" as well as where they don't. We want teachers to be able to articulate the nature of media bumps so that they can teach students how to avoid them and so they can assess student work in ways that are helpful to students, parents, and others who want to understand DST's value in education.

Many of the media grammar traits I address in this chapter were derived from my own experience as well as the discussions I've had with teachers about digital stories, an experience I covered in some detail in Part I. When assessing media grammar traits, feel free to use whatever scoring method works for you: a scale from 1 to 10? narrative critique? "in progress/satisfactory/exceeds expectations?" Up to you.

A number of the media grammar rules that I present will seem obvious to you after they're pointed out. But on the basis of viewing numerous digital stories over the years, I can assure you that these rules are abrogated as often as subject and verb agreement in student writing. After a while, bad media grammar are going to stick out so bad it's going to feel like you am slapped in the face—the way you feel slapped in the face by this sentence because of its poor grammar.

I want to reiterate what I feel is the most effective way to see the grammar and technical aspects of new media production: watch it twice. Watch it once for the story and then watch it immediately afterward. The second time, you won't be interested in the story and will be able to watch it from a technical point of view. Feel free to pause, take notes, rewind, and replay—whatever helps you "see" the new media grammar employed by your students.

Always keep in mind that there can be reasons why digital storytellers break grammatical rules. Poets do it all the time with words. Recall the discussion in Chapter 2 about digital stories being essays versus poems. When you're in doubt, it's up to you to decide whether you're looking at multimedia poetry or an essay that needs more work.

Most important, make sure that what you're watching aligns with assignment expectations. If you were expecting an essay, then insist on essaylike clarity. If students are creating poetry, then feel free to ask them to defend their choices. It's what artists are often asked to do in art school.

Grammar of Using Images in Digital Stories

If a picture is worth a thousand words, imagine the amount of grammar that implies. That's why we should help students use images as effectively as possible. The traits I describe in this section are those that most often make me go bump.

Bear in mind that there are entire university degrees offered in image creation. For those interested in more advanced image techniques, there are many resources on the Web about topics such as "the rule of thirds" of photo composition and "leading the talent" in video recording. As always, consider having professionals work with you to take your students to the next level of professionalism if the project warrants it.

But the purpose here is to address basic image grammar for content-area teachers who are not technology specialists. For them, the goal is very straightforward: students should use pictures in their digital stories that support the story and are in focus, well lit, well composed, and well selected.

▒ A Clear, Focused Picture

Although pointing out that pictures need to be clear and in focus sounds like something Captain Obvious would say, I still bump on photos with focus problems now and again, even in this age of self-focusing cameras. Still images should be in focus; if you're squinting when you look at student work, then there's often a focus problem. Video recordings should be nonjiggly; if you're feeling slightly nauseous, then the jiggles are usually present. While students can always claim artistic license, the reality is that there are very few cases in which a blurry or jiggly picture is desirable. Don't be afraid to ask students to defend their decisions in these situations.

This doesn't mean students should never move the camera when shooting either still pictures or video footage. In fact, a number of camera techniques these days require movement. Instead, it means that in the absence of trying to produce a motion effect, pictures should be steady and clear. Above all, when movement effects are used, they need to support the story. Impact without a good reason typically doesn't work. Many cameras have auto focus that can help with some of the issues identified here. Also, using tripods when movement is not required will greatly reduce blur and jiggle.

By the way, there is actually software now that will deblur pictures. One day in the not-too-distant future, you'll have to decide whether your students should use it—just the way you might expect them to use spell checking today to clean up their writing—or whether they should be prohibited from using it because it denies them an important skill-building experience.

Bottom line: Are you squinting? Dizzy? Either is analogous to going bump when you read poor writing. In both cases, you have to work harder than you should at understanding what the student is trying to convey. You want to get to their ideas, not bump on the interface. Have students reshoot, select a better image, or do their best with photo editing software to clarify the picture.

▒ A Well-Lit Picture

Poorly lit subjects in still pictures and video are quite common and harder to rectify after the fact than one might suspect. Observing the following basic rules helps: (1) make sure windows are behind the photographer rather than behind what they're shooting and (2) adjust the lights in the room where you're shooting; typically, you want as many lights on as possible without producing shadows.

I recommend students look for bright areas within their classroom or building to shoot pictures; there are always some places that are brighter than others. I also recommend that districts consider buying a good set of lights that can be shared between schools for serious media production.

Bottom line: Are you squinting? If you are, is it because of poor lighting? Have students reshoot, select a better image, or do their best to lighten the image with photo editing software.

▓ An Appropriately Composed Picture

The subject of the photo or video footage should at least be evident if not obvious. If the story is about a dog, and the dog is hard to see because it's sitting behind a tree, then the picture isn't well composed. (If the story happens to be about a dog that is hard to see, well then maybe the picture works.) Even though the dog should be central to the picture, this doesn't mean it needs to be in the center of the picture. It simply means that the dog figures prominently. You want people to look at the image, not squint, and think to themselves, either consciously or unconsciously, "That's a dog." Sound obvious? I bump on stuff like this all the time.

What detracts from the composition of the picture? One thing is unwanted visual information. It's not uncommon for students to use pictures in which the subject of a digital story—like a dog—is mixed in with what amounts to visual clutter. Perhaps a student uses a family photo in which the dog is one of many competing subjects or is crowded by all the stuff on the boat dock. Or perhaps a student uses an image in which the subject is too small in relation to the rest of the visual information in the picture, perhaps surrounded by too much space above it or on the sides; that is, perhaps the dog is so small in comparison to the lawn the dog is sleeping on that it might be mistaken for a cat. All of this makes the viewer's mind squint. Consider having students crop or reshoot the material or make the subject clearer by highlighting it or pointing to it graphically.

Background is another element of composition to consider. If the digital story is about living on a boat and students take pictures of each other standing in front of a bookcase, then they haven't thought through the composition well enough. I'm not suggesting they find a boat; I always assume that production needs to happen within a school day on school grounds. Instead, I'm suggesting that storytellers use their imagination to approximate a boat, given the materials on hand. Perhaps they could stand in front of a chalkboard or sheets of construction paper on which they've drawn simple waves. Even standing in front of a blank wall that allows viewers to fill in the background with their own imagination might work. But not a bookcase.

Bottom line: Are you squinting, wondering what the subject of the picture or video footage is? Are you confused or disoriented, bumping on extraneous visual information? You shouldn't be. The picture should be clear enough that its relationship to the narrative is not in doubt. Have students reshoot, find a better image, or use cropping and other techniques to make the subject clear.

⌘ Appropriate Use of Image

This applies particularly to the images that students import from the Web. Students can't be assessed on the quality of the images they download, because they had nothing to do with their creation. But students can be assessed on their selection and use of images.

We're back to the story of the dog. If it's about a sad little white dog, and the storyteller uses a picture of a happy big gray dog, then the picture selection needs work. The picture may be of a dog, but it's the wrong dog. Sound obvious? Yet I see this kind of thing far too often. Given the number of pictures of dogs on the Web, my guess is that the storyteller got lazy, ran out of time, or perhaps didn't have the search skills needed and gave up. When students look for pictures, they should spend time reflecting on what they use the same way they should wrestle with words in order to find the best way to say something.

Bottom line: Does the picture or video footage make you go bump because it seems at odds with the story? If so, then the student needs to find a more accurate image to use.

⌘ Supportive Image Changes

Every time the picture changes in a digital story, viewers implicitly look for a connection between the new image and the story. If they don't find it, then bumping and mind-squinting occurs. A common infraction is displaying images before the narrative occurs that they're intended to support. That is, the picture of the dog appears while the narrative is still talking about the cat. Another infraction is the "slide show" effect. That is, images appear in a way that would make sense as part of an independent slide show but not within the context of the story as it's been shaped. Ideally, image changes should happen without viewers noticing them—without going bump on them. How images change and interact with the story impacts story flow and is addressed later in this chapter.

Bottom line: Are you squinting because the images or video arrives too soon or too late and therefore conflict with rather than supports the narrative? Then the piece needs to be reedited and/or remixed.

Appropriate Shooting Angle

Camera angles are typically the domain of the professional photographer and may be beyond your concern. However, this aspect of image capture is worth pointing out because it's highly manipulative. Whether a picture is shot straight on, from above, or from beneath can impact viewer perception greatly. If the clarity, lighting, and composition are the complete, clear sentences of camera work, then camera angles are the adjectives and adverbs. If nothing else, this topic should be discussed as a media literacy topic. Resource E addresses specific angles and their meaning in some detail.

Final Note

Visual literacy and Art the 4th R. Basic image editing is part of Art the 4th R (www.jasonohler.com/fourthr). Through thoughtful image selection and placement and by using highlighting, cropping, and other simple techniques, students can clarify a picture's role in a story and ensure that story listeners don't bump on what they're watching. As with all media components, the visuals need to support, not detract from, the experience of the story.

If you're interested in taking some next steps in the area of visual literacy, I recommend anything by Robyn Williams (2003). I've consulted her *Non-Designer's Design Book* for years. I also like *Visual Literacy* by Lynell Burmark (2002). She does a great job of explaining the vast world of visual literacy in practical terms.

The Grammar of Using Audio in Digital Stories

A true story. Long before flat screens and cable TV, I used to have an ancient TV—the kind that had knobs the size of saucers and huge glowing tubes inside that could heat an entire house. It was one of those TVs that you had to whack every so often to get going, even though doing so ran the risk of hurting the flimsy rabbit ears draped in tin foil that were perched precariously on top of the TV's dark walnut cabinet. Readers who aren't old enough to belong to AARP will have to watch old movies, or talk to their grandparents, to verify that such TVs existed.

For the most part, the TV worked, except for one serious flaw: every now and then the screen would go blank. I could still hear the audio, but otherwise it looked like the TV set had been turned off. Usually, I would just wait about 10 seconds and the picture would return. Aliens? Government espionage gone awry? Who knows.

As annoying as this was, it helped me realize the importance of the audio component of media. Losing the picture for short periods didn't ruin what I was watching, because so much of TV programming is carried by the music and dialogue. On the other hand, if the audio had been dying on me instead of the picture, I would have been disoriented and confused. Prove this to yourself. Put on a movie, a TV program, or a digital story. Kill just the visual. Now kill just the audio. It's amazing. Without the visual, you're annoyed. But without the audio, you're lost.

Well-produced audio is essential to successful digital stories. DST gives students a voice, and the voice needs to be clear.

If your ears are squinting, then you're going bump. The result is that you can't understand, enjoy, or learn from the story as well as if you weren't squinting. The audio needs to be clear and well mixed, and the voicing needs to be well paced. If these basic grammatical rules are observed, the story has a good chance of being a success, even if the visuals aren't great. In this section I consider some specific grammatical issues involved in producing the audio portion of new media narrative.

▓ Clear Audio

Captain Obvious here, making the point that not being able to hear or understand the audio is like trying to read an essay printed on a printer with an empty toner cartridge. I wouldn't make this point except that I've heard way too much weak and unclear audio in my day.

By the way, students can avoid poor sound by conducting the all-important sound check before producing final audio. Record a little bit, listen to it, and adjust the audio settings as needed. Resources B and C contain information about mikes and miking techniques that can help students produce better audio.

Bottom line: Does the digital story make your ears squint because the voice is weak or unclear? If so, then the narration needs to be rerecorded or remixed.

▓ Well-Mixed Audio

Poorly mixed audio is a specific kind of unclear audio that warrants its own category because it's such a common grammatical infraction in digital stories. It takes a few forms, typically music drowning out the spoken narrative or music lyrics interfering with the spoken words of the story. The voice narrative is supremely important and should always be clear and accessible.

Table 14.1 Guidelines for Mixing Audio

Guidelines for mixing audio in digital stories

Audio rule #1:	Use music without lyrics when narrative is present.
Audio rule #2:	Only one audio source at a time should dominate. During narrative, turn the music off or way down.
Audio rule #3:	Field-test your audio to determine whether the narrative is clear and prominent.

The audio should be mixed so there is no conflict. When in doubt, storytellers should turn everything else off so that the narrative is clear. See Table 14.1 for some specific guidelines.

Bottom line: Are your ears squinting because you're trying to hear the narration among the audio clutter? If so, this usually means that better music accompaniment needs to be considered and/or the story needs to be remixed.

Voice Pacing and Inflection

Students have a tendency to hurry through their narrative, whether speaking into a mike or performing, often because they lack confidence as speakers. The result is that their narration can lack the inflection and nuance that gives a story texture.

Practice helps students gain confidence. As they gain confidence, they tend to slow down and inflect their voices. This is why renarration and retelling are important parts of the story development process.

Bottom line: If you find yourself wanting to say "Slow down" or mentally are trying to catch your breath as you listen to a digital story, then the narrative is too fast. If you find that you're bumping on the speaker's sense of timing or that you're bored or confused because of a lack or misuse of voice inflection, then the delivery needs work. This can be extended easily to performance by including considerations of body movement and facial expression.

Final Note

Helping students hear themselves. It's hard for any of us to develop an accurate sense of what we sound or look like when we're speaking or performing. Having students listen and/or watch recordings of themselves can help immensely in this regard. Doing so gives them a chance to identify and address their own challenges in the areas of pacing, inflection, and expression. This is the same strategy that dancers, athletes, and speakers use to improve their performances.

❄ The Grammar of Using Music in Digital Stories

The **Jaws** theme can make **Bambi** appear evil... that's the power of music...use it wisely.

Narrative is often developed as a result of editing and reflection, resulting in a professional relationship between creator and product. This relationship usually doesn't develop between students and the music they use because they rarely create their own music. Instead, they usually rely on familiar music that has personal emotional appeal.

Emotional appeal can be a double-edged sword. In my media literacy classes, we talk about strategies advertisers use "to pierce the neocortex," that is, to grab listeners (or consumers) beneath their judgmental minds where they are often helpless to use critical thinking to evaluate what they're experiencing. Music is the most powerful tool in their toolbox for achieving this. Like it or not, sappy music tends to make us feel sentimental (even if we don't want to), while the *Rocky* theme makes us feel powerful and conquering, even if we aren't. What's more, the effects of music are usually very predictable over a very wide range of audience members. That is, play the *Rocky* theme for a diverse crowd, and many people will have similar reactions to it every time. That's power.

In a sentence, music must support the story and not overwhelm the narrative. In the next section we consider assessment traits that can help keep the use of music in perspective.

❄ Appropriate Music Choices

Feel free to ask students, "How does the music relate to the story?" I do. Sometimes what I find out is that the connecting factor is the student, not the story. That is, the music and story are both very important to the storyteller; therefore they go together. I question this approach, because this means that the story has then been created for the storyteller rather than an audience. For the most part, I think stories should be created for audiences. This is your call.

Bottom line: Does the music fit the story and support the narrative? Does it have a compelling and authentic reason for being included in its current form? If not, then rethink the music or at least remix the audio so the music is less prominent.

❄ Appropriate Role of Music

In Part I, I talked about how the inherent emotional impact of music can overwhelm a story. When I'm conscious of being manipulated by music, especially during a bad movie, I consider it a cheap shot and an indication that the story isn't very good. I've watched digital stories that would seem shallow or disconnected if the music weren't there. If the assignment is a music video, then this might be fine. If not, then perhaps music has been given an inappropriately dominant role.

As I mentioned above, there is also the problem of the music conflicting with the spoken narrative. Again, the rule here is simple: the music should not compete with the narrative.

Bottom line: Does the music drive the story, or is it the other way around? An interesting litmus test to consider: if the music were removed, how would the story fare? If not well, then the role of music may be inappropriate. As always, if the music conflicts with the narrative, then remix the audio so that it doesn't.

☰ Final Note

Teaching the power of music. Have your students shoot 30 seconds of video of a simple activity, like walking into class and sitting down or getting out of a car and walking into a building. Then have them put different music behind the video to change the story and mood using the music they listen to or perhaps music they create with GarageBand. The results are amazing and make the persuasive power of music very apparent. I have an example of this kind of project on my Web site (www.jasonohler.com/storytelling).

☰ Grammar of Editing, Transitions, and Titling in Digital Stories

A part of every digital story is the use of editing features like transitions, effects, and titling that come standard with iMovie, Movie Maker, PowerPoint, and a number of other programs. As explained earlier, transitions help the flow between two images. A common example is fading in and out between scenes. Effects are like transitions but happen only to a specific image rather than between images. A wide variety of effects and transitions are available these days, from the subtle (like soft focus) to the purposely obtrusive (pictures flipping end over end). Titles are the words that appear on the screen, usually at the beginning and the end. It's a rather unique trait of digital stories that titles often appear during the story as well.

For many first-time users, transitions and effects are a wonderland of distraction. They can't help themselves as they make pictures and titles spin, ripple, overlap, and do all sorts of things. Personally, these kinds of effects make me dizzy. I quickly lose my focus on—and interest in—the story. That is, they make me go bump in a big way. In a sentence, the goal in using effects is to make sure they're supportive and unobtrusive. In this section I address traits that I consider when assessing this aspect of digital stories.

▓ Seamless Transitions, Unobtrusive Effects

Basically, viewers shouldn't notice editing unless there's an overwhelming artistic reason to do so. In professional movies and TV programming, transitions happen seamlessly, the same way flowing from one paragraph to another happens seamlessly in good writing.

When is an unsubtle effect okay? When it supports the story so well that you don't notice it. Here's a recent example. A workshop participant created a story about a very personal trauma. In his story he displayed a twirling expletive for about 10 seconds at just the right moment. It worked, especially because it was the only time he used such an effect. Even though I noticed it at first, it supported the story so well that the bump quickly disappeared, while the impact remained.

Bottom line: Do you notice the effects in a sustained way? Do they seem unsupportive of the story? If so, then you've bumped on them and they need to be changed or eliminated.

▓ Clear Titles

I've seen many titles that I couldn't read because they were zooming in from outer space or flipping end over end. Professional video programming rarely does this with titles. Titles need to be clear and stable long enough to read.

Bottom line: Do you squint and find yourself running out of time as you try to read the titles? Do you find yourself wishing they would stop moving so you could see what they say? Then the titles need to be modified.

▓ Clear Citations

Every digital story needs a clear citation page that cites the sources for all the images, sounds, music, and other media used in the story that are not original. It's up to each teacher to decide what citation format to use. But to me, new media projects that don't have citations are incomplete.

Bottom line: Is everything that is not original accounted for? Are citations explicit and complete?

Final Note

Overcoming effectitus. True story. I was evaluating a high school digital portfolio that included a picture of the author in which his head continually rotated 360 degrees. I requested an air bag—I really was that nauseous—before I asked him why on earth he was doing that. His reply? "I don't know—but isn't it cool!" If I had a dollar for every time I heard that, I'd be a rich man.

It can be hard to keep students from using all the transitions and effects at their disposal. In fact, one of the best ways to have them get "effectitus" out of their systems is to have them experiment with effects until they burn out on them. But if you want students to appreciate the place that effects have in the world of new media, have them watch professional movies, TV programming, or animations in "active viewing mode." Students should see fairly quickly that effects are largely absent or unnoticeable. Of course there are always exceptions—like that sound that *Law & Order* uses.

Of all the places I go bump when I watch digital stories, the misuse and overuse of transitions and effects are some of the bumpiest.

The Grammar of Organization in Digital Stories

Most teachers know the joy of receiving student writing that is well organized and flows smoothly from one thought to the next. The joy comes in being able to relax and enjoy the writing, rather than bumping on the interface, in this case the words. There are similar considerations with digital stories. If a media piece flows unobtrusively and doesn't leave viewers feeling lost or assaulted, then the audience gets to relax and enjoy the story.

I recommend that teachers focus on two basic elements that contribute to this experience: structure and pacing. As we shall see, they are closely related. In a sentence, a digital story that observes sound organizational grammar is well paced, employs effective rhythm, and is unobtrusive in the way it's structured. In this section I discuss traits that should help teachers assess this aspect of digital stories.

Structure

The hallmark of a disorganized digital story is that it causes viewers to ask, "How did I get *here?*" This often happens because of poor editing choices. Nonsupportive image or scene changes, extraneous information and subplots, and poorly edited narrative can also easily destabilize structure.

But the most serious infraction of structure is simply a weak or poorly constructed story. If the story development process I described in Part II is followed in any sense, and at least some of the story-planning instruments I described are used (story maps, storyboarding, scripts, etc.), then students' digital stories can't help but be somewhat structured. While that doesn't ensure that they'll be well structured, it improves their chances in this regard. Briefly, in terms of the story core, all problems and questions should be clearly connected and solved by the end of the piece, and the role of transformation should be clear and play a significant role in the story. In the absence of a compelling artistic reason to lose viewers—such as inspiring them to discover where they are—the audience shouldn't notice the structure. For the most part, cause and effect should move the story along without forcing it along.

Bottom line: By the end of the story, are you still wondering how you ended up at certain places? Did you feel lost, or bump on the flow of events? If so, then the story needs to be restructured and/or reedited. Students should revisit their story maps or storyboards for the project to see if there are ways to strengthen the story structure.

▓ Effective Pacing

Good organization doesn't ensure flow. Instead, flow is primarily dependent upon good pacing, which, as Lambert (2003) explains, is often one of the most transparent but most important elements of a successful story. A story's pacing and rhythm often determine the audience's interest and direct viewers' sense of expectation. When a digital story doesn't flow, it's the new media equivalent of writing in which paragraphs follow logically but awkwardly, causing the viewer to stumble along the way.

Good pacing doesn't mean consistent pacing; after all, changing pace is often an effective way to support the action of the story. Like so many things in media, when it's good, it's unnoticeable, even when it changes, because it supports the narrative so well.

Infractions come in a number of varieties. For example, a digital story can spend too much time on one part of the narrative, leaving little time for other parts. The result is that students hurry to the finish, causing viewers to feel lost as they unconsciously struggle to find the story line. As always, a story can move disconnectedly to achieve effect, and it will be up to you to determine whether obtrusive pacing is an effective execution of poetic license or simply a project that needs more work.

Bottom line: Does the story hurry or linger inappropriately in places? Is there more description than necessary? Do the images change in ways that are at odds with the narrative? Does your mind squint as you try to figure out how you got where you are in the story? Ideally, you should not notice the pacing or rhythm unless there are overwhelming artistic reasons to do so. Instead, you should ride the story's rhythm unconsciously. So, do you bump on the rhythm?

▩ Final Note

Model what you want, be open to what's new. It's important for teachers to keep in mind that they will need to model the media grammar they want students to use. An easy, effective modeling approach is building a short digital story on the spot with students as a group activity, purposely using "bad grammar." This doesn't take a lot of time or technical expertise. And it's fun and enlightening.

Teachers also need to keep in mind that unlike traditional grammar, media grammar is evolving at a perceptible rate. This puts them in the exciting but uncomfortable position of actually being in the midst of a language whose rules are changing. However, one thing doesn't change: the goal is always effective communication. My advice? Stay open to the changes while always valuing clear communication that supports the story. Generally speaking, if you notice a technical event, then you've bumped on the media. If you've bumped, then you've encountered a problem—or a potential growing experience for you.

15

Copyright and Fair Use in Education

Living in the Gray Zone, Doing the Right Thing, and Protecting Yourself

The Day the Lawyer Came to Town...

I will never forget the day a lawyer came to my institution to explain the implications of the Technology, Education, and Copyright Harmonization (TEACH) Act, a vague enactment of government intended to explain the legalities of using electronic material in education. Although the TEACH Act was created specifically to address issues related to the use of materials in distance education, it effectively updated copyright and fair use law for anyone wanting to use electronic material for teaching or learning, on-site or at a distance. Many of us looked forward to having the TEACH Act in place, because we believed it would finally answer the question on every teacher's mind: Can students download materials found on the Web and use them in their own work (such as digital stories)? Like everyone else who attended the lawyer's presentation, I looked forward to finally getting some clarification on this issue.

"Fair use" is a legal term that refers to what educators can fairly use of other people's material without infringing on their protections under copyright.

The presentation was short and vague at best. Afterward, she asked for questions. While there were plenty of them about a number of different topics, her answers all seemed to begin in the same way:

"Well now, that's sort of a gray area . . ." In short, we all came for clarity and left with gravity. Had the Q&A session been a Monty Python skit, it would have been hilarious.

> "...well, now, that's sort of a gray area..."

My intention is not to criticize the lawyer. After all, everything was a gray area, owing largely to the fact that things change overnight. A few short years ago it was too difficult to include someone else's photo in a school assignment. Now it was too easy. The larger issue that loomed behind all fair use in the digital age was simply this: in an age in which just about anyone can create and distribute his or her own media via the Web and in which just about anyone else can download it and include it in his or her digital stories, presentations, Web sites, and other digital creations, what is legal and ethical? If nothing else, the lawyer's difficulty in explaining specifics about the TEACH Act made us all feel better about being confused ourselves.

However, that was a few years ago. Fortunately, since then the TEACH Act has been a topic of much discussion in many circles. As it has been reviewed, debated, and interpreted, I have developed approaches to using it with and explaining it to students that I share here. However, I want to stress that I'm not providing legal advice and should not be construed as doing so. Rather, I'm sharing my attempt as a layperson to understand a vast,

> Whenever in doubt, ask a lawyer. Your school district should have legal counsel on staff who can help you understand fair-use issues.

evolving area of law and public policy that impacts teachers. Bear in mind that there are lawyers who do nothing but interpret this area of the law for a living, and often disagree on what the law says. Therefore, it's understandable that we would be confused about it. If you're ever concerned about the legality of something, ask your administrator or school district's legal counsel for advice.

▓ What Teachers Want to Know

▓ What's Copyright Protected?

The first thing that teachers typically want to know is this: What is copyright protected? There is a simple answer: everything.

Anything that anyone creates and publishes has automatic copyright protection without the creator having to do anything else. Publishing means committing a creation to some form of media, including posting on the Web, printing, saving as a computer file, or burning to CD or DVD. So if students can see it, hear it, or touch it, then it's copy protected.

What about the © symbol? Even if it's not present, it's always implied. Those who want ironclad proof of ownership of their material should go through the formal process of filing for copyright protection. I do this for my books and articles but not for the diagrams, pictures, or music I create and publish on the Web. The formal copyright process is time-consuming, less than free, and simply not worth it to me in many cases. If someone wants to steal my diagrams, I'll deal with it on a case-by-case basis. But in all my years as a Webster, I've never had this happen. I make almost all of my materials free to the public and request that they be cited. The public hasn't let me down yet.

Next, teachers typically want answers to specific, practical questions about using media in classroom projects, such as the following:

- Can my students use graphics, photos, movies, and other digital material they find on the Web in their digital stories, Web sites, and other new media creations? If so, are there limitations to their use?
- Can my students use music they have downloaded from commercial CDs or music sites in their media creations? If so, are there limitations to their use?
- Should my students cite works? Ask permission? Both?
- In terms of students publishing projects that include material created by others, are there legal differences between showing projects at school, distributing them via CD or DVD, and posting them on the Internet?
- What options exist for dealing with the gray area of fair use?
- What values regarding the world of creative content should I impart to my students?

Let's begin addressing these questions by using what I call "commonsense copyright."

▓ Commonsense Copyright

Using common sense, the golden rule, and respect for others' property—just like our parents taught us—is a great place to start conversations with students about using other people's material in their digital stories. It also provides a good (though incomplete) introduction to what the law actually does say.

For many students, the stumbling block in understanding the concept of fair use is the altered nature of theft in the digital age. If I take your car, I have your car and you don't. But if I take your song, you still have your copy; it seems like I haven't deprived you of anything. What I've done is a bit more vague—I've deprived an artist of royalties, recognition, and respect. Although this is a very real impact, it's conceptually less tangible, particularly to the young mind. However, asking students the following question can help them focus on the realities of fair use and copyright in very real ways: "If you were trying to make a living as a musician, how would you react if someone downloaded rather than bought your music?" If they say, as they often do, "That would be fine with me," then ask them, "And how would you buy food for your family?" The reality is that many of today's students will end up creating digital content that could well be their bread and butter. It behooves them to understand creative content protection in personal terms.

▓ Three Rules of Respect

The bottom line is respect—respect for other people's work and how they want their work to be used and credited. There are three levels of respect that help frame this discussion for students: citation, permission, and compensation.

Three rules of respect:
1. citation
2. permission
3. compensation

Citation

Students must cite all material they use in a digital story, showing the same respect for graphics, words, music, and other media that teachers expect them to show when quoting a journal article. This is the minimal level of respect and must always be observed. By the way, I would not get hung up on APA versus MLA and other considerations of format unless the students are older and really need to cite sources properly. Having third graders simply cite their sources and thank the authors is fine. The goal of citation, particularly with younger students, has more to do with being respectful and appreciative than being legal and proper. That will come later.

Permission

Seeking permission is the second level of respect. You would think that whenever possible, your students should ask permission to use other people's materials because it's the decent thing to do. Unfortunately, it's not clear whether it's also the prudent thing to do. Fair use seems to suggest that they can use someone's material, even without permission, as long as the amount they use doesn't exceed the amount established by law (amounts are addressed a little later in this chapter). That leaves teachers in an interesting situation: Should students ask permission, even if what they're using doesn't exceed legal limits? And what happens if they do ask permission and are denied? Can they use the material anyway?

Legalists in this area of copyright law have assured me that there is plenty of legal precedent to protect students if they elect to use the materials anyway. Thus the issue is really a social one. After all, in any other situation, we would expect our children to honor someone's wishes not to use something that belonged to them. Clearly, legal and social issues collide here. It's your call.

But an even thornier issue here is distinguishing between "use" and "publication." Use seems to imply a limited audience, like students creating in-house projects. Publication seems to imply something more distributed and pervasive. The problem really arises when things are put on the Web. The intended audience may be parents, teachers, and a few potential employers, but the potential audience is the entire world. So, does posting something on the Web cross the line from use to publication in every situation?

Let's test this against a typical K–12 situation many teachers are familiar with: student online portfolios. Many students are being asked to publish their work on the Web these days so that parents and community members can see it and so that the students can practice developing the digital age equivalent of a résumé. Student portfolios are increasingly going to include things like digital stories that might use digital materials gathered from the Web that are presumably used within fair-use constraints. The question arises: If students are creating digital portfolio Web sites that are intended for a limited audience and are not intended to generate much online traffic, does this constitute distribution?

The safe answer is, when in doubt, assume the worst. That is, where good intentions and common decency diverge from the law, the law wins. If school districts decide that posting a student portfolio constitutes distribution, then they would at least have to require students to either obtain permission to use materials or remove whatever parts of the digital story were in question. The degree of difficulty this imposes is directly related to how much material they need to seek permission to use. From a planning perspective, any teacher who has already decided that posting portfolios constitutes fair-use infringement would probably simply restrict students from using any materials but their own or, alternatively, build a "fair-use awareness" component into the project requiring students to seek permission for all unoriginal materials.

So where does that leave us? In the gray area. Here are some guidelines to consider about asking permission:

- If the amount of work that students want to use exceeds the amount allowed by fair use, then they must ask permission.
- If the amount they want to use doesn't exceed legal limits, then they should ask permission only if they're prepared to be denied. Once they've been turned down, they're out of luck.

- In the absence of clear district policy, teachers need to decide whether student work is being published for purposes of distribution. If they determine it is, then they should require students to obtain permission for all the media they use.

More than anything else, classroom teachers need guidance and protection in this area. The most helpful thing administrators and school boards can do for teachers is to develop a clear policy in this area and promise to protect and support those who observe it.

However, here is a brighter side of this issue that makes asking permission more attractive: no one has ever refused to let a student of mine use a picture or other piece of media for educational purposes. Often they're grateful they were asked. Contacting owners of media materials usually isn't too difficult. Just about any Web site containing materials your students want to use has a contact e-mail associated with it. I shouldn't say that I've never heard of instances in which students and educators have been turned down by content owners, but my unofficial assessment is that such cases seem to be rare.

But what happens if students try to contact someone, don't hear back, and use of the material falls within fair use? In my very unlegal opinion, they have passed the test of respect and have a fairly strong case for using it. By the way, whenever possible, they should ask the authors of the media if they want to be cited. Most do, but some might not.

Compensation

This is the third level of respect. Typically, those who require compensation for the use of their materials will be very clear about it. Feel free to ask if they make exceptions for educational use. But if they insist on being compensated, then pay them or don't use their materials. To me, it's that simple. I should note that to others, it's not that simple. Compensation is one of those issues that is handled on a case-by-case basis by the legal system. However, within a school setting I strongly encourage you not to push the limits on this. If people want to be paid for their material and you can't or don't want to pay them, then don't use the material. Period.

▓ Four-Factor Fair-Use Test

Another approach to determining fair use is what is commonly called "the four-factor fair-use test," which consists of the four criteria explained below.

If you want to know more about the four-factor test, I suggest consulting the University of Texas's site devoted to this topic. It's a great resource and offers far more detail than I provide here. I provide the URL to this and other copyright sources on my Web site (www.jasonohler.com/storytelling).

- *Factor 1:* What is the character of the use? Nonprofit, educational use is better than commercial use. That is, using graphics in academic digital stories will raise fewer red flags than using them for a school Web site that sells T-shirts, even if the T-shirt sales support the swim team.
- *Factor 2:* What is the nature of the work to be used? Factual, published material is less problematic than imaginative, unpublished work. That is, using research findings raises fewer red flags than using someone else's music.
- *Factor 3:* How much of the work will you use? Captain Obvious here, pointing out that using a small amount is less controversial than using more than a small amount. One of the issues involved here is whether a student is using so much of a work that potential customers might not feel the need to buy a copy of it themselves.
- *Factor 4:* If this kind of use were widespread, what effect would it have on the market for the original or for permissions? The less your use of the material competes with or takes away from sales, the better. Of course, this is very hard to determine. But it should be fairly clear that distributing someone else's music has a much more deleterious impact on the market for that material than including a small part of it in a student's new media project that doesn't exceed fair-use constraints.

❖ What the Law Says

I don't like giving specific advice about fair use for the same reason I don't like giving out advice about brain surgery: I don't have the professional background required to provide the advice, and I'm afraid of what might happen if I'm wrong.

Disclaimer

I'm not a lawyer and I don't play one on TV. Any information in this chapter should not be construed as legal advice. When in doubt, and even when you're not in doubt, consult legal counsel.

Having said that, what follows is my limited understanding of what the TEACH Act says and what fair use implies about using digital materials in school projects such as digital stories. Below are points that specifically relate to using material in projects:

- *Music, video, animation:* Students can use 10% or 30 seconds of songs, movies, and other works, whichever is shorter.

- *Words*: Students can use 10% or up to 1,000 words from a text, whichever is smaller.
- *Illustrations, photos, graphics*: This is more vague. Students can use no more than five images from one artist; they can use 10% or 15 works from a collection, whichever is smaller.

▓ Avoiding the Gray Zone of Copyright and Fair Use

Teachers and students do have options. Here are some ways to avoid the gray zone:

- *Be perpetually paranoid.* The easiest way to avoid the gray area is to be paranoid. Whenever in doubt (which is almost always), just don't use something and don't publish on the Web. Your intended audience might only be parents, but your potential audience is the world. While it's the safest approach, I don't recommend it. The laws are there to serve both groups of people: artists as well as teachers, students, and the rest of us who would like access to material. I say, "When in doubt, seek permission."

- *Use what you find on the Web, observing the three rules of respect.* Again, these rules are (1) cite sources always, (2) ask permission when possible, and (3) compensate when necessary.

- *Create your own material.* The problems associated with fair use create a wonderful opportunity for students to become creative-content developers themselves. The challenges posed by fair use indirectly support the need to teach art as the fourth R, a topic addressed in some length in Part I of this book.

Fortunately, the tools are so good now that it's possible for students to create good materials within the time constraints of a typical project-based curriculum. Software like GarageBand makes creating original music not only doable but also easy, quick, and fun. Even a rudimentary grasp of a program like PhotoShop or the many other image-editing programs that are available makes preparing visual information very doable. And don't forget—students can create and scan their own artwork, take their own pictures, and shoot their own video. As long as the subject matter doesn't require permission, it's theirs to use however they want.

- *Use your friends' material.* You would be surprised how many of your friends, and your friends' friends, make music, take photos, and create other digital media. They're typically amenable to you and your friends using it as long as it's cited. I use my friends' original music and let others use mine. It's a great arrangement. But better yet, encourage your friends to use the Creative Commons license, discussed a little later. This gives the material a much wider audience.

• *Subscribe to media services.* There are a number of graphics subscription services that offer unlimited access to a database of materials. For example, I subscribe to a service for about $150 per year and gain access to over a million graphics and photos. It's a great deal.

• *Use only material provided on free-use or limited-use sites.* Many places on the Web advertise the use of their material for free or with less restricted access. I've provided a list of Web sites featuring cheap or low-cost resources on my Web site (www.jasonohler.com/storytelling). Read the disclaimers, cite your sources, but use them. That's why they're posted on the Web. But, as always, assume nothing. Web sites, as well as the rules under which they operate, change.

• *Use the Creative Commons.* There is one particular source of educator-friendly media resources that is unique, helpful, and gaining ground, called the Creative Commons. It's important enough to warrant its own section in this chapter.

❈ Creative Commons

Copyright tends to be an all-or-nothing affair—in fact, that's what the term "all rights reserved" means. Yet most of us personally know artists and musicians who would gladly let teachers and students use their material if there was just a mechanism that could allow them to do so. That's what the Creative Commons provides.

Specifically, the Creative Commons is a copyright license that facilitates two things: it allows creative content developers to post their materials and specify how they can be used, and it allows the public to access their materials within those constraints. Rather than all-or-nothing, developers have options. They can specify whether a work can be used commercially as well as noncommercially, whether they will allow modifications to their work for purposes of remixing, and so on. The Commons takes a lot of the gray out of the gray area of fair use by providing access to great resources that teachers and students can use with peace of mind. It also shows that dedicated people can tackle an important problem and provide a win-win situation for everyone involved. For more information about this, go to www.creative commons.org.

Bottom line: Show respect, do your homework, follow the fair-use laws as best as you know them, and ask for legal help when you need it. You'll do fine.

🏛 Special Note of Thanks

At a recent presentation to teachers on the topic of digital storytelling, someone asked a question about copyright. When I asked the audience who was interested in this area, every hand went up. Copyright is now on the minds of many teachers. This is why I wrote this chapter.

However, keep in mind that I am just a layperson trying to sort through a very gray, complex area and present it without bias. Despite my best efforts to do so, I am sure I have presented enough material in this chapter for readers to find something they believe to be in error or that they simply disagree with. Regarding those things in this very complex area of the law that I have unintentionally misunderstood and/or misrepresented, my apologies. I am not a lawyer, nor do I play one on TV, and any information found here should *not* be construed as legal opinion or advice. When in doubt, ask your school's legal counsel.

I would like to thank those mentioned in the Acknowledgments section of this book, as well as the many Web sites dedicated to providing information about this area, for their help with this chapter. Particularly helpful were the following Web sites:

- The Copyright Management Center
  http://www.copyright.iupui.edu/fairuse.htm
- The University of Texas Intellectual Property Site
  http://www.utsystem.edu/OGC/intellectualProperty/copypol2.htm
- Stanford University Library Copyright and Fair Use Site
  http://fairuse.stanford.edu/web_resources/articles.html

As always, comments are welcome.

Epilogue

If I Had a Time Machine . . .

If I had a time machine, one of the many things I would do is visit "schools" 20 years from now, perhaps even 50 or a hundred years, if I were truly courageous. In my time travels I would expect to observe many wondrous things. Here are three of them.

First, the word "school" would be used much like the word "album" is used today to identify a music collection—more metaphor than reality. Like music collections today, schools would come in a number of forms in the future. They would be integrated into the communities that support them, involving students in using local resources and expertise to solve local problems in very real and personal ways. Schools would also be virtual, interactive, multisensory environments that are global in scope and nature. These environments would help students balance personal, local, and global perspectives and needs, and be a lot of fun too. And then there would be those schools we can't even imagine right now that would totally surprise me.

Second, telling stories would be an important part of how we teach and learn. Storytelling would be appreciated as an effective way to combine academics, thoughtful reflection and analysis, emotional engagement, and active problem solving. It would rescue literacies that are currently undervalued in our educational system, such as art and oracy, and make them as basic as the three R's are today. Storytelling would once again become prized as a highly efficient information organizer and one of the most effective ways to remember and pass on information, knowledge, and wisdom. Lesson plans and units of instruction, both formal and informal, would strive to use the story form for this reason.

Third, debates about the language of media would be prevalent and spirited. Media technique and grammar might look very different from what I describe in this book, but they would still address the same concern: how to use media to communicate effectively. Like the generations before them who have been raised on the printed word, students would also be expected to be articulate and facile with the media of their day. Debates about effective approaches to teaching reading and writing still rage today. Debates about teaching the effective use of media are just beginning.

I sincerely hope that I would also find curricula in place that are based not so much on subject areas but rather on solving real problems that face our planet and its people. Imagine students taking a course today called Introduction to Climate Change and Global Warming that integrates all the content areas currently taught as separate subjects in order to understand the science, history, and politics of this phenomenon. Or imagine a course called Our Multicultural Global Village: Valuing What's Unique and Universal that uses a similar interdisciplinary approach. No doubt the future will need a different version of these courses as problems and opportunities grow and the world becomes smaller. But that's the subject of another book.

Everyone has a story. I look forward to hearing yours.

—Jason Ohler
www.jasonohler.com

Resource A

Teaching Oral Storytelling

Here are some of my favorite oral storytelling exercises to do with participants. All of them require one or more volunteers at the front of the class. Be prepared to have lots of fun with these. For more information about teaching oral storytelling technique, I recommend reading "Sound, Motion and Expression" in *Visual Portrait of a Story* (Dillingham, 2001) at www .brettdillingham.com.

- *Show us your emotion.* I put a sheet of white paper in front of a volunteer's face and have the class call out an emotion. When I lift the paper, the volunteer needs to display a facial expression depicting that emotion. I do this for four to six emotions (Dillingham, 2001). I then expand this to the rest of the class. I ask everyone to put their hands over their faces and count to three and then show an emotion the class has decided on.

- *Show us how big and small.* New storytellers will often just stand and talk, ignoring their bodies as storytelling tools. To help them become aware of using their bodies as implements of expression, I give them a situation to describe that even shy people would use body movement to describe. Typically, I have them describe something panoramic and beautiful, like a mountain range or a scene from a beach, with one catch—they can't use their arms. To ensure this, I walk behind the volunteers and hold their arms at their sides. As the volunteers struggle to describe the scene, I release their arms and tell they're free to use them. The volunteers' arms immediately spring to life, making them look like they're trying to fly! If I really want students to stretch, I have them use body movements to describe something like a pencil or a speck of dust. The results are always interesting.

- *Tell and show.* Stories are much more powerful when storytellers combine words and movements to describe events. To drive home this point, I have a volunteer describe a mundane event, such as making a sandwich, by telling and showing each step of the process in great detail. This is often hilarious as well as very informative.

- *Two voices.* Differentiating characters within a story is often problematic for new storytellers. To help storytellers with this, I set up a two-person situation in which a volunteer plays both parts. My favorite situation consists of a parent downstairs calling upstairs to a teenage child to come down for dinner. The volunteer is directed to have this conversation at three different emotional levels: (1) amiable, (2) touchy, and (3) confrontational. To differentiate the characters, the volunteer needs to use different voices, vocabulary, and body movements that are in character for each character. Warning: this exercise tends to uncover unresolved issues within families!
- *Sound effects.* This comes straight from Drew Carey's wonderful show, *Whose Line Is It Anyway?* I ask four to six volunteers to come to the front of the class and spread out so they have enough room to move around. Then I make up a story on the spot that calls for lots of sound effects, which they then have to make.
- *Motion effects.* This is similar to *Sound effects* except that volunteers have to move in ways suggested by the story.

Resource B

*Audio Techniques for Video
Recording Oral Storytelling*

Miking a Performance

If you're using taped oral storytelling or taped performance as part of your digital story, one rule above all: do *not* rely on the mike built into the video camera. If you rely on those mikes the audio often sounds like amateur video shot at a birthday party. For one or two performers, use wireless mikes. For a group, try dangling a mike over the performers and out of the camera shot.

Mike Technique for Speaking Into Your Computer

For the most part, digital storytellers assume they need to sit when recording their narrative. Not so. Experiment with audio delivery. How you sit, stand, and move will determine what your audio sounds like. Here are some options.

- *Sitting.* This seems to be the default for recording narrative for digital storytelling. Good mike technique says "Talk directly into the mike." And because you're reading, you're sitting still at a desk. This works, but it can restrict expression.
- *Standing.* This means putting your mike on a mike stand and plugging it into your computer. A lot of radio theater is done this way. It's easier to move your body, which in turn helps you inflect your delivery.
- *Wearing a headset.* Using a headset (combination mike and headphones like those telemarketers wear) allows you to move your head without having to worry about not speaking directly into the mike. Your natural inclination is to be more expressive.

- *Wearing a wireless.* Clip the mike to your shirt and plug the receiver into your computer. This allows you to move your entire body; your natural inclination is to be more expressive. This is ideal for spontaneous, unscripted speaking. Or you can hold the narrative in your hand as you act out your narration.

Bottom line: What you do with your body as you record your voice-over narrative will greatly affect what your narrative sounds like. Use your body to help you tell your story.

Resource C

Audio Techniques for Interviewing People

Ideally, you would use two wireless microphones, one attached to you and the other to the interviewee. This is how they do it on TV and in other professional interviewing situations. It allows you to edit each speaker separately in postproduction if, for example, one is a lot louder than the other. To get the interview from the mikes into the computer, you can plug the mike receiver into the computer. If you're video recording the interview, then you need a receiver plugged into your video camera that can receive two wireless signals. These are common and fairly cheap.

But if you don't have wireless microphones, here are some other options:

- *Use a flat mike.* These are microphones that plug into the audio input in your computer and are specifically made to be put on a table to capture everyone in the room. Do a test run. Where you place the mike can make a big difference in terms of how the voices are picked up. Also, desks can pick up background hum coming from the building. Doing a test run might reveal that you should put something soft under it, like a scarf or a hat.
- *Use a portable recorder.* These are the handheld recorders that reporters use. They tend to be cheap and durable, and almost everyone has a friend who has one. While recording quality is not the best, it's an all-in-one solution. Be sure there's a way to get the sound from the recorder to the computer; usually an "audio out" or "headphone" jack will do it. Note: if you're using a portable recorder, then you don't have to be present to conduct the interview. You can leave a list of questions with your interviewees and pick up the tape when they're done.
- *Use a regular mike.* There are lots of mikes that plug directly into a USB computer port these days. Experiment with where people sit in terms of picking up audio. It's really the only variable you can control.

Bottom line about using mikes: Theory and reality are often at odds when it comes to voice recording, so always do a trial run. Make sure that whatever method you use, the sound is good *after* it's in your computer. Test it on the spot, because after the interviewee has left, there is usually no second chance.

A word about interviewing technique: bad interviews make for difficult listening. Typically, bad interviewers make the following mistakes: they ask boring questions, they don't give interviewees time to say what's important to them, they feel a need to jump into the conversation and add their two cents, and they think being antagonistic toward the interviewee is a good way to generate listener interest.

Bottom line about interviewing: Be respectful. Interviewees have graciously offered their time. Ask clear questions, let them respond, listen to what they say so that any follow-up questions you ask make sense, and thank them when the interview is over.

Resource D

Freytag's Pyramid

This diagram can be found on L. Kip Wheeler's (2004) Web page, web.cn.edu/kwheeler/freytag.html. It appears here with his permission.

Resource D Figure

Freytag's Pyramid
adapted from Gustav Freytag's
Technik des Dramas (1863)

The Structure of Tragedy

Climax

Reversal

Falling Action

Catastrophe

Complication

Rising Action

Exposition

Inciting Moment

Moment of Last Suspense

Traditionally situated in the third act of a play, the climax is the moment of greatest tension, uncertainty, or audience involvement. The climax is also called the *crisis*.

The moment of reversal is also called the *peripeteia*. In classical tragedy, the reversal is that moment in which the protagonist's fortunes change irrecoverably for the worse. Frequently, the very trait we admire in a tragic hero is the same trait that brings about the hero's downfall.

At some point after the reversal, the tragic hero realizes or verbalizes his tragic error. This moment of tragic recognition is called the *anagnorisis*.

During the falling action, the earlier tragic force causes the failing fortunes of the hero. This culminates in the final catastrophe and invokes *catharsis* (emotional purgation) in the audience.

The catastrophe often spirals outward. Not only does the hero suffer for an earlier choice, but that choice causes suffering to those the hero loves or wants to protect.

After the suspense ends, the *denouement* unwinds previous tension and helps provide closure.

Rising action is an increase in tension or uncertainty developing out of the conflict the protagonist faces.

Exposition consists of early material providing the theme, establishing the setting, and introducing the major characters and sometimes early hints of the coming conflict.

SOURCE: Adapted from Freytag (1863) by Dr. L. Kip Wheeler. Used with permission.

211

Resource E

Grammar of Camera Angles

Media is a filter while pretending to be a clear window.
—Steve Goodman (2003)

The word "medium" (singular of the word "media") means "in the middle of." Life in the digital age means adjusting to the media filters that sit in the middle of and between us and our experience of the real world. Our senses are the first filter we need to take into consideration. After all, our eyes and ears are fairly limited input devices that can perceive only certain things. A camera further restricts our abilities to experience life as it is and adds a twist: by deliberately shooting things at particular angles, a photographer or videographer can influence how viewers think and feel about the things, events, and people being captured or recorded.

Camera Angle Persuasion

Here is a short list of camera angles and other biases implicit in the technology and techniques of photography and video recording:

- *Shot from above.* Shooting from above looking down on a subject tends to diminish the stature of the subject. It can have the effect of belittling the subject and/or making viewers sympathize with or think less of it.
- *Shot from beneath.* Shooting something from beneath looking up at, say, the chin of a human subject, tends to make the subject seem larger than life. It can have the effect of making something seem superior, overly important, or menacing.
- *Shot straight on.* You'd think this is the only honest camera angle, and in some ways it's more honest than others. But we all know the effect of holding a still shot of a subject face on and not moving. We tend not to

look at people this way because it makes us and them feel uncomfortable. When the camera shoots a subject dead on without wavering for more than a few seconds, it tends to make us, the viewers, squirm. We are left with our discomfort, which is easily projected onto the subject.

- *Moving the camera.* Short, jerky coverage of a subject often makes the subject seem strange, untrustworthy, or confused because it implies that the subject is trying to dodge coverage.
- *The bias of the moving subject.* Standard fare in media literacy courses are stories about news coverage that favors scuffles over quiet discussion, regardless of how unrepresentative the video bite is. If there's a peaceful demonstration that has 15 seconds of scuffle, the video lens and the television medium favor the movement of the scuffle. That is, we, the viewers, are much more apt to stay interested if there is such movement.

Bottom line: How we hold, position, and move a camera can in large part determine how viewers think and feel about what they see. Camera angles are the adjectives and adverbs of video grammar.

Resource F

What's Scannable?

Here is a list of potential image sources from Bernajean Porter's (2004) book on digital storytelling called *DigiTales*, reprinted here with her permission:

- Old photos
- Greeting cards
- Watches
- Report cards
- Fabrics
- Jewelry
- Postcards
- Letters
- Personal papers
- Flowers, leaves
- Wallpaper
- Book covers

By the way, even some 3-D objects are scannable, such as a spice bottle or a toothbrush. Be imaginative.

Bottom line: The scanner is your friend. Most small objects can be scanned. Using scanned objects adds authenticity to your story.

▦ Resource G

Joseph Campbell's
Story Adventure Diagram

Resource G Figure

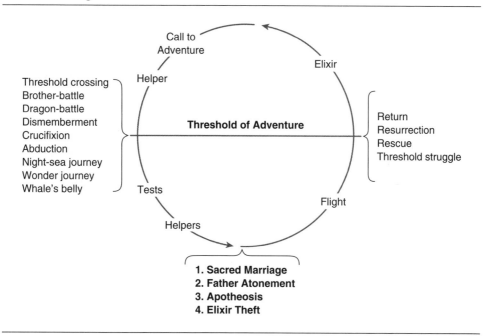

SOURCE: Campbell, Joseph. *The Hero With a Thousand Faces.* New Jersey: Princeton University Press, 1973. Reprinted here with permission from Princeton University Press.

 Resource H

Visual Portrait of a Story

Resource H1 Figure

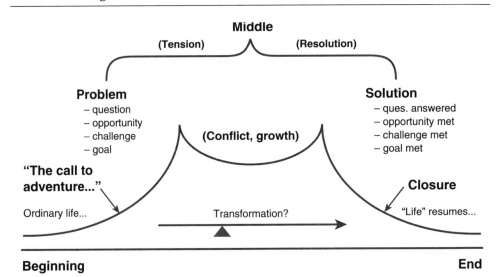

SOURCE: Adapted by Ohler (2001), from Dillingham, B. (2001). *Visual portrait of a story: Teaching storytelling* [School handout]. Juneau, AK.

Resource H2 Figure

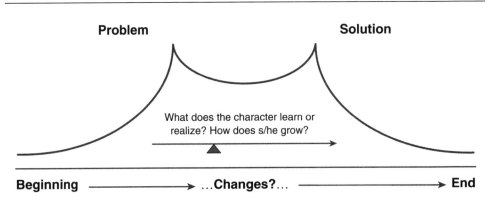

SOURCE: Adapted by Ohler (2001), from Dillingham, B. (2001). *Visual portrait of a story: Teaching storytelling* [School handout]. Juneau, AK.

216

Resource H3 Figure

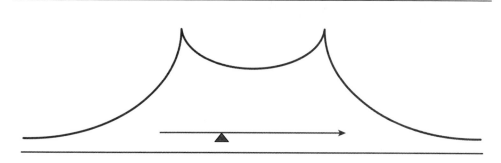

SOURCE: Adapted by Ohler (2001), from Dillingham, B. (2001). *Visual portrait of a story: Teaching storytelling* [School handout]. Juneau, AK.

References

Adams, K. (1990). *The story spine* [Language template]. New York: Story Net.

Altman, R. (Director). 2006. *A prairie home companion* [Movie]. United States: GreenStreet Films.

Assembly of Alaska Native Educators. (2000). *Guidelines for respecting cultural knowledge*. Anchorage: Alaska Native Knowledge Network.

Beckett, S. (1954). *Waiting for Godot*. New York: Grove Press.

Bloom, B. S. (Ed.). (1964). *Taxonomy of educational objectives, Book 1: The cognitive domain*. New York: Longman.

Bloom, B. S., Krathwohl, D. R., & Masia, B. B. (1964). *Taxonomy of educational objectives, Book 2: The affective domain*. New York: Longman.

Burmark, L. (2002). *Visual literacy: Learn to see, see to learn*. Alexandria, VA: ASCD.

Campbell, J. (1973). *The hero with a thousand faces*. Princeton, NJ: Princeton University Press.

Christenson, M. D. (2005). *Adapted VPS* [Student work]. Juneau, AK.

Coleridge, S. T. (1817). *Biographia Literaria*. Self-published.

Davis, H. (2003). *Adapted VPS* [Student work with parental permission]. Juneau, AK.

Dillingham, B. (2001). *Visual portrait of a story: Teaching storytelling* [School handout]. Juneau, AK.

Dillingham, B. (2005). Performance literacy. *The Reading Teacher, 59*(1), 72–75.

Dillingham, B., & Ohler, J. (2002). *Visual portrait of a story with transformation* [School handout]. Juneau, AK.

Dillingham, B., & Stanley, N. (2007). *Performance literacy: Reading and writing through storytelling*. Gainesville, FL: Maupin House.

Egan, K. (1989). *Teaching as story telling*. Chicago: Chicago Press.

Faulkner, W. (1956). *The sound and the fury*. New York: Random House.

Freytag, G. (1868). *Technique of the drama* (E. MacEwan, Trans.). New York: B. Blom. (Original work published 1863).

Gardner, H. (1983). *Frames of mind: The theory of multiple intelligences*. New York: Basic Books.

Goodman, S. (2003). *Teaching youth media: A critical guide to literacy, video production & social change*. New York: Teachers College Press.

Green Day & Armstrong, B. (2005). Boulevard of broken dreams. On *American idiot* [CD]. New York: Reprise.

International Reading Association and the National Council of Teachers of English. (1996). *Standards for the English language arts*. Retrieved March 27, 2007, from ncte.org.

Joyce, J. (1957). *Finnegan's wake*. New York: Viking Press.

Kafka, F. (1964). *The trial*. New York: Alfred A. Knopf.

Kay, A. (1996). Revealing the elephant: The use and misuse of computers in education. *Sequence, 31*(4), 1–2.

King, T. (2005). *The truth about stories: A Native narrative.* Minneapolis: University of Minnesota Press.

Kohlberg, L. (1984). *The psychology of moral development: The nature and validity of moral stages.* San Francisco: Harper & Row.

Lambert, J. (2003). *Digital storytelling cookbook and traveling companion.* San Francisco: Digital Diner Press.

McKee, R. (1997). *Story: Substance, structure, style, and the principles of screenwriting.* New York: Reagan.

McLuhan, M. (1964). *The medium is the message.* New York: New American Library.

Mellon, N. (2003). *The art of storytelling.* Cambridge, MA: Yellow Moon Press.

Momaday, N. S. (1999). *House made of dawn.* New York: Harper Perennial.

Ohler, J. (2003). *Then what? Everyone's guide to living, learning, and having fun in the digital age.* Juneau, AK: Brinton.

Ohler, J. (2004) *Digital storytelling* [PowerPoint presentation]. Juneau, AK: Brinton.

Ohler, J. (2005) *Telling your story.* Juneau, AK: Brinton.

Oreilly, T. (2005). *Web 2.0: Compact definition.* Retrieved from http://radar.oreilly.com/archives/2005/10/web_20_compact_definition.html

Pitler, H. (2006). Creative commons: A new tool for schools. *Innovate, 2*(5), n.p. Retrieved March 21, 2007, from innovateonline.info/index.php?view=article&id=251

Porter, B. (2004). *DigiTales: The art of telling digital stories.* Sedalia, CO: Porter.

Prensky, M. (2001). Digital natives, digital immigrants. *On the Horizon, 9*(5), 1–2.

Silko, L. M. (1977). *Ceremony.* New York: Penguin.

Telford, K. (1970). *Aristotle poetics, translation and analysis.* Chicago: Regnery.

Theodosakis, N. (2001). *Director in the classroom.* San Diego, CA: Tech4Learning.

2004 Elders Forum on Traditional Values. (2004). *Southeast traditional tribal values: Our way of life.* Alaska: Central Council Tlingit and Haida Indian Tribes of Alaska, Circles of Care, SAMHSA Substance Abuse Planning Project, Elderly Nutrition Program, Johnson O'Malley Program and Alaska Rural Systemic Initiative, and Alaska Association of School Boards.

Wheeler, K. (2004). Freytag's Pyramid Chart. *Dr. Wheeler's Homepage.* Retrieved March 21, 2007, from web.cn.edu/kwheeler/freytag.html

Wiggins, G., & McTighe, J. (2001). *Understanding by design.* Upper Saddle River, NJ: Merrill/Prentice Hall.

Williams, R. (2003). *Non-designer's design book.* Berkeley, CA: Peachpit Press.

Further Readings

Birch, C. (1996). Who says? The storyteller as narrator. In C. L. Birch & M. A. Heckler (Eds.), *Who says? Essays on pivotal issues in contemporary storytelling* (pp. 107–128). Little Rock, AR: August House.

Breneman, L., & Breneman, B. (1983). *Once upon a time: A storytelling handbook.* Chicago: Nelson-Hall.

Bruchac, J. (1996). The continuing circle. In C. L. Birch & M. A. Heckler (Eds.), *Who says? Essays on pivotal issues in contemporary storytelling* (pp. 91–105). Little Rock, AR: August House.

Denning, S. (2001). *The springboard: How storytelling ignites action in knowledge-era organizations.* Boston: Butterworth Heinemann.

Eisner, W. (1996). *Graphic storytelling and visual narrative.* Tamarac, FL: Poorhouse Press.

Kroeber, K. (2004). *Native American storytelling.* Malden, MA: Blackwell.

McLuhan, M., & McLuhan, E. (1988). *The laws of media.* Toronto, Ontario, Canada: University of Toronto Press.

Pink, D. (2006). *Whole new mind.* New York: Penguin Books.

Simmons, A. (2001). *The story factor.* Cambridge, MA: Perseus Books Group.

Toelken, B. (1996). The icebergs of folktale: Misconception, misuse and abuse. In C. L. Birch & M. A. Heckler (Eds.), *Who says? Essays on pivotal issues in contemporary storytelling* (pp. 34–63). Little Rock, AR: August House.

Tyner, K. (1998). *Literacy in a digital world: Teaching and learning in the age of information.* Mahwah, NJ: Erlbaum.

Index

CORWIN PRESS

The Corwin Press logo—a raven striding across an open book—represents the union of courage and learning. Corwin Press is committed to improving education for all learners by publishing books and other professional development resources for those serving the field of PreK–12 education. By providing practical, hands-on materials, Corwin Press continues to carry out the promise of its motto: **"Helping Educators Do Their Work Better."**